DISAPPEARANCE OF THE DOWRY

MURIEL NAZZARI

Disappearance of the Dowry,

WOMEN, FAMILIES,
AND SOCIAL CHANGE IN
SÃO PAULO, BRAZIL
(1600-1900)

STANFORD UNIVERSITY PRESS
STANFORD, CALIFORNIA 1991

Stanford University Press
Stanford, California
© 1991 by the Board of Trustees of the
Leland Stanford Junior University
Printed in the United States of America

CIP data appear at the end of the book

TO THE MEMORY OF BESSIE ARCHER SMITH,
MY MOTHER

ACKNOWLEDGMENTS

This project could not have been carried out without the encouragement, economic support, and outright help of many persons and organizations. A grant from the Tinker Foundation permitted me to make a preliminary trip to Brazil in the summer of 1981 to locate the necessary documents. Research in São Paulo during 1982–83 was partially supported by a Woodrow Wilson Research Grant in Women's Studies.

I thank George Nazzari, without whose moral and economic support the project would have been impossible. My children and grandchildren have backed me all along, and my appreciation and love go to them.

I remember with gratitude my months of research in the Arquivo do Estado de São Paulo, where D. Maria Gloria Martinelli and Azoardil Martinelli gave me friendship and invaluable aid. During the months I spent at the Arquivo do Ministério de Justiça at Vila Leopoldina, its director, Sr. Benedito Chaves, greatly facilitated the location of documents. I also appreciate the help of the personnel of the library of the Facultade de Direito of São Paulo, the Arquivo da Curia Metropolitana in São Paulo, the library of the Instituto de Estudos Brasileiros, the Museu Paulista, the Biblioteca Municipal, and, in Rio de Janeiro, those of the Arquivo Nacional, the Biblioteca Nacional, and the Arquivo Histórico da Secretaria de Estado das Relações Exteriores.

I thank Linda Lewin who, in São Paulo in June 1981, gave me invaluable advice on where to find documents, on what books to consult in the library of the School of Law, and on the bureaucratic procedures necessary to get permission to work in the archive of Vila Leopoldina. I owe a debt of gratitude to Heleieth Saffioti of the University of Araraquara, who listened patiently to the development of my ideas and graciously lent me her apartment for several weeks. Other scholars I thank for allowing me to share my concerns while in São Paulo are Bela Biancho, Ruth Cardoso, Ralph della Cava, Mariza Corrêa, Peter Fry, June Hahner, Miriam Moreira Leite, Maria Luiza Marcílio, Laima Mesgravis, Fernando Novais, and Robert Slenes.

Fellow researchers in Brazil helped by providing hours of conversation where ideas could be discussed. I thank Serafina Traub Borges do Amaral, John French, Kathy Higgins, John Monteiro, Mary del Priore, and Julio Caio Velloso. In the United States I received encouragement and moral support from Vaneeta D'Andrea, Carolyn Cooper, Jean Hein, and Catalina Stroll.

I am most grateful to Emilia Viotti da Costa, who directed the dissertation, providing an insightful critique at every stage of the work. I also appreciate the encouragement I received from Nancy Cott.

Though I have not followed their advice in every instance, I especially thank Silvia Arrom and Richard Graham, who carefully read and commented on subsequent drafts of the book. My choice of topic owes much to Silvia Arrom, who encouraged me to continue my research on marriage by investigating the practice of dowry, and who suggested the sampling technique that would permit such a longitudinal study. Richard Graham provided the challenge that spurred my final analysis of nineteenth-century change in the family, and he carried out detailed, thorough, and questioning readings of the manuscript.

M.N.

CONTENTS

TABLES AND FIGURES

NOTE ON CURRENCY

During the sixteenth and seventeenth centuries, the Portuguese and Brazilian monetary unit was the *real*, plural *réis*. During that period, 400 réis were called one *cruzado*. By the middle of the nineteenth century, the monetary unit was becoming the *mil-réis* (one thousand réis), written 1$000. One thousand mil-réis were called one *conto* and written 1:000$000.

INTRODUCTION

§EVERAL YEARS AGO, while searching for material on marriage in the twentieth-century United States, I came upon the suggestion that a wife's entry into the paid work force gave her power within the marriage similar to that conferred in the past by bringing a dowry to marriage. If the dowry had in fact helped wives, I wondered why the custom no longer existed, and why parents in the nineteenth and twentieth centuries, who undoubtedly loved their daughters as much as those in earlier centuries, stopped giving dowries. An answer to that question became possible when I discovered in Brazil the kind of documents that permit the study of change in the practice of dowry. This book is the result.[1]

The dowry was a European institution that the Portuguese, who colonized Brazil in the sixteenth century, brought with them, along with Christianity and other European cultural trappings.[2] According to Portuguese law and custom, giving a daughter a dowry was a parental duty, similar to the duty of feeding and caring for their children, and was only limited by the extent of parents' resources. In seventeenth-century São Paulo, most property owners gave their daughters such large dowries that wives contributed the majority of the land, cattle, agricultural tools, and Indian slaves necessary for the support of the newly married couple. Today dowry no longer exists in São Paulo, though people still remember talk about their grandmothers' or great-grandmothers' dowries.

The practice of dowry disappeared elsewhere, too. In England it was abandoned around the end of the nineteenth century, whereas in parts of Germany it may have continued until after World War I.[3] Although the dowry
has practically disappeared in Europe, there are some localities, usually rural
areas, in Greece, Ireland, Italy, Spain, Portugal, and Malta in which dowry
still appears to be practiced.[4] Dowry also persists in several other parts of the
world, notably India.[5] Regarding Latin America, Asunción Lavrin and Edith
Couturier documented a decrease in the giving of dowries in Mexico between
the middle of the seventeenth and the end of the eighteenth century, and
Silvia Arrom shows that the decline continued in the nineteenth century.[6]

In Brazil, not only did the practice of dowry disappear by the beginning of
the twentieth century, but opinions about the importance of a bride's taking a
dowry or other property to marriage changed radically. In 1623 São Paulo
resident Pero Nunes stated in his will, "I command my heirs not to interfere
with what I gave my daughter Maria or my curse will fall on them. I gave her
everything during my lifetime because she is my only beloved daughter [and it
is] for her marriage and for her well-being in life."[7] He clearly believed that
providing property for his daughter to take to marriage would ensure her happiness. By the beginning of the twentieth century, the opposite point of view
was being voiced. A Brazilian congressman commented in 1907 on the continued existence of "marriages of pure exploitation, of dowry hunters, those
who run after rich girls, not in order to share their destiny or future but simply
to share their property."[8] He obviously thought a dowry would attract the
worst kind of husband, condemning a woman to life with a fortune hunter
instead of with a man who treasured her personal qualities. Opinions about
the way to ensure a daughter's welfare had been reversed.

METHODOLOGY

To find out why the dowry disappeared, I had to study its practice while it
still persisted, looking for patterns of change over time that could help explain its disappearance. Since the time period covered had to be long enough
to reveal changes in practice, I elected to start the study of documents with
1640 and end it with 1869, when dowry still existed, as attested by legal articles on dowry published in São Paulo in the 1870's and 1880's.[9] The period
covered by the book is somewhat longer, however, from approximately 1600
to approximately 1900. I chose 1600 to represent the fact that documents
from 1640 describe the practice of dowry during the lifetime of the deceased,
in many instances at least 40 years earlier. I chose 1900 as a round figure to
end the study because I include an analysis of laws passed in 1890 and 1917
and assume that the dowry disappeared around the turn of the century.

I used *inventários*, Brazilian judicial processes of settlement of estates. They include not only the inventory of an estate but also the will of the deceased (if there was one), all litigation among heirs, lists of debts owed the estate, the demands of creditors, receipts of payment, the reports and accounts of guardians of minor heirs, and the final apportionment of the estate among the heirs. Inventários are invaluable for the documentation of change because the format changed little over three centuries and all provide approximately the same kind of information, thereby permitting comparisons among siblings, families, and periods.

What makes inventários so useful for examining the practice of dowry is that, according to Portuguese and Brazilian family law, dowry was considered an advance on a daughter's inheritance.[10] Since all legitimate children were necessary heirs—that is, they could not be disinherited—an inventário that listed married daughters or their children among the heirs to the estate usually included references to daughters' dowries, unless they had received none, a circumstance the inventário would also document.[11] Even if there were no explicit mention of a dowry, the documents themselves reveal whether a dowry had been given or not. If the married daughter inherited equally with her brothers and single sisters, it meant that she had received no dowry. If, on the other hand, she inherited nothing or declined to inherit (which was the most frequent practice for endowed daughters in the seventeenth century), it meant she had received a dowry that she and her husband considered at least the equivalent of her inheritance. At the time of each of her parents' deaths, an endowed daughter and her husband could either refuse to inherit, or enter *à colação*—that is, bring the dowry back into the estate, adding its value to the net estate before the division among heirs. If she exercised this option of colação, the dowry would be subtracted from her share of the inheritance, and she would receive the difference, or, if she and her husband had overestimated the value of the estate, and the dowry was larger than her inheritance, she was expected to return the difference to her siblings. Since a dowry was given by both parents, only half the dowry came in à colação at the death of each parent, whereas the dowry given by a widow or widower came in à colação entire.[12]

In Portuguese law the word for dowry, *dote*, has at least two meanings. In the first, dowry is seen from the point of view of its donor and defined as the property that parents and other relatives or nonrelatives give a woman at marriage. This study is principally about the dowry given by parents. In the second meaning, dowry is seen from the point of view of its recipients, the married couple, and is defined as the property that a woman brings to the marriage partnership. In this meaning, dowry can be the dowry a bride receives from her parents, property she previously inherited and brings to the marriage, or property she owns as a widow and brings when she remarries.[13]

Within the marriage, however, dowry in Brazil usually disappeared into the couple's pool of goods. The law code decreed that, unless a prenuptial agreement was signed, a valid marriage effected by the church resulted in a system of complete community property between the spouses.[14] Under this law the dowry merged into the community property, and the wife was guaranteed no fixed sum upon widowhood, as she was in Spanish law.[15] But since she owned half the couple's property, she retained her half in widowhood, and when she died, whether as a widow or while her husband was alive, her half of the community property went to her necessary heirs, her children, or, if she were childless, her parents.[16]

To study the changing practice of dowry over such a long period required that I take measures to make the study manageable. In the first place, I limited the geographic area to the city of São Paulo and its surroundings.[17] Second, I concentrated mainly on inventários dated in the middle two decades of each century.

With the purpose of eliminating subjectivity in my choice of inventários, I created a sample that comprises *all* inventários in which the deceased had married daughters (or their descendants) in a certain collection of documents within a predetermined time period.[18] The sample for the seventeenth century therefore consists of all 48 published inventários that have married daughters or their heirs for the period 1640–1651 in *Inventários e Testamentos*, 44 vols. (São Paulo: Arquivo do Estado de São Paulo, 1921–1975).[19] The eighteenth-century sample consists of all 68 manuscript inventários with married daughters or their heirs for the period 1750–1769 in "Inventários Não Publicados" at the Arquivo do Estado de São Paulo.[20] The sample for the nineteenth century consists of all 178 manuscript inventários with married daughters or their heirs for the period 1850–1869 in "Segundo Ofício da Família" at the Arquivo do Ministério de Justiça in Vila Leopoldina.[21]

The date of an inventário does not correspond, of course, to the date when the deceased parents gave a dowry to their daughter. So depending on the age of the deceased and the age at which daughters were married, an inventário dated in the middle of the century could describe dowry as practiced up to 50 years earlier. The comparison made in this study is therefore between the practice of dowry in approximately the first half of the seventeenth century, the first half of the eighteenth, and the first half of the nineteenth.

THE PROBLEM

Why did a practice that had been considered a duty stop being a duty, or, conversely, why did daughters lose the right they had previously enjoyed of receiving from their parents the wherewithal to contribute to the support of their marriage? Despite the many historical and anthropological studies about dowry, to the best of my knowledge this is the first analysis of its disappearance. My hypothesis at a general level is that the institution of dowry was among the many fetters to the development of capitalism, such as entail, monopolies, and the privileges of the nobility, of churchmen, and of army officers, that disappeared as the influence of industrial capital spread worldwide. Yet entail, monopolies, and privileges were abolished legally, whereas the dowry was not abolished legally, it disappeared in practice. Thus the question remains: what led individual families to change their customs regarding dowry?

And they changed remarkably. I found that, in the seventeenth century, practically all propertied families in São Paulo endowed every one of their daughters, favoring them by giving dowries far exceeding the value of what their brothers would inherit later on. By the early nineteenth century, in contrast, long before the custom of dowry had disappeared, less than a third of the propertied families in São Paulo were endowing their daughters, and those who did gave comparatively smaller dowries, with a very different content, while some families endowed only one or two of several daughters.

How to explain this transformation in customs? I will argue throughout this book that the practice of dowry altered because of changes in society, the family, and marriage. Since dowry is a transfer of property between family members, changes in the concept of property, in the way property is acquired and held, or in business practices are relevant to an understanding of change in the institution of dowry, as are changes in the function of the family in society, the way it is integrated into production, and how it supports its members.

The changes experienced by Brazilian society that help explain the decline and disappearance of the dowry are many of the same transformations that have been observed in more central regions of the Western world. Through a long process that started in the eighteenth century and continued into the early twentieth century, Brazil changed from a hierarchical, *ancien régime* type of society in which status, family, and patron-client relations were primary to a more individualistic society in which contract and the market increasingly reigned.[22] A society divided vertically into family clans changed gradually into a society divided horizontally into classes.[23] As the state grew stronger, it took over functions previously performed by the family, which in seventeenth-century São Paulo's frontier society had included municipal government and defense.[24]

Between the seventeenth and the late nineteenth centuries, a new concept of private property developed.[25] The family changed from being the locus of both production and consumption to being principally the locus of consumption, while "family" and "business" became formally separate.[26] The

power of the larger kin declined and the conjugal family became more important, and marriage was transformed from predominantly a property matter to
an avowed "love" relationship, the economic underpinnings of which were
no longer made explicit.[27] At the same time there was a change from the
strong authority of the patriarch over adult sons and daughters to their greater
independence, and from arranged marriages to marriages freely chosen by the
bride and groom.[28] These transformations took place in Brazil starting in the
eighteenth century and continuing throughout the nineteenth century in a
gradual and complex manner so that both old and new characteristics often
coexisted at a given time, sometimes even within the same family.[29]

As these changes occurred, the practice of dowry altered. This book traces
the transformation in São Paulo and attempts to answer how alterations in
family practice were connected to broader social changes. Why did property-
owning families modify their behavior regarding sons and daughters? And
what were the consequences for the women of these families?

Part One

THE SEVENTEENTH CENTURY
(1600–1651)

CHAPTER I

THE FAMILY AS THE BASIS
OF SOCIETY

N 1554 a group of Jesuits founded São Paulo near the settlement of several shipwrecked Portuguese men who had long been in Brazil, having married the daughters of local Indian chieftains who were converted and given Portuguese names. Their families constituted the nucleus from which all great Paulista families would descend.[1] Since São Paulo was far from Salvador, the administrative and judicial center of the colony until the eighteenth century, and did not produce anything of special interest to Portugal, it was mostly left to its own devices. Paulistas therefore developed much independence and on occasion even outright bravado against official intervention.[2]

In the absence of a strong state presence, society was controlled by extended families or clans.[3] Large kin groups, ruled by a patriarch or occasionally a matriarch, dominated most phases of social life (except perhaps the regular orders of the church), including local government, productive and commercial activities, and the large Indian slaving expeditions, *bandeiras*, that were the basis of São Paulo's prosperity—or even its existence. The clan's power resided not only in its wealth and physical assets but also, and perhaps even more significantly, in the human resources it could command: relatives, African slaves, and Indians. Thus the marriage of its children expanded and strengthened the clan.

As there were no companies or formal business partnerships in seventeenth-century São Paulo, the propertied family itself was the structure through which economic activity was carried out. Marriage was the way a new productive enterprise was formed, with the wife's dowry providing most of the means of production necessary to start the new unit. Marriage to a woman with a dowry was also one of the few ways a young man acquired independent means. Thus dowry was an important economic institution, and marriage was not a private matter of interest only to the individuals concerned, as it was to become in the nineteenth century. Because of the public importance of dowry and marriage, wives and daughters in propertied families occupied a far more important position than traditional historiography has accorded them. This chapter will describe and analyze this family-based society as a key to understanding its practice of dowry.

THE CLAN-BASED SOCIETY

By the beginning of the seventeenth century, the population of São Paulo included the descendants of the original settlers, some newly arrived Portuguese, the Jesuits with their native recruits settled in villages around the town, and countless other Indians who were subject to personal service to the settlers.[4] São Paulo developed a two-tiered society; the elite was composed of the mestizo descendants of the first Portuguese plus later Portuguese newcomers, while the Indians and a sprinkling of African slaves made up the underclass.

We have only an approximate idea of the size of the town in the seventeenth century. When the municipal council wrote the governor general of Brazil in 1589 to ask for a vicar for São Paulo, it estimated the number of households at 150, which were only those of white or mestizo settlers.[5] Some 60 years later, in 1648, Father Antônio Vieira reported that São Paulo had 700 heads of household—proprietors—and several thousand Indians.[6] All property owners lived the year round on their farms where they could better oversee their Indians, but the wealthier families also owned a house in town where they stayed when participating in urban activities such as religious processions or the meetings of the municipal council.[7]

The feud between the Pires and Camargo clans in the middle of the seventeenth century illustrates the power of the extended family in São Paulo and the concomitant weakness of the crown. In this feud, private clan vengeance took the place of public state justice.[8] The feud apparently started in 1640 when Alberto Pires killed his wife, Leonor Camargo, and later murdered the man he claimed was her lover. The Camargo forces pursued Alberto to his mother's farm and encircled it. Alberto's mother, the matriarch D. Ignez

Monteiro, called *a Matrona*, came to the door holding a crucifix on high and negotiated with the attackers, who agreed not to kill Alberto on the spot but to accept the verdict of the high court in Bahia, to which they would conduct him immediately. D. Ignez followed with her armed retainers, but on the way, Alberto's escorts assassinated him, causing the matriarch's undying thirst for revenge, which led to a confrontation between the clans that lasted at least twenty years and included not only murders and revenge but also full-fledged battles between the forces of each side.

An important part of the feud was played out within the municipal council, demonstrating that the clan or extended family was itself the structure of government at the local level. The two clans competed for political power in such an unruly way that they finally asked the governor general of Brazil to mediate, and he had them sign a peace agreement by which each clan would thereafter hold half the seats in the council.[9]

The Pires-Camargo feud demonstrates not only the political and military power of the clans but also the corporate character of the family. A sense of collective rather than individual responsibility permeates the feud, for murder and reprisal were seen as familial rather than individual affairs. This is vividly demonstrated in a legal document dated 1658 in which Anna de Proença, represented by her son, solemnly pardoned Maria Gonçalves, widow of Pedro Leme do Prado, for the latter's murder of another of Anna's sons.[10] Here we see relatives of the victim pardoning, not the murderer, but his family, his widow.[11]

Another example of corporate family responsibility, of heirs responsible for their father's actions, is that of Manoel Pinto Guedes, who took the great Indian expeditionary, João, to the wilderness without his owner's permission. When they both died on the expedition, João's owner sued Manoel's heirs for his loss.[12] Some might argue that this case is different from the preceding one because Manoel's heirs were sued for loss of property instead of for loss of family. But the property in question was a man, who could provide services similar to those of a son; it could be argued that the differences between losing a man-servant or slave and losing a son is only emotional or concerned with questions of lineage.

In any case, the family was held responsible for individual acts, and, conversely, certain individuals could represent all other members of the family. For instance, the final peace treaty between the Pires and Camargos was signed in 1660 by the chief representatives of both families "in their own names, and in the name of their families, relatives, friends, and allies, both present and absent."[13]

Moreover, family allegiance was paramount and was believed to determine individual actions. For example, Judge Dom Simão de Toledo did not think he could be objective in settling the estate of Anna Luiz because his wife was a distant relative of one of the grandsons and heirs of the deceased, and he therefore disqualified himself from continuing the process without the presence of a municipal councilman as a check.[14]

The corporate character of the extended family or clan was also evident in business relations. Although recorded business transactions appear to be between individuals, especially when it was the patriarch or his widow who carried them out, this individualism is belied by the frequency with which they were represented by other members of the family, much as present-day employees represent a firm. Pedro Vidal, for example, noted in his 1658 will that he owed the tax collector a sum "according to the agreement I made with his son."[15] The tax collector's son clearly had a modern manager's authority to negotiate.

Thus, families functioned as business units in which different members represented the family. Usually it was sons who represented their father or widowed mother, but there are numerous instances of men representing their fathers- or mothers-in-law, indicating that the business relation was as important between relatives by marriage as between blood relations. For example, when Domingos Machado was named appraiser of an inventário in 1640, he sent his son-in-law to do the job.[16] Similar cases include sons-in-law who received payment of debts owed to their fathers-in-law, or who signed the receipt for the inheritance of a father-in-law, or else a case where it was the father-in-law who collected the inheritance of his son-in-law.[17]

Marriage alliances were therefore business alliances. It is probable that a man born in São Paulo was identified either as a son or as a son-in-law depending on which family he was representing at that moment. Newly arrived Portuguese men, however, since they had no family of origin in the region, were probably always identified with their in-laws.

The alliance between two families created by a marriage did not disappear with the demise of the daughter who had been the link between the families. For example, in 1610 when Clemente Alveres escaped after committing a crime, the municipal council warned his second wife not to heed his request that she send him his forge, while similarly warning Braz Gonçalves, the father of Clemente's first wife, that neither he nor his sons should take it to Clemente.[18]

Patriarchs were represented in their business dealings not only by sons and sons-in-law but also by their wives. Despite the fact that most women proprietors in seventeenth-century São Paulo were illiterate, they frequently substituted for their husbands.[19] For instance, on many occasions it was the wife who received or made payments.[20] On other occasions, wives made major decisions independently, such as Anna Tenoria, who married off and endowed her eldest daughter while her husband was on a bandeira.[21] Wives' roles as their husbands' representatives were recognized by the authorities.

This was clearly the case when, during the absence of a child's guardian, the *juiz dos órfãos* asked the guardian's wife to come to court in his place and report on the orphan's estate.[22]

Not only did wives represent their husbands in occasional business transactions, but they also administered their estates for long periods of time. Although it was only when a woman became a widow that she legally became the head of household, wives administered the family property while their husbands, sons, and sons-in-law were away for years at a time on slaving expeditions. For instance, the judge placed Henrique da Cunha's inheritance in his wife's hands for her to administer during her husband's absence, and he suggested that she immediately put her cattlemen to oversee the new cattle.[23] Governor Antônio Paes de Saude confirmed this role of Paulista women when he described them in 1698 as "beautiful and manly, and it is customary there for husbands to leave the administration of their property in their wives' hands, for they are very industrious."[24] Such positive opinions of women's ability are found from time to time in inventários; for instance, when the judge gave Miguel Garcia Velho's widow her children's property to administer, he commented that she was very capable and would see to its increase.[25]

BANDEIRAS AS FAMILY ENTERPRISES

Not only did families carry out ordinary business transactions as a corporate unit but it was also families that organized the large slaving expeditions, which were the most important enterprise of seventeenth-century São Paulo. Both blood and marriage relatives formed bandeiras together. The relatives who went to the *sertão* (wilderness) together were mostly male, however, for legitimate wives and daughters stayed in São Paulo, and it was frequently remarked that during an expedition there were few adult men left in São Paulo. (A majority of the adult male Indians also went along as auxiliaries, as well as some Indian women.)[26]

Bandeiras were military expeditions that functioned as contractual enterprises in which some members of a family invested their capital (money, arms, supplies, or Indians) while others invested their labor.[27] For example, in the will Luis Dias made in the sertão, he stated that he came under an arrangement with his father-in-law whereby the captives would be split half and half between them in return for his father-in-law's contribution of one female and two male Indians, a shotgun, a pot, and an axe.[28] What investment was made in a bandeira by members of a family depended on their status and on their capital. The patriarch usually had begun going on expeditions during his youth and continued during his maturity, investing his person and as much of the joint capital, goods, and Indians as he and his wife could afford. In his old age he remained at home and he and his wife received Indians brought back from the wilderness in proportion to their investment in goods and men, that is, both Indians and sons. His widow continued the practice.

Bandeiras were family enterprises. The more wealth a family had, and the more Indians it already possessed, the greater the amount of supplies and Indian auxiliaries it could invest in a bandeira and the greater the rewards in captives. Since dowries always included Indians, marriage to an endowed woman increased a man's possibilities on a bandeira. Moreover, the number of male family members to join an expedition also helped guarantee the expedition's success, making it advantageous for a family to recruit not only sons but also sons-in-law, sending them on expeditions as junior partners of the patriarch or his widow.

Thus marriage and the alliances it produced gave strength to bandeiras. An example of this banding together of male relatives is the bandeira of Antônio Raposo Tavares, which attacked La Guaira in 1628 and included his brother, his father-in-law, his son-in-law, and four grandsons. Also on the expedition were Fernando de Melo and his son-in-law; Baltazar de Morais and two of his sons-in-law; Simão Jorge and two sons; Mateus Neto and two sons; Amaro Bueno and his son-in-law; Francisco Rondon and his two brothers; Calisto da Mota and his brother; Antônio Luiz de Grã and his son and son-in-law; Antônio Raposo Velho with two sons; Pedro Madeira and his son; Gaspar Velho and his son-in-law; and Baltazar Lopes Fragoso and his brother-in-law.[29] Another example is Fernão Dias Paes's famous bandeira in the latter part of the seventeenth century, from which he wrote that he had "taken arms with his relatives."[30] The relatives who went on the expedition included his nephew, his son, his son-in-law, his illegitimate son, and his brother as chaplain.[31]

Unemancipated single sons, filhos-família, went on bandeiras as their parents' representatives and received a cut of the rewards only if their parents so wished. Boys as young as ten or twelve accompanied their relatives on bandeiras. For example, while Fernão Dias Borges was away on an expedition, his wife, Isabel de Almeida, sent their nine- or ten-year-old son, Simão, to his godfather's home with instructions that he was to accompany him on the next bandeira, probably to gain in the field the knowledge he would use throughout his lifetime.[32]

As the young men's expertise—and, therefore, their value to the expedition—increased, they were allowed to keep as their personal property a share of the Indians coming to the family. Since young single men who had not already inherited owned no property, they did not act on their own when they joined a bandeira but as employees or junior partners of the family enterprise that had provided the necessary arms, ammunition, supplies, and Indian auxiliaries. For example, the widow Maria Vitoria declared in her will that she had outfitted her unmarried son, Gervazio de Vitoria, when he went to the sertão with the understanding that the Indians he brought back would be half hers and half his.[33] Francisco Borges said the same in his will, stating that his sons should only receive half the captives they brought back because he had invested in their expedition and they were still filhos-família and under his control.[34] Likewise, some of Catharina do Prado's heirs insisted that the Indians brought back from the sertão by two of her sons while they still lived with her were not theirs, as they claimed, but belonged to her estate and should be divided among all heirs.[35]

Raphael de Oliveira, however, seems not to have believed he had the right to as many of the Indians his single sons brought back as was customary. In his will he was careful to differentiate between the Indians who belonged to him and those he had allowed his sons to retain as their personal property because, as he said, they had risked their lives in procuring them. He stated that he felt it was only while he had been young enough and healthy enough to go himself to the sertão that he should receive a cut of the captives. Nevertheless, Raphael felt the need to enumerate the ways in which his sons had otherwise contributed to the growth of his estate so as to justify his decision to deprive his other heirs by allowing these sons to keep the Indians they had captured.[36]

Besides marrying a woman with a dowry, joining a bandeira was therefore the other way a young man could commence to accumulate independent means. Not only sons or sons-in-law could receive a cut of the captives. A young male orphan raised in the home of Clemente Alveres returned from the wilderness after the latter's death with a large contingent of Indians. He demanded and received two of the new captives as his reward—or payment—because he had risked his life alongside the Indian auxiliaries provided by Clemente.[37]

Once Indian captives were brought back from the wilderness, they entered the family's pool of property and were transmitted by inheritance or dowry. As any asset, Indians could be kept for income or sold for immediate profit. They provided income by working to sustain themselves and their owner's family, and by growing crops or raising pigs, sheep, or cattle that were commercialized to provide their masters with the wherewithal to buy the costly Portuguese imports, such as clothes, that symbolized their status, and to pay the tithes owed to the crown as representative of the church (see Table 1 for the diversity of production).[38] Indians became weavers, carpenters, shoemakers, sailmakers, goldsmiths, silversmiths, or blacksmiths, thereby processing primary products to increase their resale value.[39] They were also the porters who carried the commodities to Santos over the steep mountain range

TABLE I
Production (Seventeenth Century)

	Estates producing	
Product	Number	Percentage
Subsistence crops (mainly manioc, beans, and corn)	47	98
Cotton and cotton cloth	26	55
Pigs and pork	31	65
Cattle[a]	18	38
Horses[b]	10	21
Wheat and flour[c]	17	35
Sugarcane[d]	7	15
Rum	6	13
Vineyards and wine	8	17

SOURCE: Sample, 48 estates.
[a]Eighteen estates were raising cattle, owning from one to 220 head of cattle per estate, for a total of 597 head.
[b]Ten estates owned horses, from one to ten horses per estate, for a total of only thirty horses in the sample. The availability of Indians as porters may help explain the paucity of horses.
[c]Mostly, but not exclusively, estates in Parnaíba, three of which owned flour mills. See Monteiro, "São Paulo," pp. 109–10, for a discussion of flour mills in Parnaíba.
[d]Included five *trapiches*, or sugarmills, run by animal traction.

that separated it from São Paulo, and they were the auxiliaries and guides on the bandeiras organized to capture more Indians.[40]

Besides providing their masters with an income through their labor, Indians themselves could be used as commodities and sold for a one-time capital gain. Wealthy families probably profited in both ways in the course of building their family enterprise, and the number of Indians in an inventário depended on which method was being used when the family head or his wife died. This would explain why some famous *bandeirantes* left good-sized estates but few Indians.

Thus, the Indians captured on bandeiras, inherited, or received in dowry became the principal asset of São Paulo proprietors, as they well knew, remarking that their Indians were "the most profitable property in this land."[41] However, Indians were not legally slaves. In a 1609 law, the crown decreed that Indians could not be bought or sold, nor obliged to work for anyone against their will, and that they must be paid for their work.[42] As soon as the new law was known, however, Paulistas persuaded the governor to declare that, though free, Indians could still be inherited or received in dowry.[43] Indians continued to be traded throughout the seventeenth century, however, though not openly. Legal documents such as inventários constantly reiterated that Indians were free but simultaneously provided hints that Indians were still sold.[44] Some historians therefore maintain that the principal source of revenue for Paulistas was the sale of Indians rather than agricultural surpluses to other captaincies.[45] According to my sample, however, most propertied Paulistas appear to have diversified their efforts, also using Indians to produce subsistence crops and commodities for sale (see Table 1).

THE CLAN-BASED ECONOMY

The amount of money involved in commerce was so small that the famous Paulista clans were poor when compared to plantation and sugarmill owners in the northeast. At the end of the sixteenth century, it took 10,000 cruzados to set up a sugarmill in the northeast, and there were at least 100 planters in Pernambuco with yearly incomes of 5,000 cruzados, whereas in 1653 the whole estate of Pedro Fernandes of Parnaíba was worth only 1,300 cruzados, though he was held to be a wealthy man.[46] The total value of the gross assets held by 41 Paulista estates between 1640 and 1651 was just over 15,000 cruzados. That 41 Paulista estates together owned a total only one and a half times the value of just one sugarmill in the northeast confirms this comparative poverty.[47]

Nevertheless, seventeenth-century São Paulo was a society in which two of the most important assets a family could own were given no monetary value at all in inventários: land and Indians. Land was customarily not included in the assessment of an estate. If they existed, titles to land were added to the inventory, but no value was given to the land nor was it usually explicitly divided among the heirs, as were all other possessions. A monetary value was given only to improvements on the land such as planted crops or houses or barns, and these were divided among heirs.[48] Most land titles that appear in the inventários were received from the crown by way of *sesmarias* or from the municipal council through *cartas de datas de terra*.[49] Since any married man with children or widow with children could receive such grants, land had more of a use value than an exchange value. Land was probably not appraised because it had been received in a grant.

A market in land was, however, beginning to develop in the early seventeenth century. For example, Ursulo Colaço says in his will that he had sold some land to his uncle 25 years before, and though he gave him title to the land, his uncle had not yet paid him.[50] In 1624 Lucrecia Maciel and her second husband sold the land received in sesmaria by her first husband for 18$000.[51] By the end of the century, moreover, even land received in a grant appeared in inventários with an appraised value, having become a commodity.

The poverty of São Paulo's elite was therefore relative. Although the monetary value of their estates was small, they controlled a wealth of resources. This explains why heirs found it necessary to spend money on having an inventário made in nine estates in my sample that were technically bankrupt. Although their liabilities were greater than the assets that were given a monetary value, these estates all had important assets that were given no monetary value; they all had Indians. The total number of Indians owned by the nine bankrupt estates was 210; one estate had 73 Indians, while only two had fewer than 10.

Despite the apparent ease with which settlers could acquire Indians and land, the society of early seventeenth century São Paulo was not egalitarian, even among property owners. It was already stratified, pointing to some accumulation of capital.[52] Table 2 demonstrates that over half the Indians were owned by only 20 percent of the estates and that over half the total appraised wealth (houses, horses, cattle, cultivated fields, tools, household effects, and extremely expensive clothes) was owned by only 12 percent.

The greater concentration of appraised property than of Indians suggests that it was easier to accumulate Indians than other kinds of property. Of the forty-five estates in Table 2 for which Indian ownership is known, only one had no Indians and the rest had from 2 to 137, with ten estates owning over 50 Indians each. Outside the sample, some proprietors had many more; Luzia Leme left 225 Indians in 1655; Antônio Pedroso de Barros left 500 in 1652, and in 1630 Manoel Prêto was reputed to have around 1,000 on his property in Nossa Senhora do O.[53]

The possession of numerous Indians does not appear to correlate with the possession of an estate with a large appraised monetary value. Only two of the five estates in Table 2 with the greatest number of Indians were among the five estates that had the greatest appraised wealth.[54] A family could own practically nothing else and still possess Indians, since their ownership did not entail the outlay of capital that ownership of an African slave did. Cristovão Diniz and his wife, who owned 110 Indians, were among the largest owners of Indians in the sample, but when he died he had so many debts that his estate is in the bottom third with regard to monetary value.[55] Yet he was an important man in the history of São Paulo; not only was he a well-known bandeirante, but his wife was the daughter of Pedro Fernandes, another famous bandeirante who founded the nearby town of Itu and with whom Cristovão founded a chapel. His daughters were married to the sons of Anna Luiz, whose estate was one of the five largest in my sample, both in appraised wealth and in the number of Indians owned. And all his sons and daughters owned large tracts of land from the sesmarias Cristovão had received.

The size of a particular estate depended on inheritance and successful marriage as well as on the business skill of selling commodities and Indians. Seventeenth-century Paulista society was constantly dividing and regrouping property at the moments of death and marriage. When young husbands, for example, died away in the sertão or young wives died in childbirth, half their

TABLE 2

Concentration of Wealth by Assets and Indians Owned
(Seventeenth Century)

Estates (ranked by wealth)[a]			Assets owned[b]	
Top	5	(12%)	1:433$900	(51.6%)
Next	5	(12%)	577$000	(20.8%)
	5	(12%)	345$800	(12.5%)
	5	(12%)	234$600	(8.5%)
	5	(12%)	114$300	(4.1%)
	5	(12%)	58$400	(2%)
	5	(12%)	13$000	(0.5%)
Bottom (bankrupt)	6	(14.5%)	0[c]	(0)
TOTAL	41		2:777$000	
+ 7	(unknown assets)			
SAMPLE	48			

Estates (ranked by ownership of Indians)			Indians and African slaves owned[d]	
Top	5	(11%)	547	(33%)
Next	5	(11%)	350	(21%)
	5	(11%)	215	(13%)
	5	(11%)	172	(10%)
	5	(11%)	128	(8%)
	5	(11%)	85	(5%)
	5	(11%)	73	(4%)
	5	(11%)	55	(3%)
Bottom	5	(11%)	17	(1%)
TOTAL	45		1,642	
+ 3	(number of Indians and Africans unknown)			
SAMPLE	48			

NOTE: Percentages have been rounded off.

[a]The value of the estate used here and in subsequent tables is the whole net estate of a widower or widow and half the net estate owned jointly when the first spouse died. This was done to more fairly compare the estates of individuals, since, because of the community property law, a widower (or widow) owned only half the estate previously owned jointly with his or her spouse.

[b]Rounded off to hundreds of réis.

[c]Liabilities greater than assets (not counting Indians or land, which were given no monetary value).

[d](Indian ownership not corrected for marital status.) Four of the 45 estates whose ownership of Indians is known also owned a few African slaves, which did have monetary value, so they are included as assets in the first part of this table and as slaves here.

estate passed to their heirs, leaving the widower or widow with only half the estate the couple had previously owned, and increasing the property of children or of parents (the necessary heirs of a childless person). Then the survivor usually remarried, again uniting two different properties and enlarging the unit of production.

Since the nuclear family in seventeenth-century São Paulo belonged to the closely knit kin group or clan that structured society, it was not a wholly independent unit of production. Thus the dividing and regrouping of property brought about by death and marriage did not affect the clan, only the individual. For example, the estate of Cristovão Diniz was probably so small in relation to the number of Indians he owned because he had married off his daughters advantageously to the sons of a wealthy family, endowing them handsomely. As his estate decreased, the property administered by his sons-in-law increased, and his daughters went from a status in which they owned no property to one in which they had title to half of the couple's property. Though his individual property had decreased, the clan of Cristovão Diniz had experienced no loss; on the contrary, it had been strengthened by marriage alliances and the formation of new productive and reproductive units. Thus, when patriarchs and their wives substantially reduced their own property to marry off their daughters, it was because they viewed the future of the clan as more important than their own personal fortune.

Family *was* society in seventeenth-century São Paulo, but the organizing principle was not the small nuclear family but the large kin group, the family clan. The clan conducted business, fought feuds, vied for political power, and organized bandeiras. The nuclear family was the smallest unit of production within the clan—a branch of the enterprise, as it were—set up initially with the wife's dowry. And marrying a woman with a dowry was an important way a young man could acquire the property he needed to set up his own productive unit. In seventeenth-century São Paulo, dowry was therefore not a peripheral institution of interest only to women, but was instead a vital element in the economy of society as a whole.

CHAPTER 2

THE IMPORTANCE OF DOWRY

OWRIES WERE significant in the lives of seventeenth-century Paulista proprietors, for they usually provided most of the labor and means of production necessary for a couple to start up their new productive unit. When their daughters married, parents divested themselves of substantial amounts of property for dowries, often giving dowries that were several times larger than what sons would inherit. Furthermore, sons were expected to work hard to contribute toward their sisters' dowries.

The importance of the dowry a wife brought to marriage is illustrated by the words in Angela de o Campo's will: "I am the legitimate daughter of João Baptista Troche and Joanna de o Campo who married me to Diogo Guilhermo and *so that the marriage should take place* gave my husband a list of the things they promised us."[1] Angela's words touch on three characteristics of the marriage system in seventeenth-century São Paulo. First, they indicate that dowry was a requisite for marriage—that is, that marriage was a matter of property. Second, her words show that marriage was arranged, though not by the father alone, but by both parents. This is especially clear in the Portuguese version of Angela's will, for all verbs are in the plural. Third, the dowry was given, not to the daughter alone, nor to her husband, but to both. This was, of course, the only possible way under a community-property system.

Thus the daughters of propertied families never went into marriage empty-handed. Most received a dowry. Parents had endowed their daughters in 43 out of 47 families with married daughters, 91 percent of the seventeenth-century sample.[2] And every one of the married daughters in those 43 families had each received a dowry, no matter how many daughters there were.

The four families that did not give explicit dowries were of widows or widowers whose daughters still took property to their marriage, their maternal or paternal inheritance. Anna Cabral's daughter provides an example of this pattern. When Anna's husband died, their daughter Maria was only fourteen and single. She had married, however, by the time her mother died four years later. Although Anna's *inventário* shows that she had not endowed her daughter, Maria had not gone into marriage empty-handed, for she had already inherited from her father.[3] Every one of the four families who had not given any dowries were families of widows or widowers whose daughters had married with their inheritance.[4]

SIZE OF DOWRIES

Such a large portion of a family's property was spent on dowries that when Martim Rodrigues Tenório promised a dowry to his third daughter and her husband, he listed several of the items as fractions of his possessions. He promised a third of the fields he had planted, a third of the pigs he owned, a portion of his land, half his stock of tin, the house where he lived on the farm plus his house in town, and, if the houses were not acceptable, he stated he was prepared to build other ones or provide the money and land for others to be built.[5] Clearly Martim Rodrigues was willing to go to great lengths for his daughter's marriage.

Most other parents also went out of their way to give dowries, so much so that many women received dowries consisting of greater amounts of property than what their brothers would later inherit. For example, when Maria Gonçalves married in 1623, her father gave her, among other things, at least sixteen Indians. Eighteen years later, when her father died, her brother only inherited five Indians.[6] The livestock in her dowry also compares favorably with his inheritance, for she received ten head of cattle and a horse and saddle, whereas he only got three pigs. (See Table 3.)

The timing of a dowry is itself a great advantage over an inheritance. Besides receiving much more property, Maria Gonçalves had the use of her property for eighteen more years than her brother. In this way even daughters who received dowries that were equal or smaller than their inheritance had an advantage over their brothers. Yet in seventeenth-century São Paulo, most dowries were larger than the daughter's *legítima* (legal inheritance).

TABLE 3
A Dowry Compared to a Brother's Inheritance

Dowry of Maria Gonçalves (given in 1623)	Inheritance of Alvaro Rodrigues (her brother)
Her maternal *legítima** plus:	He probably received his maternal
1 chest	legítima when he married. His
1 tablecloth, 6 napkins	paternal legítima (received 1641)
6 silver spoons	consisted of:
6 plates	1 chest
2 towels	1 buffet
8 scythes	2 chairs
8 hoes	1 mattress
8 wedges	1 book
10 head of cattle	3 pigs
1 horse and saddle	Debt owed the estate, 2$000
At least 16 Indians (list of Indians incomplete)	5 Indians

NOTE: Prices found in other inventários help us to understand the value of the 2$000 credit Alvaro Rodrigues received: a mare, 2$000; 2 silver tumblers and 6 silver spoons, 6$000; 1 small house, 3$200 (no value for the land it was on); 2 *covados* (measurement equal to 66 centimeters) of imported serge, 1$000.

* Legítima was the inheritance to which a son or daughter was entitled by law, arrived at by dividing the net estate of the deceased parent equally among all children. (If the deceased had made a will bequeathing the maximum allowed by law, a third of his or her estate, each child's legítima was arrived at by dividing two-thirds of the parent's net estate equally among all children.) Thus the legítimas of siblings were always equal.

However, though quite a few seventeenth-century wills list dowries, very few were actually appraised.

The best way to demonstrate the great size of seventeenth-century dowries is therefore by analyzing the practice regarding colação.[7] Fewer than 10 percent of the families in the sample had married daughters who brought their dowry back into the estate, à colação, and many times only one or two of a family's married daughters did so. Most seventeenth-century endowed married daughters declined to inherit, indicating that they were satisfied with their dowries as their only inheritance. An example of the exercise of this option can be seen in the inventário of Catharina do Prado. Although she had eleven children, when she died there were only three heirs, two sons and her remaining single daughter, because her eight married daughters refused to inherit.[8] They clearly felt their dowries were as large or larger than the inheritance they would receive if their mother's estate were divided among eleven heirs.

Since most endowed daughters in the seventeenth century refused to inherit, dowry in such cases can be viewed as given in lieu of an inheritance. Suzanna Dias's will is quite explicit on this point. She declared that she was leaving nothing to her four daughters because in the dowries she gave them she had included everything that they could have inherited from her husband and herself.[9]

Whether the dowry was in lieu of the inheritance, however, was finally decided not by the givers but by the recipients, for they could decline to inherit or elect to bring the dowry back into the estate. This provision differed from certain dowry practices in the late Middle Ages in France, in which dowry was used as a means to disinherit a daughter.[10] In seventeenth-century São Paulo, daughters and their husbands refused to inherit because they were satisfied with what they had already received. They also refused because, if their dowries were much larger than their legítima, they would be expected to return the excess to their brothers and sisters.

Since so few daughters in the seventeenth-century sample brought their dowries back into the estate, inventários usually do not provide sufficient information for us to judge what share of the family property was given away in dowry. Though dowries were listed and dowry contracts presented, unless the dowry came in à colação, it was usually not appraised. However, in the case of João Baruel, all married daughters brought their dowries back into the estate, and we can make this calculation. He had divested himself of over a third of his property for dowries, and this fraction was undoubtedly at the lower end of the customary range because married daughters only came in à colação when they believed their dowries to be smaller than their legítimas. Adding to his net estate the three dowries João Baruel gave his daughters and two gifts to his sons, the total was then divided equally among his seven children, and each inheritance included the dowry or gift already received plus other assets to make up the difference. His three daughters' decision to bring their dowries back into the estate had been the correct one, for their dowries were in fact all smaller than their legítima.[11]

THE FAVORING OF DAUGHTERS

A discussion of the importance of dowry in seventeenth-century São Paulo is not complete without considering whether sons received equivalent gifts. The incidence of gifts to sons in the inventários is sporadic, suggesting that a gift to a son was less obligatory than a dowry for a daughter. Only 3 out of 35 families who had lay sons who were either married or over the age of majority had given them gifts.

Neither were gifts to sons as huge as dowries. The largest gift Messia Rodrigues gave a son was worth less than a tenth of the value of the largest dowry she gave.[12] Manoel João Branco had also given his son, Francisco João Leme, a gift, but it was worth only slightly over a third the value of the *smallest* of his two daughters' dowries.[13]

Priests were the only sons to receive pre-mortem gifts from their parents that were as substantial as their sisters' dowries. Priests needed property in land and Indians to give them a living, since the crown supported very few priests in colonial Brazil.[14] And though all young men in seventeenth-century São Paulo required such property to establish themselves independently, priests were the only sons who could not marry and receive that property in a wife's dowry. João Baruel, for example, gave his son, the Reverend Father Francisco Baruel, a patrimony worth 7 percent of his estate, but he gave nothing to two other sons who became mendicant friars and whose few needs were taken care of by the order.[15] The patrimony given to priests sometimes cut into the other heirs' inheritance. Such was the case of the patrimony Maria Leite da Silva had promised her son, Padre João Leite da Silva, worth 150$000. When she died, her total estate only amounted to 305$780, so that when the patrimony and other debts were subtracted, each of her three other sons received only 16$352.[16]

Dowries also depleted the family's property to the detriment of sons or single daughters, even if the dowry had not yet been paid when one of the parents died. A promised dowry was considered a debt, and all debts were subtracted from assets before dividing the estate among the heirs. For example, when Pedro de Oliveira was presumed dead after seven years in the sertão, his estate was worth 143$163, but since his debts amounted to 118$770, his wife's half share of the estate was only 12$201, and each of his minor children inherited only 2$440. However, his married daughter, Antonia de Paiva, had received a dowry, part of which was still unpaid and included in the debts. Her father still owed Antonia two and a half *arrobas* of iron plus 10,000 tiles and half the vineyard. The vineyard was given no value, but the other two items added up to 12$850. This part was therefore worth more than the entire estate left to the other children, and it was only a part of the dowry, the total of which was not recorded.[17] Antonia was therefore much wealthier than her brothers or sisters, or even her mother.

The extreme advantage of some married daughters over their siblings, especially their brothers, was common in seventeenth-century São Paulo. Another estate that was depleted by a promised dowry was that of Pedro Dias Paes Leme, who died in 1633 with a recently married daughter. Since his assets were worth 158$720 and his debts amounted to 123$440, his net estate was worth 33$530. Dividing it in half gave his widow 16$765, and each of his eight other children received an inheritance of only 2$098. But his married daughter, Maria Leite, was highly favored, for out of the sum reserved for payment of debts, she received her promised dowry of 80$000.[18]

Although it was brothers who bore the brunt of the extreme favoring of sisters, they were encouraged to think that this was as it should be.[19] Wills constantly exhorted sons to provide for their sisters' marriages. Providing for sisters was frequently given as a reason for joining an expedition to the sertão. For example, one of Estevão Furquim's sons went twice to the wilderness while still a minor "to look for a remedy for himself and for his sisters," and one of his married sisters lent him one of her male Indians to help him on the expedition.[20] Since at least half the Indians brought back by minor sons remained their parents' property, sons did in fact contribute to their sisters' dowries.

Brothers also endowed their sisters more explicitly, thereby arranging their marriages.[21] For example, Captain Amaro Alveres Tenório declared in his will that he had endowed his sister Anna do Prado. However, since he was her guardian after their father died, her inheritance may have been at least a part of what he gave her.[22] In another case, Maria de Siqueira and her husband Aleixo Jorge gave the house that they had received in dowry to her unmarried sister for her dowry, giving as their reason their wish to help their mother in view of the many debts she had to pay after her husband's death.[23] João Pedroso, on his part, gave his whole inheritance to his half-sister for her dowry.[24] Clearly the good of the family demanded sacrifices.

Only rarely did a male heir object to the favoring of his female relatives. One example is that of Ursulo Colaço, who complained in his will that his widowed grandmother gave such large dowries to her granddaughters that there was nothing left for him to inherit when she died.[25] Yet his grandmother's favoring of her granddaughters is consonant with the prevalent practice in seventeenth-century São Paulo, and Ursulo himself had probably married a well-endowed woman.

Sometimes a parent felt the need to receive the consent of the other heirs when excessively favoring a daughter. Such was the case of Constantino Coelho Leite, who declared in his will that he had endowed his second daughter so magnificently that it cut into the inheritance of his three sons, but they had agreed to the dowry and had agreed not to demand restitution.[26] On his part, Lourenço Castanho Taques asked his sons not to require their sisters to bring their large dowries back into the estate, in consideration of their current straitened circumstances.[27] And Fernão Dias Paes and his brothers told their mother to conceal certain property from the inventário of their father and to use it to give better dowries to their sisters, although that meant depriving themselves of a part of their inheritance.[28]

Endowing a daughter was so very important that it led Anna Tenorio to go rashly overboard. When her husband, Pedro Fernandes, was away in the sertão and she did not know whether he was dead or alive, she married off her daughter by her first husband and gave her a very large dowry. Since Maria was not Pedro's daughter, Anna should have had his consent to give such a large dowry, especially since she had brought only a small estate and many debts to the marriage and the dowry decreased the inheritance of the children they had in common. Pedro did not question her right to give such a large dowry when he returned, however, but her other children did so after Pedro died. The problem was resolved by having the amount of the dowry deducted from Anna's half of the estate, so that it did not cut into her children's paternal inheritance. When Anna died, Maria and her husband were expected to return a part of the dowry to Anna's other children, having had the usufruct those many years.[29] Maria had indeed been favored, though her brothers doubtless married women with great dowries.

BEQUESTS FOR DOWRIES

The favoring of daughters started early in their lives, for bequests or gifts were bestowed on girls explicitly for their dowry long before they married, even in childhood or before they were born. The phrases most commonly used when someone was making a present or bequest to a young single girl was *para ajuda de seu dote* (to help her dowry) or *para ajuda de seu casamento* (to help her marriage). For example, while Izabel de Proença was still a little girl, she received a herd of cattle from her uncle for her dowry.[30]

A good example of the explicit favoring of daughters over sons that was characteristic in seventeenth-century São Paulo is found in Pedro de Araujo's will.[31] When he lay dying in 1638, knowing that his wife was pregnant with their first child, he took into account the sex of the unborn child in his will. He declared that if the child was a girl, she was to receive not only her legítima—that is, her legal share of the inheritance—but also the remainder of his *terça*—the major portion (after funeral, masses, and minor bequests were paid) of the third of his estate that he could freely will.[32] When he left her the remainder of his terça, he was obviously thinking of the property she would take into marriage, her dowry. If the child was a boy, however, Pedro wanted the remainder of his terça to go to his wife and not to his son.[33]

Despite arranged marriages, many seventeenth-century married couples apparently cared for each other, because a majority of married testators left the remainder of their terça to their spouses. Table 4 shows that 60 percent of the married men left it to their wives, and 53 percent of the married women left it to their husbands. Most testators gave no reason for leaving the remainder of the terça to their spouses, but Ignes Dias de Alvarenga declared that she left it to her husband "because of the satisfaction he has given me," demonstrating that love or affection existed.[34]

It is especially significant that the male testators who left the remainder of the terça to their wives did so unconditionally, that is, they did not specify that their wives must not remarry to retain the bequest. This practice was surely a consequence of the sizable dowries their wives brought to marriage. Since such a large part of the couple's community property came initially from the wife's dowry, a man probably did not seek to limit his wife's option

TABLE 4

Recipients of the Remainder of the Terça by Sex and Marital Status of the Testator (Seventeenth Century)

	Married testators				Widowed testators				
Recipients	Male		Female		Male		Female		Total
Spouse	21	(60%)	12	(53%)	—		—		33
Sons	1	(2%)	0		0		3	(25%)	4
Single daughters	8	(23%)	9	(39%)	4	(67%)	5	(42%)	26
Married daughters	0		1	(4%)	0		2	(17%)	3
All children	2	(5%)	1	(4%)	0		1	(8%)	4
Illegitimate children	2	(5%)	0		0		1	(8%)	3
Church	1	(2%)	0		2	(33%)	0		3
TOTAL	35		23		6		12		76

SOURCE: Seventy-six testators whose wishes regarding the remainder of their terça are known: 41 male and 35 female.

NOTE: "Daughters" includes granddaughters, and "sons" includes grandsons. Percentages are rounded off. The widow who left the remainder of her terça to illegitimate children left it to her son's offspring.

to remarry because his bequest was not entirely of *his* property. For example, as we shall see below, Pedro de Araujo's wife had brought more to the marriage than he had, so that when she received the remainder of the terça (she had a son), it meant that after adding the remainder to her legal half of their community property, the total came to approximately what she had originally brought to the marriage. Thus his bequest was of property originally owned by his wife's family. He was giving her what was hers.

When bequeathing to their children, both fathers and mothers favored single daughters over all other children. (See Table 4.) A few mothers, however, gave the remainder of the terça to their married daughters or granddaughters or to sons. One widow whose daughters were all married left the remainder to one of her married sons to help him provide for his daughters; thus, even when favoring her son, she was thinking of her granddaughters.[35]

The bequest of the remainder of the terça to single daughters was equivalent to giving them large dowries, since these women took their legítima and bequest into marriage. Thus, bequeathing the remainder of the terça to a single daughter ensured that she would have a large dowry. But since dowry was a duty of both parents, the widowed spouse was expected to add a dowry to this inheritance from his or her property, and most seventeenth-century Paulistas did so.

When a single daughter received the remainder of the terça, it meant she took to marriage much more property than her brothers inherited. (This was especially true when there were many children, for the inheritance had to be divided equally among all the heirs.) For example, when Catharina do Prado died in 1649, she left the remainder of the terça to her single daughter, Joanna da Cunha. Each heir's legítima was 52$106, but Joanna received that amount plus the remainder of the terça, a total of 106$226, twice the inheritance of each of her brothers.[36]

When Estevão Furquim died in 1660, he also left the remainder of the terça to his three single daughters. They each received almost twice the monetary assets and four times the Indians that each of their five brothers received (24$880 versus 15$000, and four adult Indians and their children versus one adult Indian and children).[37]

The very large dowries given by seventeenth-century Paulistas and their large bequests to single daughters help explain the finding that practically all daughters of propertied families married. In 56 of 58 families with daughters of marriageable age, there were no single daughters over age 25.[38] Marriage was clearly the rule for propertied women.

In those two families where all daughters over 25 had not married, it was the youngest daughter who had not married, suggesting that she remained to care for her widowed parent. The youngest daughter of the widower Gaspar Cubas o Velho had probably not married before he died so as to accompany and take care of him, for he says in his will that he did not remarry because of her.[39] And though Manoel Rodrigues's four eldest daughters had married before he died in 1646, six single daughters remained, ranging in age from 26 to 15, but when his widow died 26 years later, all these daughters had married except the youngest.[40] Even these exceptions show that marriage was the rule among owners of property.

DOWRY WITHIN MARRIAGE

Not only the size of dowries but also the kind of property that dowries contained undoubtedly encouraged marriage. An example is the dowry of Maria de Proença, whose parents, Baltazar Fernandes and Izabel de Proença, went on May 6, 1641, to the home and office of the Parnaíba notary to register a dowry contract. Before the notary and other witnesses, they jointly promised to give the following in dowry to their daughter and her husband:

Their daughter dressed in black satin, with two other fine dresses and gold earrings and a gold necklace;[41]

A bed with its curtains and linens, a table and six chairs, a buffet, table-cloths and towels, thirty china dishes, two chests with their locks, a large and a small copper pot;

A farm in São Sebastião with a tiled house, a field of manioc, and a field
     of cotton;
A house in town;
Twenty agricultural tools;
Two African slaves;
Thirty Indians;
One boat or canoe with oars;
Five hundred *alqueires* of flour placed in Santos.

Baltazar Fernandes and his wife Izabel de Proença added that all this they
gave to their daughter and her husband forever in the knowledge that each
spouse would own half of the property.[42]

The above illustrates the principal characteristic of seventeenth-century
Paulista dowries: they all, no matter their size, contained the means of production and Indians or African slaves necessary to start a new enterprise.
Great dowries like Maria de Proença's included clothes for the bride, jewels,
bed and table linens, and other housekeeping objects that smaller dowries
lacked, but they all had means of production. For example, Antonia Dias
received in dowry a dress and four Indians, while Beatriz Rodrigues only received nine Indians.[43] Maria Vidal's dowry had one dress, a cow, two sheets
of silver, and two Indians.[44] All dowries, whether large or small, included
Indians.[45]

A wife's contribution in dowry was vital to the support of her new family,
for she brought much of what was needed to start up a productive establishment. The Indians she contributed worked to provide their own and the family's subsistence plus commodities to sell. Besides Indians, her dowry could
include land and houses and maybe one or two African slaves. Many women
contributed cattle, pigs, or horses; others brought planted fields of cotton,
wheat, or manioc, ready for harvest. Because of the lack of specie in seventeenth-century Brazil, few women brought cash to marriage; instead they
contributed commodities ready for sale, such as loads of flour or wheat, which
would be sold to supply the capital for buying cattle, tools, or supplies.

The question remains, however, whether it was daughters themselves or
their husbands who were being favored by these large productive dowries. Yet
though a man clearly profited from the establishment he was able to set up
with his wife's dowry, she benefited as much as her husband from the couple's
standard of living. And Paulistas themselves believed they were favoring
their daughters, because they always phrased bequests to single daughters in
terms of their concern for their future. Pero Nunes, for example, declared in
his will that what he had given his daughter Maria was "for her marriage and
to help her in life."[46]

A dowry not only provided materially for a woman's future, it also was a
source of pride. Though it disappeared into the pool of a couple's goods, a

wife did not forget her contribution. For example, in 1680 when Aleixo Garcia da Cunha died as a very old man, he declared in his will that certain lands he owned with his brothers had been given to his grandmother Domingas da Cunha in dowry, "as she always said."[47] That dowry must have meant a great deal to his grandmother, who was careful to tell her grandchildren about it, and also to her grandson, who remembered it so many years later.

Yet because wives did not control their dowry, marriage could appear to have been a property contract between men. For instance, Estevão Furquim, guardian of his minor brothers- and sisters-in-law, wrote in his will that he had married off his two sisters-in-law to two brothers and had handed over the women's inheritance to their husbands.[48] Although the property belonged to the woman as her inheritance, it passed from the hands of one man into the hands of another, from guardian to husband (as in other cases it went from father to husband).

However, when we consider that a widow, or a wife in her husband's absence, also married off her daughter and transferred property to the new son-in-law, we must conclude that gender was not the determining factor on the giving side, but, rather, position in the family. It was the patriarch or his representative—wife, widow, or guardian (usually a male relative, but sometimes a grandmother)—who made the deal with the son-in-law or with the son-in-law's parents. Property passed from a family of the older generation through their daughter to her new family, a younger generation.

Yet though the dowry was legally given by both husband and wife and received by both daughter and son-in-law, men frequently said "I gave my daughter a dowry" whereas their wives would invariably say "we gave," unless they were already widows when they endowed their daughters.[49] The male perception of themselves as sole actors undoubtedly reflected the patriarchal organization of the family. Although marriage was a partnership between the spouses in which all property was held in common, the husband was the legal head of the partnership, or *cabeça de casal*, and administrator of all the jointly held property, and therefore felt decisions were his alone. But precisely because property was jointly owned, the law made the wife's explicit consent necessary in any transfer of property, especially real estate.[50] Dowry was such a transfer of property and notaries always made a point of the presence and consent of the wife in the giving of dowry.

Just as men saw themselves as acting alone in the giving of dowries, they also acted many times as though the recipient of the dowry were the son-in-law. For example, when listing and appraising the dowries that came in à colação after the death of Messia Rodrigues, only the names of the sons-in-law are given. Messia herself had absorbed this patriarchal view of the dowry, for in her will she did not mention her daughters but named her sons-in-law as the recipients of the dowries she gave as a widow.

Yet wives knew they were co-owners of the community property and felt part of both the giving and receiving, though the son-in-law officially received the property as head of the family and as legal administrator of the couple's jointly owned community property, and the father officially gave the dowry as head of the family. That the wives' participation in the process was more than a formality can be seen in the frequent references made by female testators to the property they owned or to the dowries they had given. Izabel Fernandes, for example, declared in her will: "We married our daughter Izabel Ferreira to Bento Fernandes and gave her her dowry, of which we still owe a good skirt and a silk vest and headdress, and everything else we could we have given."[51] The widow Catharina Diniz said that she had married off her three daughters and had given them everything she had promised in dowry, and that she owned land in Juquerí that she had given to two sons-in-law and to a granddaughter.[52] Like many other female testators, Maria Rodrigues used strong words to assert her right to dispose of her property: "I declare that the farm on which my son-in-law, Simão da Motta, lives is his and I want nobody to meddle with him as that is my will."[53]

In one case at least, it was not the husband but the wife who knew (and therefore probably had decided) exactly what their daughter had received in dowry. When Manoel João Branco listed his daughters' dowries in his will, he said that his wife, Maria Leme, had delivered the 100 head of cattle they had promised their second daughter, and that she was the one who knew the exact number of African slaves and Indians given.[54]

Although the law made the husband the head of household, the law also specified that both partners be present and give their consent to any transaction involving the alienation of real estate.[55] Husbands and wives were therefore partners and perceived as such by the authorities in seventeenth-century São Paulo, as can be seen when the notary summoned João Baruel's endowed heirs. He first went to the home of the eldest daughter, Francisca de Siqueira, and summoned both husband and wife and reported that they both told him they did not want to bring their dowry à colação. He then went to Maria de Siqueira's house, and, learning that the couple would enter à colação, cited the husband both in his own right and in place of his wife "because she was in childbirth and could not come to the village." Then he went to the third daughter's house, and summoned her in her own right, and, because her husband was away, he also "cited her in place of her husband."[56] Thus it is clear that he viewed both members of the couple as necessary parts of the legal process and interchangeable.

The sizable dowry a wife brought to marriage may have given weight to her opinion despite her husband's legal status as head of the family. For example, when the notary summoned Messia Rodrigues, he recorded that she told him she did not want to be an heir to her mother's estate—that is, to bring her dowry back à colação. He then asked her husband, who replied that since his wife thought they should not inherit, he did not want to inherit either. Messia was more important in this couple's decision-making than we would assume, considering the long tradition of Brazilian patriarchal power.

The competence and confidence in their ownership shown by some women may have come with age, however. Young widows, even though legally competent to administer their lives and estates, still had marriages arranged for them by their parents. For example, Gaspar Cubas declared in his will that he had married his daughter Izabel Cubas to Sebastião da Costa, and that after Sebastião died, he married her to Luis Soares.[57] This example suggests that a young widow did not have the independence or authority of an older widow. It also demonstrates that women were still considered a part of their family of origin after they married.

Married women's importance to their family of origin is also shown by the prominence of their male relatives in the process of inventário when a young married woman or her husband died. Fathers or brothers usually represented young widows when their husbands died, and they were the witnesses to a young married woman's will.[58] A married daughter was therefore not on her own, but was still a part of her family of origin.

Marriage among seventeenth-century São Paulo propertied families was very different from what it was to become by the middle of the nineteenth century. Because of the process by which marriage took place, the actors who intervened, and the kind of explicit and implicit bargain made, marriage was as much a family affair as it was an arrangement between individuals, and the *sine qua non* was the transference of property from the bride or her family to the newly wed couple.

In such a marriage system, daughters were clearly privileged. Most of them received dowries, many of them several times the amount their brothers would inherit subsequently, and daughters who only married with their inheritance had been given such large bequests that they also received more than their brothers. Since dowries usually contained Indians and always included means of production, they provided a large proportion of the initial and continuing support of the newly married couple. The giving of such large dowries obviously promoted marriage, for the brothers of sisters with sizable dowries could expect to receive comparable amounts from their brides if they chose to marry. The question is, why did families want so badly to promote marriage? And what did a daughter's marriage bring to her family?

CHAPTER 3

THE MARRIAGE BARGAIN

HE EXTREME FAVORING of daughters by seventeenth-century São Paulo property owners was clearly a strategy used to enlarge and consolidate the clan, the organizing principle of military, political, and productive enterprise. Large dowries encouraged men to marry, and marriages added sons-in-law to a family while helping sons establish themselves. As a way to explain the seventeenth-century practice of dowry, this chapter will describe the marriage bargain and how it benefited each side.

In the first place, by promising good dowries, families gained leverage in the arrangement of marriages. This power is quite obvious in the case of Raphael de Oliveira, who married his son by his first wife to his stepdaughter—the daughter of his second wife by her first husband. While he gave his stepdaughter a dowry that included her maternal inheritance, twenty years later he had still not paid his son, her husband, his maternal inheritance.[1] To endow a daughter was therefore a more important duty than seeing that a son received his inheritance. Or, phrased another way, a daughter's inheritance had priority over a son's. This state of affairs could only have been due to the desire to encourage certain marriages. Certainly, if Raphael de Oliveira's son had received his maternal inheritance and thereby become independent from his father, he might not have married the girl his father wanted him to marry, or he might not have married at all, taking an Indian concubine instead. Dowry was clearly an instrument of parental control. Although most patriarchs and their wives did not control both bride and groom as Raphael de Oliveira did, his example illuminates what dowry meant for the class of property owners. When parents gave dowries to their daughters, but not equivalent gifts to their sons, which might make them independent, they were retaining control of how family and class were reproduced.

Marriage was thus not a personal affair so much as a family one, and it enhanced a family in many ways. The marriage of one's children continued both parents' lineage because in Brazil, as in Portugal, lineage was transmitted through both men and women.[2] Furthermore, the marriage of a son gave the family as a whole an alliance with the bride's family plus a new unit of production set up mostly with the bride's dowry. Conversely, through the marriage of a daughter her family gained a new partner, who could contribute to the expansion of the family enterprise.

In fact, marrying off a daughter meant not losing her, but acquiring a son-in-law. And if the family's own sons were minors, the marriage of a daughter gave a family a second adult male who could take the place of an absent or deceased father; this is possibly an explanation of why some daughters married very young. Out of thirty families in which the ages of the eldest child are known, fifteen had married daughters even though the eldest child was a minor, twenty-four years old or under (in two cases the eldest child was only fifteen, and in another two, only sixteen). For example, besides his daughter Antonia de Paiva, who was married to Affonso Dias, Pedro de Oliveira's five heirs were children aged seven to sixteen. Affonso Dias figured prominently in the process of Pedro's inventário, since he was the one who settled the matters of the estate.[3] In the case of Bernardo da Motta, mentioned above, it also was his son-in-law, Estevão Furquim, who became the tutor of his minor brothers- and sisters-in-law and administered their estate.[4] Although sons in their teens were too young to take over, a daughter in her teens was old enough to marry and thus bring another adult man into the family to perform the male role.

DOWRY AND RESIDENCE

If the bride's family was interested in acquiring a son-in-law to perform the adult male role, it would be important to have the new couple live nearby. A dowry undoubtedly helped determine the residence of the couple when it included a house or land. Of thirty-three seventeenth-century Paulista dowries, seventeen contained land, nine of which also included an urban house, while eight other dowries had only an urban house.[5] Those 25 couples who received land or houses in their dowries would naturally tend to live near the wife's family.

Captain João Mendes Giraldo of the village of Parnaíba was quite explicit about endowing his daughter with a house in order to have her live near her parents. In the document he made listing his daughter's dowry, he stated that he would give his son-in-law a house with a tiled roof in Parnaíba if the newlyweds would live in Parnaíba. If they would not, he did not consider himself under any obligation to settle a house on them.[6] This condition carried some force, considering that his future son-in-law lived in São Paulo at the time, not Parnaíba.

Besides insuring that the daughter and son-in-law lived nearby, giving land in dowry had another advantage for her family. Since a sesmaria required that the land be cultivated within three years for ownership to continue, to endow a daughter with land received in sesmaria reinforced the family's hold on that land.[7] For example, Braz Rodrigues de Arzão stated in his will that, due to arrangements he had made with his brothers, a certain piece of land was his, and he had settled his son-in-law on it and given him a part of it. Having his son-in-law living on and cultivating the land with his Indians meant the family had strengthened their claim on that land.[8] Giving land was thus not a loss to the larger family but a gain.

The more sons and sons-in-law settled on a family's land the stronger would be the family's claim to it. Most of the families that gave land therefore gave it to all their daughters or to all their children. For example, Maria Bicuda declared in her will that she and her husband had given their first son-in-law 400 *braças* of land and 100 *braças* each to their other two sons-in-law.[9] Cristovão Diniz stated in his will that he had had a sesmaria in his possession for over four years and that each one of his sons had his half league on it and so did each of his married daughters, while he had kept only half a league for himself.[10] Giving land in this context was thus a way to expand family resources, except that it was not the parents' nuclear family that benefited but the larger kin.

NOBILITY AND RACE IN THE MARRIAGE BARGAIN

There were other ways in which giving a substantial dowry benefited the larger kin. For example, a good dowry could attract noble blood, an important consideration at a time in which nobility conferred much more status than wealth. The eighteenth-century São Paulo genealogist Frei Gaspar da Madre de Deus claimed that seventeenth-century Paulistas gave such large dowries to daughters who married penniless arrivals because they wanted to incorporate noble blood into their families.[11] Noble status, even if it were only as a *fidalgo* (the lowest rank), gave newcomers the opportunity to make an excellent match, even though they had few or no other assets.

His *fidalguia* clearly helped Dom João Matheus Rendon, who married

Maria Bueno de Ribeira, a daughter of the prominent Paulista Amador Bueno, who undoubtedly gave his daughter a large dowry.[12] Yet they did not do well, and by the time D. Maria Bueno (who acquired the "Dona" because of her husband's status) died in 1646, their estate had more debts than assets (though they possessed 104 Indians and two sesmarias that were given no monetary value). The judge divided the Indians between the widower and his children and left the other assets with the widower so that he could pay off the debts.[13] By 1654 Dom João Matheus Rendon had married Catharina de Goes, the very wealthy widow of Valentim de Barros.[14] His status must have weighed heavily in both marriage bargains.

Another example in which an outsider's status undoubtedly weighed significantly is that of Simão Borges Cerqueira, who, according to Pedro Taques, had been one of King Henrique's attendants.[15] He married Leonor Leme, of the important Leme family, and became a notary in São Paulo. Thus he brought his wife's family a claim to nobility and a profession. When he died, however, their estate was much smaller than the estate of Leonor's two sisters, Maria Leme and Luzia Leme. If her family conformed to the customary seventeenth-century practice, Leonor's dowry had probably been the same size as those of her two sisters, so that the small size of Leonor and Simão's estate could only have been because her husband brought no assets to the marriage or because he had little business ability.[16]

The fidalguia and resulting status that some Portuguese sons-in-law brought into their wife's family may help explain why some parents favored some daughters not only over their sons but also over other daughters. It would certainly help explain Margarida Rodrigues's dowry, which was five times as large as her sisters'.[17] She was one of the two (out of nine) daughters of Messia Rodrigues who were given the title "Dona" by the eighteenth-century genealogist Pedro Taques, a title they must have acquired from their husbands. Their sisters had all married men from São Paulo, but Margarida and her sister Catharina married Portuguese men who, according to Pedro Taques, had claims to nobility.[18]

Since most of the men who arrived from Portugal did not have noble blood, however, their contribution to the marriage transaction was probably the infusion of white blood into the mixed-blood Paulista families. Margarida and Catharina Rodrigues may have benefited both from their husbands' nobility and from their European ancestry, for the sisters belonged to the important São Paulo family, the Pires, who descended from the Indian chief Piquerobí.[19]

The marriage of daughters may thus have become even more important than that of sons in the early years of São Paulo's history because families wished to improve their race. In 1561 the officials of the municipal council of São Paulo sent a petition to the crown asking that it "please send deportees who are not thieves to this town to help populate it, for there are many mixed-blood women here whom they can marry." [20] The mestizo women mentioned by the officials of the town council were undoubtedly the settlers' daughters and granddaughters. To them, "populating" must have meant, first of all, increasing the influence of Christianity and Portuguese culture vis-à-vis the Indians by recruiting Portuguese men who would aid in the process of gaining control. Second, it must have also meant recruiting Europeans who, by marrying the mestizo descendants of the first settlers, would whiten the succeeding generations to elevate them above the remaining mestizos and Indians. [21] The cry made by the officials of the São Paulo town council was a cry to perpetuate their families' rule of the society by whitening their lineage.

Several years before founding São Paulo, the Jesuits had already expressed their concern regarding the issue of a white population in Brazil. Father Nóbrega had written from Bahia suggesting that the crown send orphan girls and even prostitutes from Portugal. He thought that the better class of Portuguese men would then marry the orphans, while men of the lower class could marry the prostitutes. [22] He appears therefore to have been concerned not only that Portuguese men were taking Indian women as concubines (and not marrying them), but also that they were not producing white children.

Father Leonardo Nunes also showed a concern with the reproduction of the white race, viewing mestizo women as better spouses for Portuguese men than Indian women. In a letter written from São Vicente in 1551, he congratulated himself on having persuaded several single men to leave their Indian mistresses and marry the "daughters of white men," that is, women of mixed blood. [23] If his only concern had been the immorality of concubinage, he would have urged the men to marry their Indian concubines. Thus, as long as the whites who settled in São Paulo were primarily men, mestizo women had an advantage over Indian women.

Mixed-blood women also had an advantage over their brothers. As long as few or no Portuguese women came to São Paulo, it was only through the daughters of the mestizo founding families that the whitening process could come about, since sons could find no white partners and had necessarily to marry mestizo women. [24] Studying the genealogies of over a dozen of the Paulista founding families has led me to conclude that, until the end of the eighteenth century, men were the great majority of the Portuguese newcomers to São Paulo. Except for the few male and female descendants of three or four Portuguese couples who came to São Vicente in the middle of the sixteenth century, the pure Europeans who married into the old Paulista families were exclusively male. [25]

The propensity of Paulistas to marry their daughters to newly arrived Europeans was noted in 1698 by Governor Antonio Paes de Sande. He said the women of São Paulo were "industrious and more inclined to marry their daughters to strangers who would raise their status, than to local men who were their equals."[26] (This quotation also shows how mothers were seen as important actors in the arrangement of their daughters' marriages.)

That the Portuguese newcomers to São Paulo were mostly male also explains why many old Paulista families trace their lineage back to the founding fathers almost exclusively through the female line. For example, the famous late seventeenth-century priest, Dr. Guilherme Pompêu de Almeida, wrote that his ancestry went back to the founder of São Paulo, João Ramalho, through his mother, Ana Lima, the daughter of João Pedrozo and Maria de Lima, who, he goes on to say, "was the daughter of João da Costa, who had married the daughter of Domingos Luiz o Carvoeiro, who had married the daughter of Jeronimo Dias Cortes, who had married the daughter of Bartholomeu Camacho, who had married the daughter of João Ramalho" (who had married the daughter of Tibiriça, an Indian chief).[27] He only mentions male European names after his grandmother's, thereby emphasizing his European background, but a look at the resulting genealogical tree shows that he traces his lineage exclusively through the female line (see Figure 1).

That the Europeans who came to São Paulo were mostly male also helps

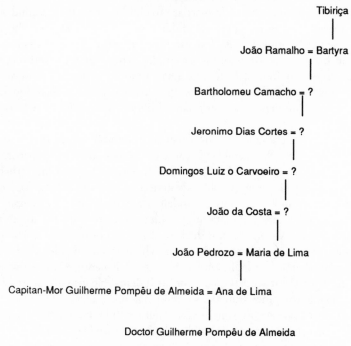

Fig. 1. *Ancestry of Dr. Guilherme Pompêu de Almeida.*

explain why throughout colonial times the surname chosen for many of a family's children was as likely to be the mother's name as the father's. (The use of different surnames for the different children of the same married couple was an old Portuguese custom.)[28] In São Paulo 45 percent of all daughters and 23 percent of all sons in the seventeenth-century sample carried their mother's instead of their father's surname. The frequent use of the mother's surname may well have been because, despite claims by eighteenth-century Paulista genealogists, most seventeenth-century Portuguese newcomers brought no claim to distinction with them, while their wives belonged to the powerful families of São Paulo and had contributed most of the couple's property.[29]

OTHER CONTRIBUTIONS OF SONS-IN-LAW

Since only a trickle of Portuguese men reached São Paulo in the seventeenth century, most Paulista families had to marry their daughters to other Paulistas. Many married them to relatives, thereby consolidating property within the immediate family. Some married nieces to uncles.[30] Some married their children to their childrens' cousins. Others, like Raphael de Oliveira, married children from their first marriage to children from their second wife's first marriage.[31] At other times the children of one family married the children of a neighboring family. For example, in 1652 Domingos Fernandes stated in his will that three of his six children (two daughters and one son) married three children of Domingos Dias o moço.[32] Three of Antonio Bicudo's sons married three daughters of Francisco de Alvarenga and Luzia Leme.[33] And Domingos Cordeiro married his two daughters to two sons of Raphael de Oliveira.[34]

Other families chose their sons-in-law for their abilities, or their sons-in-law chose to marry the daughter because of the resources and expertise the family held. When a son-in-law fit in with the kind of ventures his father-in-law was interested in, it was doubly advantageous. Captain Martim Rodrigues Tenório, for example, combined bandeirante activity with commerce and showed a strong interest in metallurgy, which correlates with the interests of his sons-in-law.[35] When Martim died in 1612, two of his sons-in-law were Clemente Alveres and Cornelio de Arzão, who both had metallurgical expertise. Besides being a prominent bandeirante, Clemente Alveres owned a forge and operated it with the labor of his Indians. He also discovered fourteen gold and iron mines around São Paulo in as many years.[36] The other son-in-law, Cornelio de Arzão, came to São Paulo with D. Francisco de Souza in 1599 for the express purpose of building foundries (see Figure 2).[37]

The complementarity of Martim Rodrigues's sons-in-law's abilities suggests parental strategy. Martim must have had a strong interest in mines and the

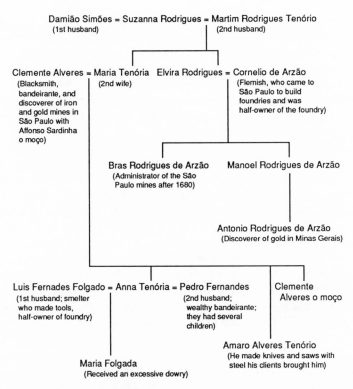

Fig. 2. Family tree of Martim Rodrigues Tenório. Note: Not all children are included in the tree. All professions were carried out principally by or with the help of trained Indians. See Appendix A.V for the dowry of Elvira Rodrigues.

future of ironworks. In 1607 he recorded the opening of a foundry in his book of accounts, and some historians have inferred it was his, although it was not listed as his property when he died in 1612.[38] Whether the foundry belonged specifically to Martim Rodrigues or not, it at least belonged to his family, for half the foundry was owned in 1628 by his daughter Elvira Rodrigues and her husband, Cornelio, when the Inquisition confiscated her husband's share of their property.[39] The other half of the foundry was owned in 1628 by Anna Tenória, Martim's granddaughter (daughter of Clemente Alveres), with her husband, Luis Fernandes, who was a smelter by profession and made tools.[40] Luis fit the family preference for sons-in-law with metallurgical expertise.[41] And Anna Tenória's brother continued operating their father's forge with the help of Indians trained as blacksmiths.[42] (See Figure 2.)

Thus, for a man in seventeenth-century São Paulo, marriage was much more than becoming a woman's spouse: it meant joining a family, with responsibilities not only to his wife but to her family as well. David Ventura is the exception that confirms this rule, for despite accepting the larger part of his wife's dowry, he never lived with her nor continued his partnership with his father-in-law, yet he did repay his debt to the family. When David married Manoel João Branco's daughter Anna Leme, he was promised a very large dowry, which included half the value of a ship for the slave trade to Angola. According to Manoel's will, David took or sent the ship to Angola in partnership with his father-in-law, but their accounts had never been settled because David wanted to buy his father-in-law's share and Manoel João would not agree.[43] Sometime after the wedding, David had left São Paulo without his bride and established himself in Bahia. The only part of the dowry he had received was the half ship, though he appears to have retained usufruct of his father-in-law's half. His wife continued to live with her parents and received another part of her dowry: cattle, Indians, two slaves whom she sold, and some houses that she rented.[44] David proceeded to build a fortune in Bahia. When he died a widower many years later, he willed his fortune to his wife's grandniece for her dowry, and she married in Bahia, starting the powerful family that came to be called the Lemes of David Ventura.[45] In this way he paid back his wife's family and enhanced their lineage.

ASSETS EACH SPOUSE TOOK TO MARRIAGE

But did men like David Ventura contribute as much economically to the marriage as their wives did with their dowries? It is difficult to determine a husband's contribution to the marriage because of the system of community property used in Portugal and Brazil, in which the dowry and any other property brought by husband or wife to the marriage disappears into the pool of goods, and is therefore not listed separately when either of the spouses dies. Nevertheless, in some mid-seventeenth-century cases we do know the wife's dowry and the estate of at least one of the parents of the groom, making it possible to arrive at an approximate idea of what each brought to the marriage.

In every one of these marriages the wife's dowry was greater than the amount of property contributed by her husband. Such is the case with Thomazia Pires and her husband, Francisco de Godoy. Let us first study the dowry, which is listed in her mother's 1665 will. It consisted of fifteen adult Indians and a young girl, a house in town, an expensive dress, a bed with its sheets and bed hangings, 44 head of cattle, and three horses.[46] Since the couple accepted the option of bringing the dowry à colação, the inventário included the amount for which it was appraised, 140$020.[47] That the whole dowry came in à colação indicates that it was given by her mother only and that Thomazia married after her father died. She therefore had also received an inheritance from her father.[48]

Thomazia and Francisco had brought approximately the same number of Indians to marriage. In 1649 the estate of Francisco's father included 137 Indians, of which 68 remained with his mother, and the nine children received 7 or 8 Indians each. Assuming that the number of Indians neither increased nor decreased by the time his mother died, Francisco would have received another 7 or 8 at her death, making the total number of Indians he inherited from 14 to 16. Thus the number of Indians he brought to the marriage by inheritance was approximately the same as the 15 in his wife's dowry.

However, Francisco brought considerably fewer appraised assets to the marriage than his wife. Except for the Indians, his parents' entire estate at the time of his father's death fifteen years before was approximately the same size as his wife's dowry. Assuming that the estate did not change its size significantly before his mother died, the most Francisco, as one of nine children, could have received in inheritance from both parents was one-ninth the assets his wife brought in dowry.[49]

Thomazia's sister, Anna Pires, also contributed more to the marriage than her husband, João Gago da Cunha. Her mother's will does not list Anna's dowry because she was endowed before her father died. But as the three smallest of the four listed dowries fall within the 140$000-to-180$000 range and include from fifteen to twenty-two Indians, and the final legítima was 143$000, we can safely assume that her dowry was worth over 100$000 and included at least fifteen Indians. Anna and João were already married when his mother died in 1649, and his maternal inheritance amounted to 52$106 and six Indians.[50] His father had died ten years before, when João was still a minor, and his paternal legítima amounted to only 4$780 plus one Indian and a half interest in another.[51] It is possible that his parents' estate was so small when his father died because they had already married off and endowed three daughters, divesting themselves of a good part of their estate. It is also possible that his mother's estate later grew with the help of her single sons' efforts. In any case, João da Cunha's total inheritance of 56$886 and seven Indians was much less than what his wife brought in dowry. And her dowry was not only larger than what he brought, but the couple received it at the moment of marriage, whereas they did not receive the bulk of his inheritance until his mother died. However, he undoubtedly helped to increase their common property in other ways, for he made several trips to the sertão.

Another example that corroborates the view that bridegrooms did not contribute as much to marriage as their brides is that of João Gago da Cunha's sister, Catharina do Prado, who was married and endowed before their father died in 1639. We do not know her dowry, since she and her husband, Mathias Lopes, refused the inheritance. Mathias declared, though, that one of the houses that had been placed in the inventory had been promised to him and his wife in dowry and should not be included in his father-in-law's inventory.[52] We therefore know that his wife had received one of two houses appraised at 12$ooo and 15$ooo, respectively.[53] The house in itself was worth approximately three times her brothers' legítimas of 4$780. And though her dowry is not listed, we have an incomplete list of the dowry of Catharina's sister, Luzia da Cunha, who had also married during their father's lifetime. Among several items that are illegible in the manuscript, she had received cotton or a field of planted cotton, several head of cattle, a field of manioc, several tools, 2,000 tiles for a roof, a few pieces of furniture, some clothes and dishes, and four Indians.[54] Assuming that Catharina do Prado received a similar dowry, and knowing that she had received the house, a very conservative estimate of her dowry is that it was worth 35$ooo and included four Indians. We do know what Catharina's husband, Mathias Lopes, inherited: 33$404 and three Indians.[55] We can safely conclude that what he brought to the marriage was either less or at the most equal to his wife's dowry.

Pedro de Araujo also contributed less than his wife to the marriage. The information we have about him is more clear-cut than the preceding cases because he died shortly after he married Izabel Mendes, daughter of João Mendes Giraldo.[56] His wife's dowry is listed in the inventário and can therefore be subtracted from the total assets owned by the couple to reveal that, though both husband and wife contributed approximately the same amount of moveable goods, Izabel contributed the land. Pedro had several fields planted with different crops, but he does not appear to have had title to any land, while his wife's dowry included title to 500 braças of land.

The number of Indians that Izabel contributed was also greater than the number her husband owned. Pedro had brought four Indians back from an expedition to the sertão that, added to the Indians he had received when his father died, made a total of eighteen adult Indians with some children.[57] His wife's dowry included thirty adult Indians: twenty to do agricultural work, equipped with the requisite tools (ten men and ten women and their children) plus ten women for service in the house.[58] Izabel therefore provided almost two-thirds of the couple's labor force.

Thus the preceding examples all indicate that, when a man established himself through marriage in seventeenth-century São Paulo, his wife's dowry provided the greater initial share of the property they held in common.[59] Frei Gaspar da Madre de Deus, writing in the eighteenth century, corroborates this finding when he comments that Paulistas in the seventeenth century could afford to give their daughters so much land and so many Indians that they could live comfortably even if their husbands were penniless Portuguese.[60]

Antonio Raposo da Silveira provides the extreme example of how well a dowry could support a couple. In his will, he stated that he was *juiz dos órfãos* (the judge who protected the rights of minor orphans—those who had lost at least one parent), having received the office from the Marquez de Cascaes with the privilege of transmitting it to one of his daughters for her dowry. He therefore named his eldest daughter, Dona Anna Maria da Silveira, as the recipient of the office, so that whoever married her would serve in his place.[61] It is significant that Antonio also had three sons yet apparently neither he nor the Marquez de Cascaes thought the office should go to one of them. Of course, his sons were and would always be a part of his clan, whereas giving the office in dowry provided the clan with an alliance and another male member.

Since a bride's dowry in seventeenth-century São Paulo was usually greater than the assets the groom took to marriage, the marriage bargain was weighted in favor of the wife and her family. Thus, the bride's family had leverage in arranging a marriage for their daughter, in determining where the couple would live, and in overseeing how the property was administered. Although brides married down economically, the bargain was evened out through the grooms' white blood, membership in an important clan, claim to nobility, ability as a warrior, technological expertise, or just hard work. Because the marriage of a daughter thus expanded the family's alliances while incorporating another male into the family's military, political, or economic projects, a daughter's dowry took precedence among the family's expenditures. Although brothers bore the brunt of the favoring of their sisters, they also had the opportunity of marrying women with great dowries; the final outcome was therefore approximate equality between married brothers and married sisters. This situation was to change in the eighteenth century.

Part Two

THE EIGHTEENTH CENTURY
(1700–1769)

CHAPTER 4

TRANSITION IN THE FAMILY
AND SOCIETY

N THE FIRST HALF of the eighteenth century, São Paulo experienced rapid changes that entailed both losses and gains for propertied families. Much of the regional autonomy enjoyed a hundred years earlier was lost through the crown's increasing control of military and political activities. After the discovery of gold in the 1690's, some of the old families' most enterprising members moved to the gold-mining regions of Minas Gerais, Mato Grosso, and Goiás, accompanied by their Indians and African slaves, but wealth trickled back and countless Portuguese newcomers took their place in the city. Agricultural markets largely disappeared, leading to a mainly subsistence economy, yet the possibility and profitability of interregional commerce increased spectacularly. The labor force changed when the virtual Indian slavery of the seventeenth century was eliminated, creating a free peasantry along with the need for propertied families to acquire African slaves.

In the struggle of individuals and families to adapt to changing circumstances, the patriarch's power was weakened, thereby altering the framework of the practice of dowry. The change from a society based on military ability and the corporate extended family to a society based increasingly on the possession of capital and entrepreneurial ability opened up opportunities that enabled sons to become more independent of their fathers, while commerce permitted men with relatively little property to make fortunes. Thus, a number of suitors entered the marriage market who did not, as other men, *need* a large dowry containing productive property. Inevitably, the presence of these self-sufficient suitors transformed the marriage bargain.

FAMILY DISPERSAL

In the early eighteenth century, Paulistas roamed far from São Paulo, but they were driven by different motives from those of their ancestors. Expeditions from São Paulo had discovered gold in Minas Gerais during the last decade of the seventeenth century, and large contingents of Paulistas remained there. As the gold rush gathered intensity, they fought unsuccessfully to preserve their exclusive rights to the discovery against newcomers from Portugal and other parts of Brazil.[1] Thereafter Paulistas continued to look for deposits of precious metals and discovered gold in Cuiabá and Goiás in 1718 and 1725.[2]

Expeditions in search of gold were much more the project of individuals than the bandeiras of the previous century. Since the discovery of gold depended more on chance than on numbers, eighteenth-century expeditions were smaller and needed less capital outlay, and their success was not contingent on the power of the clan. Thus, men with few assets were more easily included, and individual men or small groups struck out on their own, finding they could act independently of the patriarch.[3]

Distance itself precluded strict patriarchal control. It is therefore significant that quite a few heirs of eighteenth-century estates were away at the gold mines. Nineteen out of 86 inventários showed family members in Minas Gerais, Cuiabá, or Goiás. One inventário was of a man who died in the mines, leaving a wife and children in São Paulo; another was of the deceased wife of a man in the mines; and the remaining seventeen were persons who died in São Paulo but had heirs in the mines.[4] Although most of the heirs who emigrated to the gold mines were sons, a surprising proportion were daughters. Of the seventeen inventários with heirs in the mines, twelve included sons permanently or temporarily at the mines, two of whom were priests, whereas six had married daughters living there.

Some families became widely dispersed, undoubtedly making it difficult for the patriarch to control his far-flung family effectively. For example, though he died in São Paulo, Manoel João de Oliveira had himself been in the mines of Cuiabá. Of his five sons, three had died in Cuiabá or Goiás, two of whom had married and their children still resided at the mines with their widowed mothers. The first husband of his eldest daughter, Ignes, had raised money on the strength of her dowry and then abandoned her in São Paulo after only three years of married life. He later died in the mines of Cuiabá. The youngest of Manoel João's three daughters had gone to Goiás with her brother and remained there when she married.[5]

The dispersal of family members to the mines was undoubtedly greater than the inventários suggest, since an inventário is taken at just one moment in the life cycle of a family and does not necessarily show what the deceased or his heirs did in the past. Yet other information in inventários can point to a family's involvement either in mining itself or in trade with the mines. Some inventários list bars of gold or quantities of gold dust, reflecting business conducted with Minas Gerais, Goiás, or Cuiabá, while others have lists of creditors or property in the mines, or partnerships with people residing there. Adding all the inventários that show business with the gold mines to those where the deceased, spouse, or heirs were at the mines, we find that 33 percent show connections to the mines.[6]

Not surprisingly, those who had traded with, resided at, or had heirs in the mines tended to be within the wealthiest strata of eighteenth-century Paulistas. Over half the richest 25 percent of the estates studied had obvious connections to the mines, while only 11 percent of the poorest 25 percent did.[7]

Trade to the mines became the expanding economic activity of São Paulo and occupied large numbers of its men, who traveled to and from the mines. In the early years, all imported goods for Minas Gerais went through São Paulo, but a direct road from Rio de Janeiro to Minas Gerais was built in 1733, cutting off that traffic. Paulistas thereafter developed the trade of cattle, horses, and mules from the far south to Minas Gerais, and by this means they were able to accumulate capital.[8] São Paulo remained, however, the hub of commerce to the rest of the mines, and Paulistas developed a complex system of river transportation with large canoes that left in seasonal flotillas called *monções*. These monções took slaves, manufactures, subsistence goods, and salt to Cuiabá, while the overland trail to Goiás, later extended to reach Cuiabá and the other mining regions of Mato Grosso, was used to transport cattle, horses, and mules.[9]

The discovery of gold brought not only mining and trading opportunities but also possibilities of employment that weakened the patriarchal family. For example, in 1767 two Portuguese servants escaped from the house of the governor of São Paulo to serve another master in the mines for much higher wages paid in gold. Although the governor admitted that he had not paid his servants for the last six years nor did he permit them to do any outside business on their own, he sued and imprisoned the priest he claimed had enticed his "family" away. At a time in which servants were still considered a part of the family, the opportunities in the mines permitted such "family members" to act independently and to flout the patriarch's power.[10]

Not only servants but sons as well found in the mines a way to break free from complete patriarchal control. Many sons were sent to the mines by their father; others left on their own. In either case, the father's immediate control of his son's actions was broken. Antonio de Quadros, for example, was sent by his father to the Cataguás mines while he was still a filho-família; on the trip he lent a man some of the gold dust he had with him and the loan was never repaid. After the fact, his father's only recourse was to mention this independent act years later in his will, and wonder whether Antonio did not owe that money to his parents' estate.[11]

Other sons simply appropriated a part of the family's estate and took off. For example, the sons of Manoel dos Santos de Almeida loaded the family's horses with merchandise and left for Goiás without his express permission. Antonio Rodrigues Fam also left for the mines without his father's consent, taking a slave, three horses, gold dust, and cash.[12] Whatever the fathers felt about these defections and appropriations, the mines gave sons a way to act independently of their fathers' control and to forge ahead on their own.

One of the consequences of the exodus of Paulistas to the gold mines was, therefore, a decline of patriarchal power and the fragmentation of the extended family and its fortune. Distances were so great that a brother, son, or son-in-law in the mines could not be effectively controlled. Neither could a married daughter be easily protected when she lived at great distance from her parents. Although the patriarchal family still existed, Paulista society had moved a step closer to the individualism that was to develop in the nineteenth century.

INCREASING LITERACY FOR WOMEN PROPERTY OWNERS

Another change in eighteenth-century society that was related to the growth of individualism and that may have had to do with the weakening of patriarchal control is the growth of female literacy among the wealthy.[13] In the eight largest estates of the sample, either the wife and daughters or all or some of the daughters signed wills, bills of sale, affidavits, requests, or other documents in an inventário. In one case a daughter signed for her illiterate mother, something that in the past had always been the role of sons or other male relatives. Neither did eighteenth-century Paulistas use the phrase common in the seventeenth century when a woman did not know how to sign a document, "because she is a woman and does not know how to read or write." Literacy was no longer exclusively gender specific but was instead class related.

As in other parts of the Western world, people in São Paulo were beginning to believe that not only elite men but also elite women should read and write. When Pedro Taques, the great eighteenth-century Paulista historian and genealogist, described how one of his contemporaries, D. Ines Pires Monteiro, was defrauded in Portugal by her second husband because she did not know how to read or write, he was expressing concern for the education of women, at least wealthy women.[14] The case of D. Ines is also an example of how the loss of power by the extended family, in this case by distance, made a wife's literacy important in the defense of her rights to property. It is likely that she was defrauded by her husband not only because she did not know how to read and write, but also because they were in Portugal, far from the strength of the Pires clan. The constant supervision and even intervention in the affairs of a married couple by the wife's relatives, as had been common in São Paulo, was impossible across the ocean. Married daughters who were far from their families, whether in Portugal or at the mines, therefore were vulnerable and confronted their husbands without the watchful eyes of their male relatives. Literacy became indispensable as a means to protect women's property.

The drive for elite women to be educated, which was to intensify in the nineteenth century, was therefore partly a response to the weakening of the power (and protection) of the patriarch and of the extended family over the younger generation. At the same time, educating elite women empowered them individually, thereby contributing to the growth of individualism in the nineteenth century and to the further weakening of patriarchal power.

GROWING CONTROL BY THE CROWN

By the middle of the eighteenth century, the power of the extended patriarchal family or clan was further curtailed by the crown's increasing control of the region. Until the discovery of gold, São Paulo had been quite independent. The ultimate example of its independence was perhaps the unilateral measures taken by the municipal council in 1690 regarding the value of coins. Because the seventeenth-century Paulista economy chronically suffered a scarcity of specie, commodities such as cotton cloth were often used locally to pay debts. But merchants who brought goods from Portugal wanted payment only in specie, so it was pulled from all parts of Brazil to pay for imports, and a permanent shortage in the colony was the result. Despite colonial requests for the creation of a colonial coin that could not be used in Portugal, in 1688 the crown devalued the money in use and decreed that coins would have uniform value in the entire empire. This measure increased the shortage throughout Brazil, but it was only in São Paulo that countermeasures were taken. The municipal council decreed in 1690 that coins in São Paulo would be worth more than in the rest of empire, and set exchange rates for trade with other towns.[15] Three years later São Paulo reflated the value of specie even further, leading the exasperated governor general to write that the crown's monetary reform was enforced without opposition in the whole colony, "save only in São Paulo, where they know neither God, nor Law, nor Justice, nor do they obey any order whatsoever."[16]

But the independence of the great São Paulo clans did not last. In the early eighteenth century, the crown aggressively sought to gain control of the region, thereby curbing the clans' autonomy and diminishing their power. Until then the town of São Paulo had belonged to the donatary captaincy of São Paulo and São Vicente. In 1709 a wealthy Paulista, José de Góis Morais, offered to buy the captaincy from the donatary captain for 40,000 cruzados, but the crown bought it instead at the same price with the income from the tax on gold.[17] Although the crown was to elevate São Paulo to the status of a city in 1711, it progressively dismembered the captaincy, creating the separate captaincies of Rio Grande do Sul, Minas Gerais, Mato Grosso, and Goiás, and finally in 1748 it further diminished São Paulo's independence by making it a part of the captaincy of Rio de Janeiro until 1765.[18] When the king separated Minas Gerais from São Paulo, he stated explicitly that one of his reasons was to manipulate the Paulistas into discovering more gold, which they proceeded to do. They later discovered diamond deposits as well.[19]

The state also began to monopolize functions it had previously shared with the church. In the early seventeenth century, the making of an inventário was a moment of reckoning and settling of all accounts in which both secular and religious justice intervened, and people were frequently exhorted to fulfill the clauses of a will or to pay their debts on pain of excommunication. For example, when someone complained that no money had been spent for the good of Manoel de Alvarenga's soul, the ecclesiastic inspector, called visita-dor, noting that there was no property in the estate, decided that the heirs would not be required to pay for masses, saying, "I therefore declare his heirs free from this obligation for now and forever after and I command that, under pain of excommunication, no justice oblige them otherwise . . . for I have so decided in my competent judgment."[20] Or in the litigation against the brother of the deceased Lourenço Fernandes, who had retained possession of Lourenço's property, one of the heirs appealed, "I ask Your Lordship to require that everything missing that belongs to this estate be returned under threat of excommunication."[21] By the mid-eighteenth century, in contrast, though the church still had an interest in pious bequests, it was the secular authority that oversaw the fulfillment of a will.[22] And the threat of excommunication was no longer used.

The crown also moved to control the military autonomy of Paulista clans by starting two military organizations controlled by the state: a professional army, and the militia. In the preceding century, the clans and their Indian auxiliaries had constituted all military power, since bandeiras were led by clan members who funded and controlled them. The new, paid army of the eighteenth century was meant to change the situation, but it was relatively small and stationed in Santos. The militia organized all the male inhabitants of the captaincy and also served as a conduit to recruit army personnel.[23] The leaders of the wealthiest clans became officers of the militia and thus retained a degree of administrative and military autonomy, for the small professional army in Santos was not sufficient to control São Paulo.[24]

The wealthiest families in my sample, both merchants and planters, all include militia officials. For example, one of the inventários is that of Manoel Mendes de Almeida, captain major of the city of São Paulo after 1740 and reputedly one of the wealthiest people in the city.[25] He was a Portuguese merchant, married into an old Paulista family, who had seven children, three sons who became Benedictine monks, and four married daughters. Two of his sons-in-law were also officers of the militia, a sergeant major and a captain, while another was a royal judge. Captain Major Manoel Mendes de Almeida had extensive connections with the gold mines, since at mid-century his grandson, Dr. Antonio Mendes de Almeida, was the intendent of the Royal Gold Mint in Goiás.[26] When the captain major died in 1756, he and his wife owned three houses in the center of São Paulo on the Rua Direita, one of them with a shop. They also owned 98 slaves, the largest number of any estate in the sample, and, among other objects of conspicuous consumption, ornate jacaranda beds made in Bahia, ivory from Angola, china from India, and a sedan chair with gold decorations and sumptuous lined curtains.[27]

THE GROWING IMPORTANCE OF WEALTH

Whereas in the seventeenth century military power and clan cohesion led to wealth, in the eighteenth century wealth gave access to military power. Since members of the militia were required to provide their own arms, and those who belonged to the cavalry had to keep a horse and a slave to care for it, only men with substantial property became militia officers. Moreover, their private arms, horses, and slaves could not be seized for debt, giving those who joined the militia an added advantage.[28] Besides Captain Major Manoel Mendes de Almeida and Lieutenant José Rodrigues Pereira, there were officers in all of the eleven wealthiest families in the sample, including two other captain majors, one *Guardamor* or chief custodian (of mines, for example), two captains, two sergeant majors, another lieutenant, and a second lieutenant. The other 57 inventários in the sample included only six militia officers, indicating that the power conferred by a commission in the militia or the regular army usually went to the families that already had the most economic power.[29]

São Paulo's economy was affected very differently by the eighteenth-century expeditions for gold than by the bandeiras of the preceding century. The seventeenth-century expeditions had provided an infusion of labor to the São Paulo economy that led to increased production and gradual development, whereas the expeditions for gold caused an exodus of people and assets.[30] Most of the regional markets for São Paulo's agricultural products disappeared by the middle of the eighteenth century, so that agriculture was no longer the source of some capital accumulation as it had been in the seventeenth century. Families in São Paulo therefore largely reverted to producing only enough for family and local urban needs.[31]

By the middle of the eighteenth century, except for long-distance commerce, the economy of São Paulo had stagnated, and Portuguese officials, interested in the promotion of exports, described the era as a period of decadence.[32] Scholars differ over whether this was really "decadence." Maria Luiza Marcílio, for example, argues that eighteenth-century São Paulo could not have been decadent because it had not been ascendant.[33] True, seventeenth-century inventários certainly show that there was no great wealth at that time in São Paulo.[34] Yet those same inventários show that the resources controlled by the seventeenth-century Paulista elite, whether of land or labor or military might, were great compared to those of their mid-eighteenth-century descendants. Therefore, eighteenth-century genealogist Pedro Taques seems to have been accurate when he described his seventeenth-century ancestors in glowing terms as "potentates," thereby implicitly acknowledging São Paulo's later decline.[35]

It is likely that a labor shortage contributed to the early eighteenth-century decline in agricultural production. The exodus of many Paulistas, initially with large numbers of Indians and later with many African slaves, resulted in a scarcity of labor in São Paulo. The high cost of slaves and the great prices they commanded if sold in the gold mines would also have prompted Paulistas to consider the opportunity cost of keeping slaves at agricultural production in São Paulo in a period of dwindling markets.

The change from Indian to African slave labor also affected the wealth and productivity of Paulista propertied families. As long as people had been able to "administer" Indians and transmit that "administration" to their descendants through inheritance, wills, or dowries, Indians, though technically free, had been a valuable kind of property. In 1758, however, Indians finally became completely free.[36]

The principal difference for the property-owning families of São Paulo between the slavery or quasi-slavery of Indians and that of African slaves was in

TABLE 5
Ownership of Indians and African Slaves
(Seventeenth and Eighteenth Centuries)

African slaves or Indians per estate	Estates	
	17th cent.	18th cent.
0	1 (2.2%)	5 (9%)
1–4	2 (4.4%)	15 (27.3%)
5–10	4 (8.8%)	15 (27.3%)
11–20	13 (28.8%)	9 (16.3%)
20 or more	25 (55.5%)	11 (20%)
TOTAL ESTATES	45	55
Missing information	3	13
SAMPLE	48	68

the method of acquisition. Although Indians could be bought in the seventeenth century, most Paulistas inherited them, received them in dowry, or organized expeditions to capture them. Although some investment was required for bandeiras, the most important factor in their success was family-based, private military prowess and organization. To acquire African slaves, in contrast, required substantial capital. The rules of the game had changed. Indians had been like wild game, a natural resource that could be acquired directly by the use of force. African slaves, on the other hand, were a commodity that must be bought, so that the family-as-enterprise was forced to find ways to accumulate the required capital.

The labor controlled by property owners in São Paulo therefore declined between the mid-seventeenth and the mid-eighteenth centuries. The average number of Indians or African slaves owned by each family in the sample was 36.5 in the seventeenth century, whereas it was only 11.6 in the eighteenth. Over half the estates in the seventeenth-century sample had 20 Indians or more, whereas only one-fifth of the eighteenth-century sample owned that many slaves (see Table 5). And ten families in the seventeenth-century sample had more than 50 Indians each (including three families that owned over 100) whereas only one family in the eighteenth-century sample owned more than 50 slaves (though it owned 98, a sizable number). There were also fewer slaves in total in the eighteenth-century sample. Forty-five estates of the seventeenth-century sample had a total 1,642 Indians, whereas 55 estates of the eighteenth-century sample owned only 638 slaves.[37]

The large number of Indians owned in the seventeenth century meant there were always many of them available to be used as porters to carry commodities to Santos. In the early eighteenth century, in contrast, African slaves were too few and too precious to be used as porters; thus the rugged mountain chain that separated São Paulo from Santos became more of a barrier than in the preceding century, affecting the marketability of São Paulo's agricultural products. This situation was to change only after the road to Santos was improved in 1780 so that merchandise could be transported on mules.[38]

The proportion of free population in São Paulo increased in the eighteenth century with the incorporation of free Indians and the arrival of Portuguese immigrants. In 1765 slaves were less than a third of the population of the city of São Paulo.[39] This had not been the ratio in the preceding century. Throughout the seventeenth century Indians in the personal service of property owners made up four-fifths of the armed men of São Paulo.[40] If we assume that the ratio in the total population was the same as that of the armed men, and if we assume that white meant free while Indian meant unfree, we see that the ratio between the free and the unfree had gone from one free per four unfree in the seventeenth century to two free persons per slave in the middle of the eighteenth.

The ratio of more than two free persons per slave in the middle of the eighteenth century also points to an increase in free persons who held no slaves. The census of 1765 shows that 47 percent of the households in the city of São Paulo declared no assets at all, so that at least that many owned no slaves.[41] In my sample the number of property holders who held no slaves increased from 2 percent of the sample in the seventeenth century to 9 percent in the eighteenth.

Property owners without slaves in eighteenth-century São Paulo would almost surely have had to work their own land, since free men in that century rarely hired themselves out to work for others; this fact probably resulted from, among other things, easy access to land. Many of the respondents in the 1765 census who declared they made their living out of agricultural work owned no assets. They were not landless laborers, however, but mostly squatters or tenants.[42]

Despite the decline of mid-eighteenth-century São Paulo agriculture, some property owners were very prosperous. The average wealth reported in the 1765 census by the households of the city of São Paulo was 296$154.[43] Because the families in my sample were all property owners, a minority of the population, their average net estate was much higher, 2:016$000.[44]

Clearly, the surviving inventários represent the wealthiest part of São Paulo's population. Moreover, a greater proportion of estates in the sample than households in the general population are in the upper levels of wealth. Almost half the families in the sample possessed as much property as that reported to the census taker in 1765 by the richest 10.4 percent of the population. (See Figure 3.) Within the sample itself there was greater concentration of wealth than in the seventeenth century. Table 6 shows that over half the wealth was owned by only 9 percent of the eighteenth-century sample,

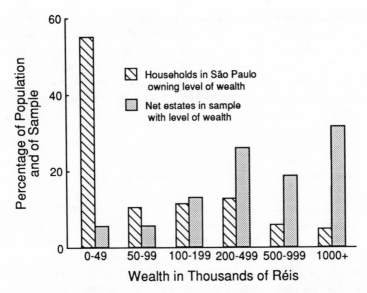

Fig. 3. *Proportion of population of São Paulo and the sample with differ-ent levels of wealth. Sources: The property of heads of household in São Paulo is from table III:3, p. 100, Kuznesof, "Household Composition" (based on the census of 1765); the property of estates, 1750–1769, is from my sample.*

TABLE 6
Concentration of Wealth Among Eighteenth-Century Property Owners

	Number of estates		Sum of net estates	
Top	5	(9.25%)	40:656$300	(53.39%)
Bottom	27	(50%)	4:154$300	(5.45%)
TOTAL	54		76:137$300	

SOURCE: Sample, 68 observations minus 14 missing information.

compared to 12 percent in the seventeenth century. The poorest half of the eighteenth-century sample of property owners owned only 5 percent of the total wealth, whereas the poorest half of the seventeenth-century sample owned 7 percent of the monetary assets and 18 percent of the Indians.[45]

There were no strictly urban property owners in mid-eighteenth-century São Paulo, since practically everyone in the sample owned one or more farms, *sitios*, even the wealthy merchants. Roughly half the families owned both rural and urban property, while the other half only owned rural prop-erty. Those who had houses in the center of São Paulo usually lived in them,

at least during a part of the year, in contrast to the seventeenth-century property owners, who used their town houses only when they had business in the
city. The families who owned both a farm and a house in town were generally
the wealthiest.[46] Only two families in the sample owned exclusively urban
property, and both of the deceased in these families were widows, so it is
probable that they had only received the town houses when the property was
divided at their husbands' deaths, having lost title to the farms previously
owned with their husbands.[47]

COMMERCE AS AN AVENUE TO WEALTH

By mid-eighteenth century, there was a visible change in the main source
of wealth in São Paulo, which was to affect family dynamics. Large-scale merchants, most of them Portuguese, had become the wealthiest residents.[48] Merchants headed 5 percent of the urban households of São Paulo and reported
an average capital of 2:250$000 to the 1765 census taker.[49] That their aver-
age wealth was only slightly larger than the average wealth of my sample,
which contains many estates not belonging to merchants, may be explained
by the tendency of some Paulistas to report less wealth to the census than
they actually possessed. For example, Maria da Silva Leite, widow of José da
Silva Ferrão, reported property worth only 10:000$000 to the 1765 census
taker, yet when her husband had died two years earlier, her half of their estate
had been appraised for 28:179$000.[50]

The four wealthiest estates of my sample were those of merchants, and the
net values of their estates ranged from 4:593$000 to 14:632$000. Three of
the four were widowers when they died and had therefore lost title, though
perhaps not control, of half of their property when their wives died. In other
words, their fortunes had been twice the amount cited in the inventory. All
these large-scale merchants had connections to the mines.[51]

Most of the merchants in colonial Brazil were Portuguese immigrants.[52]
The Marqués de Lavradio, viceroy of Brazil, maintained in 1779 that Portuguese businessmen in Brazil would not hire native-born men as cashiers or
trainees.[53] Young, single Portuguese men from any background therefore had
jobs waiting for them when they arrived in Brazil. They would work in Rio de
Janeiro for several years as the cashiers of large merchants. There they learned
the ins and outs of trade and later branched out on their own or in partnership with their former employer or another businessman.[54]

Thus a young man could build up capital through commerce even if he
started with absolutely nothing. This possibility affected the marriage bargain, since a merchant did not have to marry to receive in his wife's dowry
the property necessary to establish himself, as Portuguese newcomers to São
Paulo had done in the early seventeenth century.

Young clerks instead sought partnerships with their employers. For example, Lourenço Ribeyro Guimaraes went into a partnership in São Paulo with the important merchant Lieutenant José Rodrigues Pereira; the lieutenant provided all the capital while Lourenço administered the shop. When José died in 1769, he stated in his will that Lourenço had paid up his capital, becoming a full partner in the shop with profits divided between them equally. José Rodrigues Pereira also declared that he had a second partner who administered another shop but who had not yet contributed capital to it, and who therefore was entitled to only one-sixth of the profits.[55] It was a long, slow road to accumulate capital, however, as can be seen in the case of another of José Rodrigues Pereira's cashiers. This man was listed in the 1765 census as single, 40 years old, and with property valued at 150$000, whereas his employer is listed as owning property valued at 28:000$000.[56] The merchant with capital undoubtedly had the advantage, which could be multiplied by drawing in the appropriate partners, whether outsiders or relatives.

Once merchants had partnerships with outsiders, the extended family was no longer the sole structure for business, as it had been in the preceding centuries. Outside partners enlarged the commercial network of relatives, even permitting the formation of a business without relatives. These developments began the process of separation of family from business that was to intensify in the nineteenth century.

But relatives could still be useful to a merchant, and marriage provided some capital in a wife's dowry plus a network of relatives who either were merchants themselves or had the resources to invest in trade. In the eighteenth century, a majority of the successful immigrant merchants did, in fact, marry into established Paulista families. The interests of the immigrant merchants and those of the local families they married into were complementary. While the immigrants gained access to resources and a network of possible partners through marriage, the elite families of São Paulo maintained control of community resources with the help of sons-in-law, who, as merchants, had great possibilities of increasing their wealth.[57]

Lieutenant José Rodrigues Pereira had himself married into a family of merchants, for his wife, Anna de Oliveira, was the step-daughter of a merchant, Thomé Rabelho Pinto. Thomé owned a substantial dry goods and hardware store in São Paulo and traded slaves and other merchandise to Cuiabá.[58] Anna's grandfather, Manoel Vellozo, was another wealthy merchant with extensive dealings in Cuiabá and a son-in-law established there.[59] José Rodrigues Pereira also had a brother who died in Goiás and who had probably been his partner in business. Rodrigues Pereira thus had a strong commercial network of relatives and outside partners, and, like most other successful businessmen, he acquired local power and became a member of the city council.[60]

Although the new class of merchants brought wealth to the old Paulista families, they were nonetheless looked down on.[61] For example, one of Manoel Vellozo's granddaughters, Maria Eufrasia, was the wife of Pedro Taques de Almeida Paes Leme, the well-known genealogist and historian.[62] When Taques described the genealogy of his wife, he listed the many noble attributes of her Portuguese father and of her two clerical maternal uncles but neglected to mention her maternal grandfather. We could speculate that he made this omission precisely because Manoel Vellozo was a merchant.

It is also possible that Taques's concern with tracing the genealogies of his and other traditional São Paulo families to Portuguese nobility came from a sense of displacement because they no longer exercised the political power they had in the seventeenth century and their fortunes were small in comparison to those of the recently arrived merchants. Taques is listed in the 1765 census with substantial wealth, assets worth 3:200$000, but this amount is still not much compared to the 28:000$000 of his wife's cousin by marriage, José Rodrigues Pereira.

Although commerce was the best way to make money, the frequency with which merchants themselves had their sons follow other careers indicates that even merchants did not consider it a prestigious occupation.[63] The two sons of Manoel Vellozo, for example, became a monk and a clergyman, although at least one of his three daughters married a merchant. And Manoel's granddaughter and her merchant husband, José Rodrigues Pereira, the wealthiest couple in my sample, had one son who was a priest and one who became a captain in the army. Their third son studied in Coimbra, married a Portuguese woman, and returned to Brazil as a *desembargador*, a judge of the High Court.[64]

CHANGES IN ACCOUNTING PRACTICES

The growth of commerce brought about changes in accounting practices that affected the way business and family affairs were conducted. In the early seventeenth century, the payment and perhaps even the contracting of debts was frequently determined more by extra-economic considerations than by purely economic ones. For example, after Lourenço de Siqueira died, his creditor, his brother-in-law Jeronymo Bueno, declared that though the estate still had not paid him, he wanted the examining official to consider the debt paid. He explained his request by stating that he would negotiate with the heirs and executors as persons of his own family, and if he thought fit he would collect the money, which he had not yet done for reasons that existed between them.[65] For him the debt appears not to have been a strictly economic transaction but something within the realm of family relations in which reciprocity or duty or other noneconomic considerations played the most important part. He also appears to have considered the official support of his right to be paid redundant, and perhaps even intrusive. These were family matters.

At another level, a person's word was all that was necessary to substantiate a fact in the seventeenth century. For example, Suzanna Dias had endowed her daughters long before she died as a very old woman, yet the statement in her will that the dowries covered their paternal legítimas was sufficient for heirs and officials alike, and no further documents were needed to confirm it. Her word was enough. In reading Raphael de Oliveira's will, a modern reader would wonder if he had actually given his stepdaughter her inheritance as he claims. He stated, "I gave her in dowry that which I could from my property, with the understanding that if she could claim something from the legítima of her mother, my second wife Catharina Dorta, it must have been very little, and would enter into the dowry, as it did, and this was always my intention, so that I owe nothing of that legítima."[66] In the eighteenth century, it would have been necessary to substantiate what he stated with written documents.

Neither was bookkeeping systematic in the seventeenth century; debts in inventários were frequently not listed in monetary terms but as quantities of commodities with no price attached. For example, among the debts owed to Pedro Fernandes is one for "the share the deceased received of the Uanga farm, partial payment for which was received in the amount of fifteen hundred tiles." A debt owed by his estate reads, "He owes Pedro Leme one arroba of iron plus eighteen hundred and eighty réis in money."[67] In no place is the money value of the Uanga farm or of the arroba of iron mentioned. In another inventory, a receipt for payment reads, "I have received payment in full for 21 alqueires of flour which Anastacio da Costa owed Mathias Dias who gave me the promissory note."[68] Neither does this receipt give the monetary amount owed. (It does show how promissory notes were used as payment.)

In eighteenth-century São Paulo, in contrast, debts were always listed in monetary terms, and merchants were beginning to use double-entry bookkeeping.[69] Another change concerned the identification of and payment to creditors of an estate. In the seventeenth century there were few promissory notes; the word of the creditor or even of the debtor in his or her will was sufficient. For example, in 1659 Maria Bicudo declared in her will that "I have over 100,000 réis in the hands of my nephew, João Bicudo de Brito, or whatever he says is true."[70] Domingos Fernandes declared in his will, "If I owe any debt to anyone, especially tithes, whether those of times past or those of the present, if it is found that I probably owe them, I order that they be paid."[71] The words "he owes me whatever he says, or whatever he finds in his conscience," were very common in seventeenth-century wills.[72]

In the eighteenth century, scrupulous accounting practices were used and the original documents of dowries and loans were always presented, for no payments were made without proper substantiation. This attention to precise accounting indicates a different concern for money and property, the increasing value of the written record as opposed to the spoken word, and the state's, rather than the patriarch's, control of the transmission of property. The state monitored the practice at the local level by having the crown magistrate give the juiz dos órfãos strict instructions from the High Court justice on the correct way to carry out the inventory of an estate.[73] And individual heirs contributed to the change as well by demanding that the law be followed.

In the eighteenth century, the extended patriarchal families of São Paulo lost some of their power to the crown, which intervened administratively and militarily to curtail that power. At another level, it was the change in the way families acquired power that altered the dynamics within the propertied family. In the seventeenth century, an extended family's cohesion and military prowess brought it wealth and political power, causing marriage alliances and the acquisition of sons-in-law to be important to the clan. In the eighteenth century, in contrast, it was wealth that brought military and political power. The main ways to acquire wealth, mining and commerce, required individual entrepreneurial abilities even more than family connections, though the latter helped. As sons set off on their own to far-off regions, they achieved through distance increasing independence from the patriarchal family. The good marriage of daughters continued to be important in family strategies, however, for they could marry wealthy merchants, whose integration by marriage into the traditional elite was essential to ensure its continued preeminence.

CHAPTER 5

CONTINUITY AND CHANGE IN THE PRACTICE OF DOWRY

ESPITE DOWRY'S continued importance in early eighteenth-century São Paulo, its practice had changed. In the first place, there were now a few families who let their daughters enter marriage empty-handed, contrary to the early seventeenth-century practice in which all daughters of property owners took either a dowry or their inheritance into marriage. The majority of families, however, still favored daughters over sons by endowing them handsomely, though far fewer daughters received dowries of greater value than their future inheritance, and when they did, these expressions of patriarchal will were curtailed by the strict interpretation of the law brought about through the intervention of the state and the efforts of other heirs.

DOWRY FREQUENCY

The practice of dowry was still widespread, for most families of property owners in the first half of the eighteenth century provided their daughters with dowries, although the proportion was slightly smaller than in the preceding century. Eighty-one percent of the families in the eighteenth-century sample still endowed their married daughters, whereas in the seventeenth century 91 percent of the families had done so.[1]

TABLE 7
Dowry-Giving in Relation to Wealth (Eighteenth Century)

Wealth	Number of families		Gave dowries		No dowries	
Slaves owned:						
4 or more	39		32	(82%)	7	(18%)
3 or less	18		14	(78%)	4	(22%)
Unknown number	11		9		2	
TOTAL	68	(100%)	55	(81%)	13	(19%)
Net estate:						
Wealthiest half	27		24	(89%)	3	(11%)
Poorest half	27		21	(78%)	6	(22%)
Unknown value	14		10		4	
TOTAL	68		55		13	

SOURCE: Sample.
NOTE: All percentages have been rounded off.

Although all ranks of property owners endowed their daughters, there was a slightly greater proportion of families with large estates who did so than those with smaller estates. Of those families with four or more slaves, 82 percent gave dowries, while 78 percent of those with fewer than four slaves did so (see Table 7). In a ranking of the net estates we find the same pattern: dowry-giving in 89 percent of the families in the wealthiest half, but in only 78 percent of the bottom half. The difference is slight, of course, and the fact that over three-quarters of the less wealthy families gave dowries indicates that giving a dowry was still the usual practice.

There were some significant changes within the group of families who did not endow their daughters, however. In the early seventeenth century, the only families not giving dowries were those of the widowed whose daughters entered marriage with property, their inheritance, even though they did not bring dowries. Six of the thirteen eighteenth-century families who did not endow their daughters were also headed by widows or widowers whose daughters married simply with their inheritance. The novelty is that the other seven families allowed their daughters to marry empty-handed. They were starting a trend, for in the early nineteenth century most daughters of property owners took no property to marriage.

Some families may not have endowed their daughters because they could not afford to do so. Six of the seven families who let their daughters marry without property had relatively small estates, lying within the less wealthy half of the sample. Of these, the largest property owner was João Fernandes da Costa, who owned a farm in the *bairro* (neighborhood) of Santana, cattle, and ten slaves, yet his estate was worth less than 2 percent of the largest estate in the sample.[2] Though he had one married daughter who had not received a dowry, he also had a single daughter over 25 who was emancipated. (During colonial times, single adult children did not become automatically emancipated at reaching 25, the age of majority, but instead had to solicit emancipation juridically.) We can speculate that a dowry might have facilitated her marriage or, looked at from another angle, curtailed her independence.

The other five families with small estates who did not endow their daughters had much less property than João, and the scarcity of their assets undoubtedly determined their decision not to give dowries. The best example is Miguel Delgado da Cruz, who owned no slaves. He and his wife had three married daughters who had not received dowries, and an elderly daughter in the *recolhimento* (religious institution similar to a convent but where women do not make perpetual vows) who had been received without a dowry out of charity. Although he and his wife owned two small farms, they had so little liquidity that there was no money when he died to pay for masses or the few debts he had left.[3] His example is the most extreme, but it reinforces the conclusion that families with small estates probably decided not to give dowries precisely because of their straitened circumstances.

The illegitimacy of a daughter, especially if she was of mixed race, may have been another reason for not observing the practice of dowry. Manoel Garcia, a married merchant whose estate was in the top half of the sample, had two *filhos naturais*, children born of a free single black woman while he was single; in addition he had several younger, legitimate heirs. Although he recognized these children in his will, and they inherited equally with his legitimate children because they had been born while he was still single, he had not endowed his filha natural when she married.[4] Maybe he reasoned that her position as heiress should be sufficient encouragement for her husband, who was only a freedman.

Outside the sample there is a similar case, that of Sergeant Major Manoel Soares de Carvalho, who made his fortune trading with the mines in Goiás and Cuiabá. He left his estate to his filhos naturais whose mother was a free black woman. He had not endowed his two married daughters, despite the fact that he gave dowries to the mulatto and mestizo filhas naturais of his deceased brother. He complained in his will, however, that his nieces' husbands had run through their dowries very quickly, and perhaps he feared the same thing would happen to his daughters if they received dowries.[5]

The only other case in the sample with a married filha natural is that of the merchant Aniceto Fernandes, who did give this daughter a dowry.[6] Since nothing is said about her race, however, it can be presumed that she was white, a fact that might be the reason her father gave her a dowry almost as large as that of her legitimate half-sister. In summary, these cases illustrate that filhas naturais depended on their father's favor for a dowry even more

than legitimate daughters, just as they depended on their father's recognition
in order to inherit from him.[7]

The rest of the families in the sample who did not endow their daughters
were widows or widowers who allowed their daughters to marry simply with
their paternal or maternal inheritance. In fact, except for Manoel Garcia in
the example above, the only persons in the wealthiest half of the sample who
did not give dowries were widows or widowers.

Still, not giving their daughters dowries in addition to the inheritance
they received from their first deceased parent was a departure from customary
practice. Under the community-property system of marriage, if both parents
were alive when a daughter married, her dowry was understood to have come
from both her father and mother.[8] It had therefore been customary in the
seventeenth century for a widow or widower to give a daughter who married
after the death of the other parent not only her legítima from the half of the
estate that belonged to the deceased but also a dowry from his or her remaining half.

Several propertied widows and widowers in eighteenth-century São Paulo
did give dowries in addition to their daughters' inheritance. Besides the six
widows or widowers mentioned above, all of whose daughters married after
the death of one parent, taking merely their inheritance into marriage, there
were twelve widows or widowers in the sample who endowed those daughters
who married while both parents were still alive, but who had other daughters
who married after one parent died. Of these, seven gave a dowry in addition
to their legítima to the daughters who married after the death of one parent,
whereas the other five did not. So that out of a total of eighteen widows or
widowers who had daughters married after the death of their spouse, seven
gave those daughters dowries on top of their inheritance, whereas eleven did
not. We see here the beginning of a trend, for by the nineteenth century no
widows or widowers gave dowries from their remaining property.

Clearly widows or widowers were beginning to feel that it was not necessary to sacrifice themselves for the daughters who married after the death of a
parent, for even if they did not receive a dowry, they took property into marriage, their legítima. An example is the case of the widow Maria Bueno de
Oliveira, whose estate was in the top half of the sample. Her daughters married after their father's death, and by the time Maria died, she had paid her
daughters most of their paternal legítima, and both of them had received gifts
toward their dowries from other relatives (the eldest from her maternal aunt
and the youngest from her stepfather's remainder of terça).[9] Although her
daughters received no dowry from their mother's property, they married with
considerable assets, later inheriting their share of her estate.

A widowed parent's decision to give his or her daughter merely her legítima when she married was in reality a decision to renege on the duty of

giving dowry. Although daughters who married with only their paternal or maternal inheritance contributed to the support of their marriage, this contribution did not cost their surviving parent anything.

A significant indication of the new trend is the case of the wealthy Lieutenant José Rodrigues Pereira who did not give his daughter a dowry in addition to her maternal legítima and her mother's remainder of the terça. As a merchant with debts amounting to approximately half his assets, his decision to give no dowry to his daughter and son-in-law probably meant that his first concern was for his business. He did, however, leave this married daughter the entire remainder of his terça, despite his having other daughters who were still single. This action suggests that he was making up for not having given her a dowry from his share of the community property.[10] José Rodrigues Pereira had clearly departed from the customary practice of dowry, although he still favored one daughter over the rest.[11]

Nevertheless, families who did not give dowries were still the exception in early eighteenth-century São Paulo, and most of those who did give dowries endowed every one of their married daughters. Of the 55 families in the sample that gave dowries, 48 endowed all their married daughters. As we saw above, 5 others endowed all daughters married during the life of both parents, whereas they allowed the daughters who married after the death of the first parent to marry merely with their legítima.

Only two families in the eighteenth-century sample permitted some daughters to marry empty-handed while endowing others. One of these cases clearly illustrates the connection between dowry and patriarchal control of marriage. This is the case of Manoel Dultra Machado o velho and Mariana Machado, who endowed only four of their five married daughters. Their wills do not explain why they had not endowed their third married daughter, Ignes, and it is only in the inventário of Ignes herself that we find an inkling of what may have prompted her parents. Since her absent husband was listed in her inventário as "Antonio Correa, deported as a criminal to Africa," it is probable that her parents disapproved of her marriage and for this reason did not endow her. Yet after he was sentenced and she was left alone and without resources, they sheltered her in their home. Furthermore, both parents left her the remainder of their terça.[12]

SIZE OF DOWRIES

Although most eighteenth-century Paulista property owners continued to endow their daughters, dowries were not quite as large as those given in the preceding century. In the seventeenth century the dowries of every one of the married daughters of a family were usually greater than the legítima, but since

TABLE 8
Dowry as Percentage of Legítima (Eighteenth Century)

Size of the estate	Mean	Median
Fewer than 4 slaves	163%	123%
From 4 to 9 slaves	131%	85%
10 or more slaves	97%	57%
Whole sample	147%	102%

SOURCE: Sample. The largest dowry given by a family as percentage of
the legítima in the 47 estates in which their value and the number of
slaves are known.

most married daughters refused to inherit, we do not have precise statistics to
confirm this except in five cases where the dowries came in à colação and in
which we know the monetary value of the legítima. In those five cases, which
do not necessarily include the largest dowry given in each family, the average
dowry was 250 percent the legítima. In the following century, though dowries
were still sizable, families usually gave only one or at the most two dowries of
greater value than the legítima. Using the value of the largest dowry given by
each family in the eighteenth-century sample, I found that their average size
was one and a half times the daughter's subsequent legítima (see Table 8).
However, the richer the estate, as measured by the number of slaves or assets
owned, the smaller the proportion of the legítima represented by the largest
dowry. And in none of the inventários of my eighteenth-century sample were
there disparities such as that between Maria Leite's dowry worth 80$000 in
1633 and her siblings' inheritance of only 2$098 each.

Many property owners in eighteenth-century São Paulo gave the most
handsome dowry to their eldest daughter. Of the families in the sample who
had at least three married daughters, 48 percent gave the eldest daughter the
largest dowry, continuing with successively smaller dowries, while 31 percent
did exactly the opposite, giving successively greater dowries, the largest to
the youngest daughter. The rest, 21 percent, gave their dowries in no particular order of size.[13]

Although families did not give equal dowries to all their daughters, the
most common practice was to keep the difference small. Only ten of the
twenty-nine families with three or more married daughters gave one dowry
that was more than double the size of their smallest dowry.[14] Most families
gave their daughters dowries that were approximately equal, as did Maria de
Lima de Siqueira.[15] Each of her six daughters took property to marriage valued
between 1:900$000 and 2:220$000. These similar amounts show careful calculation on the part of the parents, especially considering that two daughters
were endowed while both parents were alive, whereas the other four married
with their paternal legítima, their share of the remainder of the paternal
terça, and a dowry given by their widowed mother.

The ten families in which there was the largest difference between dowries were mostly those with the smaller estates. One could speculate that they gave their first daughters such handsome dowries because they had expectations of growing prosperity that did not materialize, or the large dowry was given before the family's property diminished, or else a family in straitened circumstances deliberately chose to give one sizable dowry to maintain their status through the good marriage of at least one daughter.

One case of a great difference between dowries is that of Manoel Dultra Machado o velho and his wife, Mariana Machado. Their eldest daughter received a dowry three times as large as that of their second daughter, and, as the dowries decreased in size, the difference became greater, so that the dowry of the eldest daughter was six and a half times the size of her youngest sister's.[16] Even with the declining size of these dowries, by the time Manoel Dultra Machado o velho and his wife had married off all their daughters, they had divested themselves of almost a third of their estate.

Diogo das Neves Pires is an example of someone whose property appears to have diminished greatly after endowing one of his three married daughters. Diogo belonged to São Paulo's oldest families, yet he left a relatively small estate.[17] When his first wife died at least eighteen years before, his half of their joint estate was worth 101$820. When he died in 1760, having remarried, the net worth of his estate was approximately the same, 110$100, but half of this belonged to his new wife, so he left his children only 55$050. If, as seems probable, Diogo's second wife had brought a dowry to their marriage, his property must have dwindled. This may be the reason he chose to favor only two of the six children by his first wife. One of these was his only son by his first wife, to whom he gave land worth 20$000 inherited from his first wife's parents. He also favored his second married daughter, who received a dowry of 54$382, twelve times her siblings' legítima of 4$242.[18]

Diogo das Neves Pires's case suggests that, even when a family's estate was dwindling, the gift of a large dowry to at least one daughter was still considered important. Another case of a diminishing estate with a large dowry is that of Izabel Dultra and her husband Estevão de Lima do Prado, who also belonged to an old Paulista founding family. Izabel had taken a dowry worth 73$320 into her first marriage, yet when she died the entire estate she and her second husband possessed was less than that amount. Her dowry had consisted of a chest, six silver spoons, a bed and bedding, two mares, 21 head of cattle, and a piece of land in the midst of Dultra Machado property, on which the family was still living when her second husband died a few years after she did. They also still owned a herd of cattle and several horses. When their joint property was inventoried in 1748, Izabel's father sold the property and deducted debts and expenses so that each heir received a legítima of only 2$370.[19] However, Izabel Dultra had given her only daughter by her first husband a great dowry. Besides inheriting—as an only child—half her parents' joint estate when her father died, this daughter received a dowry from her mother worth 21$640, nine times the legítima her siblings would receive when their mother died.[20] This family's property had clearly dwindled as the death and remarriage of parents and the marriage of a daughter fractioned and regrouped property, at the same time that small cattle-breeders were being hurt by the weak market.[21]

Another statistic that demonstrates how essential the giving of dowries continued to be for eighteenth-century Paulistas is the large proportion of its estate a family gave away in dowry. The average divestment in the sample was 41 percent. Of course, families with many married daughters tended to divest themselves of more property than families with few daughters. Families with three or more married daughters divested themselves of an average of 48 percent of their estate. A good example of an average divestment is that of the family of Maria de Lima de Siqueira. Her husband had used 21 percent of his half of the community property for the dowries of their two eldest daughters, and his widow divested herself of a full 54 percent of her property for their six daughters.[22] Endowing daughters was obviously still a significant obligation.

These large divestments of property for dowries undoubtedly contributed to daughters settling near their parents. Elizabeth Kuznesof found in her study of eighteenth-century São Paulo bairros that families tended to live in the proximity of the larger kin, the clan. And within this general tendency, matrilocality was the rule; married couples lived near the wife's family more often than near the husband's.[23] Matrilocality permitted the bride's clan to receive the greatest advantage of the alliance achieved through the daughter's marriage while continuing to protect the daughter and her property. In this respect the eighteenth-century practice was much like that of the preceding century.

Besides giving their daughters relatively smaller dowries, eighteenth-century Paulistas appear to have helped all their children to a greater extent than they did in the seventeenth century. The percentage of families that provided gifts to sons other than priests almost doubled, going from 9 percent in the seventeenth century to 17 percent in the eighteenth. The percentage of families who loaned money to sons doubled, and that of families who loaned to married daughters and their husbands also increased. And parents continued to allow their adult offspring, especially their sons, to use their slaves and land. Conversely, married daughters and their husbands were loaning money to their parents more frequently than in the past, while sons were doing so less frequently.[24]

The picture one gets is that of difficult times, in which children, especially sons, were receiving more help from their parents than they did a hundred years earlier, thereby diminishing the advantage daughters had once possessed. Families were probably reacting to the fluid and precarious economic situation of São Paulo itself in the early eighteenth century. Money was being made only in the gold mines of Minas Gerais, Goiás, or Cuiabá, or else by merchants supplying those mines. Sons needed help to emigrate to the mines and parents increasingly outfitted them with a horse and saddle, a rifle, and, if possible, a slave or two.[25] In fact, as dowries became smaller, many sons received gifts of property equivalent to their sisters' dowries. This was the case of the sons of Mariana Machado who all received approximately what their sisters did, except for the somewhat larger dowry of the eldest daughter.[26] Daughters were no longer being favored to the extent that they had been in the seventeenth century.

Not only were dowries not as large in relation to the legítima as they had been in the preceding century, but their composition had changed as well. The bride's parents were no longer providing the greater part of the means of production needed by the newlyweds to start up a new enterprise. In the early seventeenth century all dowries contained means of production and Indians, though many did not contain the objects commonly considered part of a trousseau. In the eighteenth century the situation was reversed: most dowries contained a trousseau and jewels while a smaller proportion had means of production. Only 2 percent of eighteenth-century dowries included a house in town, as compared to 40 percent the preceding century; 20 percent included land, as compared to 40 percent in the seventeenth century. Paulistas were giving less money in dowries, too. In the seventeenth century dowries contained very little actual cash because of the general lack of specie, but I counted loads of flour placed in Santos, for example, as money. In 45 percent of the seventeenth-century dowries we find such commodities ready for sale, whereas in only 32 percent of eighteenth-century dowries was there cash, gold dust, or gold bars. Tools and machinery were included in only 10 percent of the dowries, as compared to 35 percent a hundred years before. And only 27 percent of the eighteenth-century dowries included cattle, as compared to 40 percent in the seventeenth century. The only objects that could be presumed to be means of production that were given more frequently than in the past were horses. Yet when we look carefully at the dowries, even the horses were not always means of production, for they were often riding horses meant for the bride's use.[27]

USE OF COLAÇÃO

Because most dowries were relatively not as large as those in the seventeenth century, most married daughters did not refuse to inherit as in the seventeenth century but instead brought their dowries back into the estate, à colação (see Table 9). As we saw above, according to Portuguese law, the estate of a deceased person was to be divided only among those children who had not received a dowry or gift, unless the endowed children wanted to

TABLE 9
Colação in Families with Endowed Daughters

Families in which	17th cent.		18th cent.	
All endowed married daughters refused to inherit	37	(90.2%)	11	(22.4%)
Some endowed married daughters refused and some brought dowry à colação	3	(7.3%)	8	(16.3%)
All endowed married daughters brought dowry à colação	1	(2.4%)	30	(61.2%)
Missing information	2		6	
Families who gave dowries	43		55	

SOURCE: Sample.

bring their dowries back into the estate. In the seventeenth century, most married daughters and their husbands did not want to bring their dowries à colação and therefore refused to inherit.[28] In the eighteenth century, in contrast, declining to inherit became the exception rather than the rule, for in over 60 percent of the families every married daughter brought her dowry back into the estate, while another 16 percent included some daughters coming in à colação.[29] This meant that in only 22 percent of eighteenth-century families did all the daughters refuse to inherit, compared to 90 percent in the preceding century. Moreover, the eighteenth-century practice established a trend, for by the nineteenth century there were no cases of daughters refusing to inherit; the practice had completely disappeared.

This change was one of practice, for the law had not altered. In the seventeenth century, patriarchs and their wives favored some or all daughters by giving them dowries much larger than the subsequent legítima and those married daughters refused to inherit. Despite allowing heirs to decline the inheritance, the Ordenações limited the right of patriarchs or their wives to favor one child over others with a dowry or gift. When the dowry or gift had been larger than the legítima plus the terça, even though the heir declined to inherit, he or she could be compelled to return the difference to the other heirs.[30] The underlying assumption here is that a parent had the right to dispose of only his or her terça to favor a child. A parent should not favor any child to the detriment of all others.

Eighteenth-century Paulistas observed the law regarding the size of a dowry, whereas their seventeenth-century ancestors usually had not, though they were aware of it.[31] In this regard, their ancestors put the patriarchal privilege of arranging marriages before the equality among heirs. As we saw earlier, daughters in the seventeenth century were rarely asked to return part of their dowries to their siblings. And even if the dowry had not been fully paid, daughters and their husbands retained the advantage because the debt was discounted from the gross estate before the legítima of their brothers and sisters was calculated.

Eighteenth-century Paulistas, in contrast, followed the law scrupulously, suggesting that the equal rights of all heirs were becoming more significant than the right of the patriarch to arrange a marriage. The inventário of Maria Bueno de Araujo illustrates a simple case where all dowries were smaller than the legítima and came back into the estate.[32] She and her husband, Antonio Correa Pires, were the wealthiest family in the relatively poor neighborhood of Penha, and their first son-in-law, Manoel Dias Bueno, became captain major of the bairro.[33] When Maria Bueno de Araujo died, both married daughters and the son, who was a priest, came in à colação. The net estate was divided in two, with half remaining for the widower. After discounting from her half an amount to cover masses for her soul and inventory costs (she died intestate), the value of half of each dowry and patrimony given was added to her net estate, and the sum was divided by the number of heirs, giving the legítima. Only half of each dowry and patrimony came in à colação because they had been given by both parents.[34] The second half would be discounted when the father died. After the value of the legítima was arrived at, each heir received that amount minus any value brought à colação.

The case of Maria de Lima de Siqueira illustrates the most common practice in the eighteenth century when a married daughter refused to inherit.[35] Maria was a widow whose two eldest daughters had married during their father's lifetime, and when he died they had declined to inherit, doing the same thing when their mother died. Each of their dowries was worth over two contos (2:000$000). If the two eldest daughters had brought their dowries à colação at the death of both parents, the first would have had to return a total of 462$346, and the second 300$364. We understand why they refused when we consider that the average price of a slave in the sample was 68$000, and the average price of a house in town was 168$000. Because they refused, the terça of their mother's estate was brought into the picture. Starting with the first dowry given, the legítima was subtracted from the dowry and the resulting difference was deducted from the terça. Both dowries of Maria's eldest daughters fit into their legítimas plus the terça. In cases where the dowry was so large that the terça did not cover the difference, the daughter and her husband, or even their heirs, if the daughter and son-in-law predeceased their parents, were expected to make up the difference to her siblings.

PATRIARCHAL POWER CURTAILED

The strict adherence to the *Ordenações* in eighteenth-century São Paulo limited the rights of parents to dispose of their property as they wished. They could no longer give lavish dowries. They had to consider the size of their terça and whether it would be enough to hold the excess between the dowry and legítima. And if they gave large dowries, they also knew that their terça would be diminished and would not hold as many bequests as they might want to make.

People understood this consequence of bringing a large dowry back into the estate. When Manoel Pacheco Gato died in 1715, his heirs included a married daughter, two single daughters, and five single sons, one of them a Franciscan friar. The heirs agreed among themselves that it was best if the married daughter did not come in à colação. Their arguments, which convinced the judge, were that their brother-in-law was at the moment in straitened circumstances (so he would have had a hard time returning a part of the dowry) and especially that not having him bring the dowry back into the estate would benefit the two single daughters who had received a bequest of the remainder of their father's terça (since the excess of the dowry would then not be deducted from the terça).[36] Yet it also meant the brothers' legítima would be smaller than if the dowries had been brought à colação—that is, added to the net estate before the division among heirs. Here, as in the early seventeenth century, brothers were sacrificing themselves for their sisters (both the married and the single ones), and preference was being given to the intentions of the patriarch.

There are other examples in the eighteenth-century inventários of brothers sacrificing themselves for their sisters. For example, Manoel João de Oliveira's grandson from Goiás donated his share of his father's legítima to his sister when she married, so that she received a double share. And when Ignacio Dinis Caldeyra's estate decreased and he died with only five slaves, his six heirs decided to favor their two young, single sisters, dividing the whole estate between them for dowries, and inheriting nothing themselves.[37] Their reasoning was seventeenth-century reasoning, in which daughters were invariably favored.

Even in the seventeenth century, however, some sons had tried to rebel at such seeming inequity. Let us recall, for example, the case of Manoel João Branco, whose eldest daughter, Anna Leme, received half a ship in dowry. Her husband, Captain David Ventura, moved to Bahia without her, kept the ship, and continued his trade without ever adjusting accounts with his father-in-law. When Manoel João died, his only son, Francisco João Leme, tried to have the ship appraised in a vain effort to equalize his inheritance with his sister's dowry. If he could have made her come in à colação, she would have owed him money.

Instead, his sister's rights were given priority. She was paid, at least on paper, the amount that was still owed her on her dowry even before the estate was divided in order to give their mother her half. (See Appendix D.II.)

The amount the estate still owed Anna was 107$000, and the value of half a ship was far over 200$000, so that her dowry was worth at least 307$000 and probably much more, without considering the usufruct and value of the other half of the ship that was never returned.[38] Furthermore, she also received the remainder of her mother's terça. Throughout, Francisco João had been slighted in favor of his sister and brother-in-law. His frustration is evident in his continuous litigation against his mother and, after her death, his sister; he even went so far as to steal and kill their cattle. It is significant, however, that Francisco João did not act while his father, the patriarch, was still alive, though it had been his father's decision to give such a large dowry to Anna and David Ventura. He did not presume to challenge his father.

This great respect for the patriarch's wishes had changed by the eighteenth century. That more and more married daughters were obliged to bring their large dowries back into the estate at their parents' deaths reflects the lessening of the patriarch's power over his children, as they, with the aid of lawyers and judges, attempted to enforce the law's provisions for equality among heirs. Considering that in the seventeenth century daughters were privileged vis-à-vis sons, and the tendency continued in the eighteenth century, we can see the legal battle for equality as a battle of brothers against their sisters. And since the privilege of daughters was based on the patriarch's view of what was best for the family as a whole, the eighteenth-century battles for sibling equality can also be seen as a claim for the rights of individuals—sons—over the right of the patriarch to decide what was best for the family.

Even in the seventeenth century, patriarchs were conscious of the possibility that after their death their sons would attempt to right the injustice they felt had been done. This possibility was obviously on Constantino Coelho Leite's mind when he enlisted his sons' agreement to the large dowries he gave his daughters and included that information within his will, a legal and religious document that had to be respected.[39] Pero Nunes in his 1623 will called down his curse on any son who dared to contest his only daughter's possession of the things he had given her during his lifetime.[40]

Another change that reflects diminished patriarchal control of sons-in-law regards the promise and payment of dowries. Although seventeenth-century parents promised all their daughters extremely large dowries, many times they did not pay up immediately.[41] Of the families of the sample who had endowed their married daughters, 43.6 percent had not paid the full dowry by the time of the death of one of the parents. This practice can be viewed as one of control, for as long as the dowry was unpaid, the son-in-law was dependent on his father-in-law and could be expected to consider his wishes. In contrast, by mid-eighteenth century, all parents had paid the entire dowry long before their death (see Table 10).

Obviously there had been a change in the relationship between the bride's

TABLE 10

Payment of Promised Dowries by Time of Parent's Death

Families with	17th cent.		18th cent.	
Wholly paid dowries	22	(56.4%)	54	(100%)
Partly paid dowries	17	(43.6%)	0	
Missing information	4		1	
Families who gave dowries	43		55	

SOURCE: Sample.

parents and the newly married couple. In the seventeenth century the patriarch retained control by delaying payment, whereas in the eighteenth century dowries were paid as promised, making the situation more formal and clear cut and the newlyweds potentially more independent.

Although the eighteenth-century practice of dowry shared many characteristics with that of the preceding century, such as the large percentage of propertied families who gave dowries and the large part of each family's estate that was given away, there were also changes. The most important ones were the appearance of a few families who allowed their daughters to marry empty-handed and the change in the practice of colação—from one of rarely coming in à colação in the seventeenth century to one of rarely refusing the inheritance in the eighteenth. The rights of sons were growing vis-à-vis the rights of patriarchs or their representatives to favor daughters. A stricter interpretation of the law and the litigation of siblings prevented patriarchs from giving dowries as large as those given in the early seventeenth century, so large that they cut into their sons' inheritance. These limitations on the size of dowries undoubtedly placed constraints on the patriarch's ability to choose a son-in-law, thereby leading to changes in the marriage bargain.

CHAPTER 6

A CHANGING MARRIAGE BARGAIN

SEVERAL DEVELOPMENTS contributed to a change in the marriage bargain in eighteenth-century São Paulo. Since parents were constrained from giving such relatively large dowries as they had given in the early seventeenth century, it was no longer as much a buyer's market for the bride. At the same time, the new opportunities to accumulate capital through commerce strengthened the position of merchants as future bridegrooms, changing the pool of suitors and leading to a pattern in which husbands contributed more than their wives to the couple's property. The marriage bargain had altered.

MARRIAGE STILL A MATTER OF PROPERTY

It might be thought that the male/female ratio was another cause of the alteration of the marriage bargain, since one consequence of the out-migration of males after the discovery of the gold mines was that São Paulo became a city in which women outnumbered men. In the free population of the urban parish of Sé in 1765 there were only 70 men between the ages of 20 and 39 per 100 women of the same age group. The number of men increased in older age groups, however, probably because many men migrated during their youth and adult working years, returning to São Paulo to live out their old age.[1]

In 1768 the new governor of São Paulo, Dom Luiz Antonio de Souza, showed concern with the few marriages taking place in São Paulo and reported that the laws passed by the crown to make it difficult for women to emigrate from Brazil to Portugal had not accomplished their purpose of facilitating population growth. Instead, he wrote, men roamed all over Brazil, and thousands of women remained single.[2]

The governor's perception is partly confirmed by studies made of the 1765 census that show that in São Paulo there were more than a few never-married persons and many female-headed households. Maria Luiza Marcílio shows that in the parish of Sé over 16 percent of the men and over 10 percent of the women who were over 50 had never married, though they may have formed consensual unions.[3] Elizabeth Kuznesof found that in the whole district of the city of São Paulo, 28 percent of the households were headed by women. Although these included widows and married women whose husbands were absent, many were single women, for 6 percent of the women with children had never married and were without a male companion in the household.[4] Another statistic that confirms the existence of many single mothers is that 29 percent of children baptized in the parish of Sé were either illegitimate or *expostos*, abandoned infants.[5] The census also shows that 9 percent of all households in São Paulo included *agregados*, related or unrelated adults who were not children of the head of household.[6] Some of these people were single men and women, and in view of the low ratio of men to women in São Paulo, it is likely that many more were women than men.

Yet the numerous single women in eighteenth-century São Paulo were not the daughters of property owners, for most of these married, indicating that marriage was still a matter of property. Of the 233 daughters in the eighteenth-century sample who were 25 years old or over, only 29, or 13 percent, were single. And these single women would not necessarily stay single the rest of their lives. Women may have been marrying later, inasmuch as the proportion of families who had single daughters over 25 had risen from only 7 percent in the seventeenth century to 26 percent in the eighteenth.[7] Nevertheless, most of these single women were still in their twenties so it is probable that the majority eventually married.

Governor de Souza's concern centered on the fact that few people married properly in the church. He referred to immigrant Portuguese men especially, who he believed tended not to marry and settle down but to become vagrants instead. He also believed that so few married because it was too difficult and expensive to complete the bureaucratic process required by the church to prove that someone from another part of the country or from overseas was truly single or widowed and therefore could marry. He added that only a good dowry made the expensive and time-consuming process worthwhile. If there were no dowry, he wrote, there was no marriage, and men entered a relation of concubinage with the same or another woman, and there was no "good" population growth nor did men become firmly established in the region.[8] Besides wishing the church would relax its requirements for marriage, he seemed to be calling for a system that did not require a dowry for marriage, and in this he was a harbinger of the kind of thinking that was to gather strength in the nineteenth century.

The governor obviously believed that making marriage possible for greater numbers would solve many of the problems he found in São Paulo. In his view, marriage would tie men down more firmly than concubinage and would help to eliminate the many vagrants who roamed throughout the country. And inasmuch as children are born as frequently within concubinage as within marriage, he must have been thinking about the quality of children's lives when he spoke about "good" population growth as a result of marriage. He meant the growth of the legitimate, not illegitimate, population and a rise in the number of children brought up by their family, not expostos.

The governor was criticizing the marriage system, and his criticism brings the system into relief: in mid-eighteenth-century São Paulo, marriage was for property owners and not for the poor.[9] At least one of the marriage partners had to have means simply to comply with the requirements of the church, and the church did not change its costly requirements for marriage until the early nineteenth century.[10] By that time the percentage of single persons and female-headed households in São Paulo had increased substantially.[11]

Even those who could afford dowries and marriage were affected by the difficult economic situation of São Paulo. The eighteenth-century genealogist, Frei Gaspar da Madre de Deus, maintained that Paulistas could no longer afford to give such large dowries as they had in the preceding century. In the seventeenth century, he said, people had been able to

give so much land, and so many Indians and blacks to their daughters in dowry, that they could live in luxury. Because of that, when they chose husbands for their daughters they were more interested in their future son-in-law's birth than in his fortune. Usually they married their daughters to their neighbors and relatives or else to strangers with noble blood, so that when a man with good blood arrived in Brazil he was sure to make a good marriage even if he was very poor . . . but after the laws prohibiting the captivity and administration of Indians were enforced, necessity obliged many of the most important families to seek to marry their daughters to rich men who could support them.[12]

Frei Gaspar may well have reflected what Paulista families were feeling. When he commented that the wealth of seventeenth-century families al-

TABLE II

Men and Women Who Married More Than Once
(Seventeenth to Nineteenth Centuries)

Century	Deceased women	Married more than once	Deceased men	Married more than once
17th	18	7 (39%)	30	5 (17%)
18th	32	5 (16%)	36	9 (25%)
19th	68	7 (10%)	110	27 (25%)

SOURCE: Sample.

lowed them to be more interested in a prospective son-in-law's birth than in his fortune, whereas his contemporaries had to first consider a son-in-law's fortune, he was describing a significant change in the marriage bargain. In the eighteenth century, families' options were more limited than in the preceding century. Because they could no longer afford to provide all the means of production and labor necessary for the support of the couple, they tried to marry their daughters to wealthy men, who were often merchants, superior in fortune but inferior in status. Frei Gaspar was undoubtedly bemoaning the passing of the grand old age when it was a buyer's market for propertied families with marriageable daughters.

A study of the rate of remarriage of widows and widowers confirms this change in the marriage market. A. J. R. Russell-Wood's study of 165 published seventeenth-century São Paulo wills demonstrates the tendency of women to remarry more than men: 16 percent of the female testators had married more than once whereas only 11 percent of the males had done so.[13] The percentage of women in my seventeenth-century sample who had married more than once was much higher: 39 percent versus 17 percent for men (see Table 11).[14] The higher percentage of remarriage for both sexes in my sample is probably due to its being by definition composed only of the parents of married daughters, necessarily older persons and therefore with a greater chance of having remarried. One cause of the high rate of female remarriage in the seventeenth century may have been the military occupation of most Paulista husbands, which frequently resulted in their early death and a young propertied widow.

By the middle of the eighteenth century, the marriage market had changed, for widows no longer remarried more frequently than widowers. The proportion of men who married more than once in my sample rose from 17 percent to 25 percent, while the proportion of women marrying more than once declined precipitously, from 39 percent in the seventeenth century to 16 percent in the eighteenth.[15] This decline in the proportion of widows remarrying may have been the result of several factors. There were probably fewer young widows in the eighteenth century than in the preceding century because of lower male mortality, since many more men were now solely engaged in peaceful occupations. And inasmuch as out-migration resulted in a shortage of men and a surplus of women, young single women undoubtedly competed successfully with widows. The trend for fewer and fewer widows to remarry intensified in the nineteenth century, for by then only 10 percent of the female decedents in the sample had married more than once (see Table 11).

Yet since all the widows of my sample were by definition property owners, I would argue that their declining rate of remarriage is due to a decline in the male's need to have property to marry, a change in the marriage bargain. Propertied widows remarried in such large numbers in the seventeenth century precisely because men at the time needed to receive property from their wives to be able to establish themselves, creating a buyer's market for women with assets. Thus in the early seventeenth century, a widow's property was an inducement for a man to marry her. Since fewer widows remarried in the first half of the eighteenth century, we must conclude that a widow's property was no longer sufficient inducement. Perhaps a man required that his bride not only have property but also be younger than he and beautiful.

CONTRIBUTIONS TO MARRIAGE

The economic contribution of the marriage partners had also changed by the middle of the eighteenth century. As we saw above, the daughters of seventeenth-century Paulista property owners frequently married penniless Portuguese immigrants or family friends or relatives who did not contribute as much property to the marriage as their wives. In the eighteenth century, in contrast, husbands appear to have contributed more to the marriage than their wives, especially in the case of merchants who were or became much wealthier than their wives' contribution alone would have made them.

In her study of family inheritance strategies in Parnaíba, Alida Metcalf concluded that eighteenth-century families chose one or several daughters to be favored, and these daughters and their husbands took the place of their parents in the community while their siblings either emigrated or suffered downward mobility. She studied the number of slaves owned by the children of several families of Parnaíba, first in the records of dowries and inheritance received and then in several succeeding censuses. She found that daughters who had received sizable dowries consistently showed up in later censuses with more slaves than their brothers.[16]

This result could only have come about, however, because the sons in those families had not been able to find wives with dowries as large as their

TABLE 12

The Wealth of Thomé Alves de Crasto's Family

Information from inventário[a]		Reported to census		
		Year	Age	Capital
Thomé (widowed father):				
Net estate (1772)	4:725$000	1767	80	1:200$000[b]
Francisco (eldest son):				
Gift received	200$000			
Slave received	50$000			
Owed his father	392$000			
Maternal legítima (at least)	1:630$900			
Total received	2:272$900	1765	(absent)	200$000[c]
Wife (no children living with her)			40	
Joseph (2nd son):				
Slave received	50$000			
Maternal legítima (at least)	1:630$900			
Total received	1:680$900	1767	52[d]	2:000$000[e]
Wife			28	
4 children			11 (eldest)	
Captain-Major Manoel de Oliveira Cardoso:		1765	54	8:000$000[f]
Wife, D. Manoela Angélica de Crasto (1st daughter of Thomé)			46	
(no children living with them)				
Dowry	2:099$600			
Slave received	32$000			
Total received	2:131$600			
Alferes Manoel G. da Silva:		1765	43	4:000$000[g]
Wife, D. Brígida Rosa de Crasto (2nd daughter of Thomé)			40	
Dowry	2:260$600			
Their daughter			2	
2 sons from her first marriage			21 (eldest)	

[a]Thomé Alves de Crasto, 1772, AESP, INP, #ord. 549, c. 72.
[b]DI, vol. 62, p. 306.
[c]DI, vol. 62, p. 28. Since her husband was absent, his wife was living with her mother.
[d]From the age of his eldest child it appears he may have married at 40, maybe right after his mother died.
[e]DI, vol. 62, p. 305.
[f]DI, vol. 62, p. 9. Also in 1767 census, p. 257.
[g]DI, vol. 62, p. 71.

sisters'. The situation was therefore the reverse of that in the seventeenth century. Seventeenth-century men married women who brought more property to the marriage than they did; thus, even if daughters were favored with handsome dowries, sons could make up their disadvantage by marrying women with equivalent dowries. In the eighteenth century, this was no longer the case, for though dowries were large and daughters were still favored over sons, daughters married men of equal or superior means.

Parents' initial favoring of daughters resulted in permanent advantage for them, thereby bringing about an imbalance between siblings that probably contributed to the increased litigation visible in eighteenth-century inventários. The children of the merchant Thomé Alves de Crasto are a good example of the continuing inequality that favored daughters (see Table 12). Thomé died at age 85 in 1772; through his inventário, we know the value of his daughters' dowries and the gifts he made to his sons, and through the censuses of 1765 and 1767 we know the declared capital of two sons and two daughters.[17] Thomé Alves de Crasto's daughters had undergone upward mobility, while his sons at best had remained at his level.

Yet his daughters' wealth came not from their dowries but for the most part from their husbands. It is obvious that the fortunes of his daughters and sons-in-law were not dependent on the dowries they received, which were respectively only half and one-fourth of their declared capital. And if they had underdeclared their capital to the census taker as Thomé did, their property was even greater.[18] Furthermore, his eldest daughter had married the captain major of the city of São Paulo, a prominent merchant reported to be one of the richest men of the region.[19] The disparity between the capital declared to the census by his daughters and his sons suggests that his sons had not found wives with dowries as large as their sisters'.[20]

The case of three of Maria de Lima de Siqueira's children also demonstrates the new marriage bargain in which men took much more property to marriage than their wives, or else acquired it through a life of commerce (see Table 13).[21] Although her two daughters contributed more to their marriages than her eldest son, the difference is too small to account for the difference in their fortunes. Captain Ignacio Soares de Barros, the husband of Maria's fourth daughter, Martha de Camargo Lima, was an important planter who owned 81 slaves and had a partnership for the transportation of horses from Curitiba. He and his wife lived on a sitio inherited from his mother and owned other land inherited from his father. When he died they had recently bought a house in the center of São Paulo.[22] With the property Martha took to marriage, she contributed only 1:982$194 to their community property, which was worth 6:617$194 in 1759. The rest was property he had inherited and property he had acquired through business.

The husband of Maria's eldest daughter, Maria de Lima de Camargo, also

TABLE 13

Comparison Among the Estates of Three Heirs of Maria de Lima de Siqueira

Heir	Amount received from parents	Net estate with spouse
Joseph Ortiz de Camargo Lima (d. 1785), eldest son:		
Paternal legítima (1742)	884$254	
Maternal legítima (1769)	872$092	
His mother's bequest to his wife	45$000	
TOTAL	1:801$346	2:656$933 (1785)
Licenciado Manoel José da Cunha (d. 1746), husband of Maria de Lima de Camargo, eldest daughter:		
Her dowry, received 1740	2:218$640	14:829$388 (1746)
Captain Ignacio Soares de Barros (d. 1759), husband of Martha de Camargo Lima, 4th daughter:		
Her paternal legítima (1742)	884$254	
Her share of the remainder of the terça left by her father to his four single daughters	605$581	
Her dowry (given by mother alone)	492$340	
TOTAL	1:982$175	6:617$194 (1759)

SOURCES: Maria de Lima de Siqueira, 1769, AESP, INP, #ord. 545, c. 68; Joseph Ortiz de Camargo, 1785, AESP, INP, #ord. 689, c. 77; Licenciado Manoel José da Cunha, 1746, AESP, 1° Of., no. 14.123; and Ignacio Soares de Barros, 1759, AESP, 1° Of., no. 14.328.

took significantly more property to marriage than his wife, undoubtedly because he was a merchant. He died six years after their marriage, leaving a fortune seven times Maria's dowry, and more than twice the size of her sister and brother-in-law's fortune.[23] Since the sisters' dowries were approximately the same size, the simplest explanation for the difference between their wealth is the amount contributed by their husbands, whether initially or as the years went by.

The case of their brother, Joseph Ortiz de Camargo Lima, demonstrates that men were no longer marrying women who brought much more property to marriage than they did. When he died in 1785, his estate was worth only a little more than the amounts he had inherited and was roughly one-fourth the size of Maria's fortune and half the size of Martha's (see Table 13).[24] Since the inheritance he took to his marriage was almost the same amount that his sisters took to theirs, the difference in the siblings' property must have been the result not only of the larger contributions of his brothers-in-law but also of his wife's smaller (or perhaps nonexistent) dowry. Thus, although siblings inherited or received in dowry approximately equal amounts of property, sisters married up economically and brothers married down.

The fortune of a daughter who received a dowry was therefore no longer, as in the seventeenth century, mainly a function of her dowry. Not only did her husband now probably contribute at least twice the value of her dowry, but his profession and ability also made a difference. This was especially true of the wives of merchants, who appear to have consistently experienced great upward mobility in the eighteenth century. The best example is that of Anna de Oliveira, who married militia lieutenant José Rodrigues Pereira, a prosperous merchant. Her dowry had consisted of one male slave in his prime and some jewels, two gold chains and a ring, for a total of 198$400. Yet many years later, José Rodrigues Pereira reported an estate worth 28:000$000 to the census.[25] Their large property had obviously not been created solely on the basis of her dowry.

Anna had, however, contributed something else to the marriage that was more significant to a merchant than a dowry, for she came from both an old Paulista family and a family of merchants. Her stepfather, Thomé Rabelho Pinto, was a merchant, and her maternal grandfather, Manoel Vellozo, was a Portuguese merchant who had married into an old Paulista family, the Maciéis.[26] Anna therefore provided her merchant husband with a network of merchant relatives and an entry into one of the founding families.

That José Rodrigues Pereira's mercantile success was of consequence to the family history can be seen in an analysis of what happened to his and Anna's children and their descendants in comparison to the absence of record for her nieces and nephews. Three of her five siblings had no descendants, and though Silva Leme mentions the other two in his genealogy, he has no information about their spouses or children, so that they simply disappear from the public record. In contrast, José and Anna's daughters all married very well, two to Portuguese men, another to a relative, and the fourth to a member of a well-known Paulista family. Their first son became a priest, the second an army captain, and the third went to the University of Coimbra, married a Portuguese woman, became a justice of the High Court, and *desembargador do paço*, and was a member of the constitutional convention of the new empire of Brazil in 1822.[27]

Marrying a daughter to a merchant was therefore a practice that enabled old Paulista families to increase their wealth and thereby successfully maintain their status in a period in which wealth was increasingly the determining factor. Yet if we analyze the chosen professions of the sons of merchants, such as José Rodrigues Pereira or Manoel Vellozo, we see that none became a merchant.[28] So that while marrying a daughter to a merchant was an acceptable way to maintain the family fortune, for a son in the family to become a merchant clearly was not.

However, since not all men in São Paulo were merchants, propertied women also married cattle raisers and planters. For these marriages, the dowry was still important, inasmuch as it frequently included the means of production that could make the difference between failure and success in the family enterprise.

Yet Izabel Dultra's case, as we have seen, shows that a woman's dowry did not always ensure her upward mobility. Another example is that of Catharina de Siqueira, who had received a dowry of 153$000 but at the time of her death owned with her husband property worth only 157$000.[29] Most of these cases were of small planters who owned few slaves and whose daughters married men of the same kind, at a time when it was difficult to make money with agriculture or cattle breeding in São Paulo.

PROBLEMS WITH THE DOWRY

These examples confirm that there was always some risk in the giving of dowries. In a system of community property, where the dowry disappeared into the pool of goods owned by the couple and administered solely by the husband, a dowry could be lost if the husband was inept, dishonest, or just unlucky. An example of the risk incurred giving a dowry during those uncertain times is that of Escolastica Vellozo, who received a dowry worth 500$000 when she married her first husband. When he was robbed and murdered on his way back from Cuiabá, their remaining assets were fewer than their debts, so she lost her entire dowry.[30] Her father must have felt it important to marry her off a second time, for he gave her a second dowry to make the marriage possible.[31]

Another woman who lost her dowry was Ignes de Siqueira, the eldest daughter of Manoel João de Oliveira. She had received a sizable dowry, worth almost as much as the entire estate of her parents when they died years later. When her second husband refused to bring her dowry back into the estate following her parents' death, his excuse was that she had brought nothing to their marriage, because her dowry had been auctioned for the debts owed by her first husband. He added that his wife should not be obliged to bring her dowry back à colação:

She only enjoyed her dowry three years because her first husband went to Cuiabá and left her alone on the farm with no supervision, and her father went to get her and brought her back to his house when she was only nineteen, and she lived under his control without being the mistress of the dowry she had received, and he only gave her board but no clothes . . . and since she had not enjoyed the usufruct [of the dowry] she should not be obliged [to come à colação] if only in consideration of her services during the fourteen or fifteen years she lived under her father's control.[32]

Because her dowry had been so large and because her parents' property had probably diminished, the end result was that Ignes de Siqueira, who had already lost her dowry, was still expected to pay her four siblings the amount of 118$105 (the difference between her dowry and her legítima plus the terça). This situation is precisely the opposite of what happened to Manoel João Branco's daughter in the seventeenth century; she had received a very large dowry in relation to her siblings' legítima but she was not required to bring it back into the estate nor repay her brother.[33]

The preceding examples illustrate some underlying assumptions of the Portuguese inheritance and dowry laws and reveal how such laws were fast becoming invalid in eighteenth-century São Paulo. The law had a static view of property, assuming that property was conserved, always retained its value, and was unfailingly productive. Both the parents' property and the dowry were expected to remain unchanged for 20, 30, or 40 years. Thus, only at the moment of the parents' deaths did the law on dowry settle the inequalities that arose between sons and daughters because of the practice of dowry. The basic assumption was an unchanging economic scene upon which outside market forces did not impinge.

An unchanging scenario was certainly not the case in eighteenth-century São Paulo, where the gold market had turned everything upside down. The influx of gold, which bought slaves, land, and imported merchandise, developed the market economy, while agricultural production found few outlets and reverted practically to subsistence agriculture. Depending on the way property was used, profits could be either high or nearly nonexistent. Slaves, for example, could be very productive in successful mines or in the transportation of merchandise, whereas their work in agriculture in São Paulo itself might barely feed the family and produce a small surplus to be sold in town to buy expensive salt and clothes.

Under these conditions, the protection built into the law for the siblings of endowed daughters may not have worked. For example, let us return to the case of Ignes de Siqueira, whose first husband went off to Cuiabá. When she was commanded to make restitution, did she actually pay her brothers and sisters? It is most probable that she and her second husband did not have the means to do so. Although there were legal measures that could have been taken to enforce payment, would her brothers and sisters have taken them against her?

The static view of property in the Portuguese laws concerning dowry and inheritance was also evident in the laws that made it possible to have a spendthrift declared incompetent. Arguing that the crown had the responsibility to see that owners used their property wisely in the interest of future heirs, the law allowed the naming of an administrator for the property of a spendthrift.[34] Reflecting on this law, it is clear that any decline in the size or value of property was assumed to be caused by the inexperience, ineptitude, or character of the administrator, and could be corrected by changing the administrator. It was a law like the dowry law that did not take market forces into account.

But it was the market that made or destroyed fortunes in eighteenth-century São Paulo. For example, though Ignes de Siqueira's husband was certainly inconsiderate when he left her to go to try his luck in the gold mines after raising money on the strength of her dowry, he may not have been a spendthrift. Instead, when he went to the only place where money was being made, he was a man responding to market forces. His lack of success was more likely due to general economic circumstances or bad luck than to personal inadequacy.

The *Ordenações* treated property more as a trust or responsibility than as a privilege. It limited the freedom to use property by declaring that parents should conserve and augment their estate for the good of their heirs. Parents must not dissipate their property or give away more than a third, the *terça*, whether during their lifetimes or in their wills. This concept was so ingrained in eighteenth-century São Paulo that Thomé Alves de Crasto apologized to his children in his will for having spent more than his *terça* during the last years of his life, deciding therefore not even to specify the masses he would like said for his soul.[35]

In the seventeenth century, this part of the law was not observed. Lourenço Castanho Taques, for example, after marrying off his sons and endowing his daughters, dedicated most of his remaining property to the founding of the Recolhimento de Santa Thereza.[36] He would not have been able purposely to diminish his estate to such an extent if he had been following the strict interpretation of the *Ordenações*.

Thus, the strict interpretation of the law in the eighteenth century was a limitation of parents' right of choice in the way they disposed of their property and a defense of the rights of heirs. The new rigor in the application of dowry law in particular was a defense of the rights of sons, because daughters had traditionally been favored.

The favoring of daughters with large dowries or bequests had functioned well to reproduce the propertied class according to the patriarch's design—so long as sons were able to marry women with dowries as large as their sisters'. The growth of commerce, however, permitted some men to accumulate capital mainly through their own entrepreneurial skills, giving merchants leverage in the marriage bargain, not only because of their wealth but because they did not *need* to marry to receive a dowry in order to establish a productive enterprise. Thus they were able to marry women with comparatively small dowries. The entrance of merchants into the pool of suitors of Paulista brides changed the marriage market so that it became difficult for other men to continue, as in the seventeenth century, to marry women with dowries of greater value than their own assets. Men who were not merchants therefore lost economic status compared to that of their parents, whereas the status of their sisters rose with marriage. The changing marriage bargain led to the lifetime inequality of brothers and sisters, a situation that could not last.

Part Three

THE NINETEENTH CENTURY
(1800–1869)

CHAPTER 7

THE GROWTH OF INDIVIDUALISM

RAZIL EXPERIENCED great changes during the early nineteenth century. It became an independent empire, integrated into world markets, with a constitution and with new criminal and commercial laws. The concept of property altered as land became primarily a commodity. Greater individualism led to a decline in the corporate character of the family, while the economic role of the family was transformed from one of production to one of consumption. These changes were reflected in data from the sample of inventários, which showed marked differences from those of the colonial period.

A DIFFERENT SAMPLE IN A CHANGING ECONOMY

During the last quarter of the eighteenth century and the first half of the nineteenth, the economy of the captaincy, or (after independence) province, of São Paulo developed considerably. The decline in agriculture and the primacy of commerce described for the first half of the eighteenth century was reversed during the last half of the century; production in the gold mines declined, diminishing commerce to and from Minas Gerais, Cuiabá, and Goiás, while in São Paulo the production of sugar grew and was increasingly exported through the port of Santos.[1] Exportation accelerated in the 1770's with the improvement of the road over the rugged, steep hills that separate Santos from the São Paulo plateau.[2] In the early nineteenth century, cotton was again grown and exported from São Paulo, followed in the northeast of the province by the first coffee plantations, which thereafter expanded throughout the northwest as well.

Thus the basis for the economic preeminence of São Paulo in Brazil had been created by the last quarter of the nineteenth century.[3] A network of rough roads crisscrossed the captaincy, expanding after independence as coffee was planted farther north and west. Mule trains transported the sugar, cotton, and coffee to Santos. But the economic importance of the city of São Paulo itself was to become paramount only after the first railroad connecting the port of Santos to São Paulo was built in 1864—that is, at the end of the period this chapter will examine.[4] Although São Paulo's greatest demographic and business growth were to take place in the last third of the nineteenth century, its population had increased somewhat from around 20,000 in 1765 to 30,000 in 1872.[5]

After independence in 1822 the city of São Paulo experienced many changes. The city's government functions expanded when it became the legislative capital of the province. Further, with the creation of the School of Law, intellectual life flourished and students became a significant component of the population. Theaters were established, a postal service was created, and, after the royal family moved to Brazil in 1808, the crown permitted the printing press in Brazil, leading to the publication of newspapers and journals in São Paulo, as elsewhere. The government formed a national guard and enlarged the army, continuing the process of professionalization of the military.

The growth of a strong market economy altered the characteristics of property owners studied in our sample. Small proprietors are in the majority, on the one hand showing greater concentration of wealth and on the other making it less of an elite sample. In the eighteenth-century sample, families who did not own slaves constituted only 9 percent of the sample, and those who owned fewer than four slaves, 33 percent; in the nineteenth century 38 percent owned no slaves, and 65 percent owned fewer than four (see Table 14).[6]

The decrease in the number of slaveholders in the nineteenth-century sample corresponds to the trends in the total population. In the urban areas of the city of São Paulo, the percentage of households without slaves increased from 47 percent in 1778 to 54 percent in 1836, while in the rural bairros the increase was even greater, from 52 to 72 percent. Not only did the percentage of slaveholders decrease, but so did the percentage of slaves in the total population of the city, from 35 to 28 percent.[7] It is probable that the further decline in the actual numbers of slaves in the city of São Paulo, from 6,872 in 1854 to 3,828 in 1874, resulted from the prohibition of the slave traffic in 1850, which made slaves much more expensive.[8]

TABLE 14
Ownership of Slaves (Eighteenth and Nineteenth Centuries)

	Number and percentage of estates	
Slaves owned	18th cent.	19th cent.
20 or more	11 (20%)	11 (6.4%)
10–19	10 (18.2%)	19 (11%)
4–9	16 (29.1%)	31 (17.9%)
½–3	13 (23.6%)	47 (27.1%)
0	5 (9.1%)	65 (37.6%)
TOTAL	55 (100%)	173 (100%)
Number of slaves unknown	13	5
SAMPLE	68	178

NOTE: Ownership of half a slave occurs when one slave is owned jointly by two persons or families.

The nineteenth-century sample may also have become less elitist as a result of a change in legal requirements. In the eighteenth century, only estates that included minor heirs were required to go through a judicial inventário; when all heirs were adults, it was legally possible to have a friendly division of the estate without official intervention. Property owners without minor heirs who avoided having a judicial inventário because of the large expense involved did not therefore appear in the sample. In contrast, the growing interest of the nineteenth-century state in taxing bequests and inheritances led to the requirement that all estates be settled judicially. Accordingly, all property owners, not only those with minor heirs, are represented in the sample of nineteenth-century inventários.[9]

The less elitist character of the nineteenth-century sample is also revealed when looking at literacy, for no longer were all male proprietors literate. In the seventeenth century sample, practically all the men—but none of the women—knew how to sign their names.[10] In the eighteenth century all the men of the sample knew how to read and write, and so did the daughters (and occasionally wives) of the wealthiest families. In the nineteenth-century sample, in contrast, there were many male proprietors who were as illiterate as their wives or sisters; over a third of the families included some male members who were illiterate (see Table 15). Nevertheless, this was a much smaller rate of illiteracy than in the general population, for in the 1872 census in the city of São Paulo, 68 percent of the men and 83 percent of the women were illiterate.[11]

The rise in the proportion of illiterate men in the sample seems to correspond to the rise in the proportion of small landowners, demonstrating that class was the variable that defined the level of literacy. The illiterate male property owners were usually from the rural bairros, and their lack of learning

TABLE 15
Literacy in Property-Owning Families (Nineteenth Century)

Who signs in family	Sample			
	Poorest third	Middle third	Wealthy third	Total
All men and women	9 (25%)	10 (24%)	29 (66%)	48 (40%)
All men, some women	3 (8%)	6 (15%)	3 (6%)	12 (10%)
Only men	6 (17%)	6 (15%)	5 (12%)	17 (14%)
Only some men	9 (25%)	15 (36%)	6 (14%)	30 (25%)
No one	9 (25%)	4 (10%)	1 (2%)	14 (11%)
TOTAL	36 (100%)	41 (100%)	44 (100%)	121 (100%)

NOTE: In only 121 out of 178 inventários was there information on the literacy of all adult members of the family: 36 in the poorest third of the sample, 41 in the middle third, and 44 in the wealthiest third. All percentages have been rounded off.

was undoubtedly connected to the distance from school and the need to work on the farm. For example, although the immigrant German farmer Cristiano Gotfriet knew how to write, none of his sons or daughters did.[12] And the son of José Pereira never learned because after his father died, he was the only son left to take care of his mother and work on the farm.[13] An 1858 report says that only one in ten school-age boys was enrolled in school in the province of São Paulo.[14]

The correlation between literacy and wealth in the sample is far from perfect, however. What is most surprising is the relatively large proportion (25 percent) of families in the poorest third of the sample in which all members, both men and women, knew how to write, while in seven of the wealthiest forty-four families at least some of the men and all the women were illiterate. These anomalies suggest processes of downward and upward mobility.

A NEW CONCEPT OF PROPERTY

The difference between the eighteenth- and nineteenth-century samples can also be explained by changes in the evolution of private property itself. Because an inventário records the possession of property, a change in the kind of property most valued can result in a change in the kinds of people whose property is recorded. One of the simplest changes relates to land and clothes. Because in the seventeenth century land was free and accessible to all, whereas clothes that gave status could cost more than a house, land was not important in inventários but clothes were always included. It is therefore possible that people who owned land but no expensive clothes would not even have had an inventário drawn up, and consequently would not appear in the sample. By the nineteenth century, in contrast, clothes had completely disappeared from inventários, while land and other real estate became their most significant component.

Moreover, land was being transformed from mainly a use value to an exchange value; it became a full commodity. Property rights over land became more rigid and exclusive in the nineteenth century, as the availability of land decreased and its value increased. Land in the seventeenth century was freely settled and received in grant, and families treated its title casually; although titles were presented at the time of inventário, no monetary value was given to land. However, the improvements made on land, whether the family held title to it or not, were considered property and duly appraised.

In the eighteenth century, sesmarias were still granted, but most land, and all land in the sample, was acquired through purchase, inheritance, or dowry. Very few proprietors declared improvements on land without having title to the land itself, unlike many proprietors in the seventeenth century.[15] Furthermore, as we saw above, half the inhabitants of eighteenth-century São Paulo owned no slaves or land whatever, and they worked and lived on land they did not own. They were not landless laborers, however, but squatters or tenant farmers, whose property was probably not sufficient to warrant a judicial inventário.[16]

A change also came about in the relative importance of slaves and land. In seventeenth-century São Paulo, custom, though not the law, made Indians significant property, so that an inventário was made even if Indians were the only property owned. By the mid-eighteenth century, Indians were no longer considered a part of property, but African slaves were and would be until 1888, when the law abolished property rights over people. The decline by mid-nineteenth century in the number of slaveowners in the sample probably signals a decline in the relative importance of slaves as compared to land. Real estate was certainly becoming a much more significant part of Paulista property: land and houses averaged 50 percent of the gross estate in the nineteenth-century sample, as compared to only 19 percent in the eighteenth century.

By the middle of the nineteenth century, not only had the law regarding land ownership changed, but a stronger market economy had further increased the monetary value of land. The granting of sesmarias had ceased at independence, but a legal process still existed by which squatters could acquire title to the land they had worked and lived on. But after the Land Law was passed in 1850, public land could be acquired legally only by purchase. The transformation of land into a commodity was thus complete.[17]

The processes by which land became a commodity went hand in hand with a change in the concept of private property itself. Not only was the colonial sesmaria acquired by grant and not by purchase, but in the early eighteenth century it was not supposed to be alienated without permission from the crown.[18] A sesmaria was also conditional property, given on condition that it be worked, or exploited.[19] A 1798 law, reiterating previous rulings, specified that "when a sesmaria is not cultivated it will be lost, and transferred to abler hands that have sufficient capital."[20]

Hence the concepts that prevailed throughout colonial times were that property entailed not only privileges but duties and responsibilities as well and that the final arbiter was the crown. As we saw above, the crown believed that one of its duties was to see that "no one misuse his property" and therefore had the power to deny rights to persons it categorized as spendthrifts—namely, those who spent their capital recklessly and thus did not fulfill their responsibility and duty toward property and their families.[21]

After independence, however, land stopped being royal patrimony and became private property, and property was no longer a duty but only a privilege, which included the right to make unwise decisions regarding one's property. Not only did the new laws of 1821 and the Imperial Constitution of 1824 abolish all personal privileges and guarantee individual liberty against the power of the state, but they also protected private property against the power of the state.[22] Henceforth only in special cases was the state allowed to expropriate private property.[23] Neither could the state limit the rights of spendthrifts, because as the nineteenth-century Brazilian jurist Candido Mendes de Almeida wrote, the old law against spendthrifts "is contrary to the principle in the Constitution that a citizen has the full right to private property, including the use and abuse of such property, only limited by the harm he could do to third parties."[24] In order for market relations to function, people had to be able to make mistakes.

CONCENTRATION OF WEALTH

The preponderance of small proprietors in our nineteenth-century sample may also indicate that the privilege of owning private property was being acquired by more and more families. Most were probably descendants of those persons listed in the mid-eighteenth-century censuses as people who worked the land but did not own it, for the majority were born in the parish where they lived or in a nearby parish.[25] In the intervening years they had acquired the land they worked. João Soares de Camargo, for example, acquired his land by proving that it had been in his possession and cultivated since 1838.[26] A few of the small proprietors in the sample were German immigrants.[27] Other small proprietors may have experienced downward mobility, having descended from more prosperous families whose property was repeatedly fractioned through inheritance.

The preponderance of small property owners in the sample is, in addition,

TABLE 16

Comparative Size of Estates (Seventeenth to Nineteenth Centuries)

Century	Largest gross estate	Smallest gross estate	Ratio
17th	1:190$500	6$800	175:1
18th	26:196$200	43$700	668:1
19th	231:245$500	142$000	1628:1

SOURCE: Sample. There were larger estates outside the sample; for example, in the seventeenth century, João Baruel with 4:358$600 (ratio 641:1), and in the nineteenth century the Barão de Limeira with 2,766:874$000 (ratio 19,485:1).

a reflection of the fact that, despite growing land concentration in the province of São Paulo, the city's rural bairros did not experience concentration.[28] The great money-making crops were planted in other parts of the province. Although sugar had been cultivated in the district of the city of São Paulo in the eighteenth century, the great plantations that exported sugar toward the end of the century and during the first half of the nineteenth century were formed in newer agricultural regions where bush still existed.[29] Neither was coffee much cultivated in the rural bairros of São Paulo, for in 1836 there were only three coffee plantations in the area.[30]

Many of the small and some of the large proprietors in our sample raised mules and worked mule trains, the principal form of commercial transportation in the province until the inauguration of railroads in the 1860's. Forty-eight estates of the sample (34 percent) possessed mules, and in 34 of these, the principal occupation was raising mules and running mule trains.[31] Fully 78 percent of the sample owned horses, mules, oxen, or cattle.[32] Fifty-nine percent of the families in the sample planted beans, manioc, or corn for subsistence and sale to the urban areas.[33]

Although land concentration did not occur in the city of São Paulo and its outskirts, wealth from all sources became much more concentrated by the middle of the nineteenth century than it had been in colonial times. In the seventeenth century the top 10 percent of the sample owned 43 percent of the total wealth of the sample; in the eighteenth century it owned 53 percent; and in the nineteenth century, 60 percent.

The greater possibilities for accumulation in the nineteenth century are revealed as well in the increase of the ratio between the gross estate of the largest property owner and that of the smallest in each sample. The ratio went from 175:1 in the seventeenth century to 668:1 in the eighteenth to 1,628:1 in the nineteenth, showing a tenfold increase. (See Table 16.)

Furthermore, the methods of accumulation altered. Agricultural production for export was the engine that moved accumulation in the early nineteenth century, and large planters, not merchants, were the wealthiest persons. Although the number of merchants in São Paulo increased by 1836, the extremely wealthy merchants who had dominated the mid-eighteenth-century elite had disappeared, and merchants now tended to be less wealthy than large planters and professionals.[34] Nevertheless, many of the great planter fortunes, such as that of the Prado family, had been founded by merchants.[35]

There was also a new category of property owners whom contemporaries called *capitalistas*. These were individuals whose income derived mainly from financial instruments such as shares, stocks, and bonds and from the lending of money at interest, even though many of these men owned plantations as well.[36] For example, the Barão de Antonina was listed in the almanac as a capitalista, and though he had countless properties (houses, land, and plantations), over 50 percent of his net estate consisted of shares.[37]

The composition of the nineteenth-century sample is much more varied than that of the preceding century. The rural contingent consists of many small and some middle-sized or large rural proprietors within the district of São Paulo, plus a few wealthy planters who lived much of the year in the center of São Paulo and perhaps owned a *chácara*, or fruit farm, in a rural bairro, but whose more important plantations were elsewhere in the province.[38] Merchants, large and small, professionals, and some strictly urban families complete the picture.

A market had developed for renting urban real estate. Some of the urban families in the sample rented the house they lived in, and others owned several houses for rent or else strings of rooms, *quartos*, adjacent to their houses, which were also rented out.[39] This practice sharply differentiated the first half of the nineteenth century from the early eighteenth century. In both the seventeenth and eighteenth centuries, houses had been rented, but some houses that were offered for rent languished unoccupied for long periods. In colonial times most people owned their own house and few had regular cash incomes that would permit them to rent. But by the middle of the nineteenth century, free land on which to build had disappeared and opportunities for paid employment or petty commerce increased, so that the number of people without homes of their own but with the ability to pay rent grew. Not only urban owners but also rural residents responded to this demand, renting, for example, a small house on their property at the side of the road to serve as a store and the storekeeper's quarters.[40]

EMERGENCE OF A MIDDLE CLASS

One of the most striking developments is the appearance in the sample of urban families who owned little property, perhaps renting their house in the center of São Paulo, yet who evinced elite status through their education, furniture, and connections; they were the beginning of a middle class.

The families in this incipient middle class were usually supported by the income from the father's profession or army career. A good example is that of José Gomes Segurado and his wife, Donna Anna Benedicta de Azevedo Segurado, who owned no real estate whatever but who had distinguished sons. One son was a lieutenant in the army, and another son and a son-in-law both bore the title of doctor. The couple's joint *inventário* was only carried out when the widow died thirteen years after her husband (a way to limit judicial costs). At that time she owned only three female domestic slaves and the income from a *montepio* (annuity fund), 25$000 a month until her death, probably left to her by her husband. Despite their relatively few assets, the family's status was high because of the sons' and son-in-law's professions; the furniture was also of excellent quality, and the daughters had beautiful calligraphy, indicating that they had been well educated.[41]

Another example of this new kind of family was that of Dr. João Thomaz de Mello, a homeopathic doctor who lived and had his office on the Rua Direita.[42] The property he and his wife owned when he died in 1859 consisted only of a great deal of very expensive furniture, a horse, and seven slaves. They had more debts than assets, yet their standard of living was so high that when he died, his wife had no compunction in spending 62$000 to return from Rio de Janeiro for the funeral in São Paulo, plus 87$000 on clothes for mourning. The family undoubtedly lived on the income from the doctor's profession in addition to the income from renting out their slaves. (One slave was a stonecutter, for whose skill they would be well paid.) The family probably continued to live well after the father's death, for the son-in-law was a doctor of law with an important position in the Imperial court in Rio de Janeiro, and the judge permitted the widow to retain all assets with the commitment to pay all debts.[43]

The significant characteristic of the above families is that they were units of consumption rather than production. The husband did produce, since he provided services, but he produced as an individual; the family *as a unit* only consumed. And the status and level of consumption was not based on the ownership of the means of production, or capital, but on the exercise of a profession, human capital. In this characteristic these families were truly "modern." They differed sharply from families of the seventeenth and eighteenth centuries, as well as from the families of the small proprietors in the rural areas of mid-nineteenth-century São Paulo, who were still primarily units of production.

Yet because they had so little property, the future of these families' sons depended entirely on their ability as professionals (with the help of connections), while the future of single daughters depended either on their brothers' generosity or on finding a husband to support them. Marriage could not be a property arrangement in these families of professionals because they had little or no property. It is in this context that the drive for female education and literacy can well be understood as a substitute for dowry.

If the families of professionals were mainly units of consumption, what were the families of wealthy plantation owners? I have concluded that, though they *owned* units of production, the families themselves were gradually losing their function as units of production. Instead of living most of the time on their rural properties, as Paulistas had done in the past, most now lived in São Paulo a great part of the year.[44] This residence and the fact that they accumulated properties in many different parts of the state made it difficult for individual men of the family to be a part of the productive unit, even if only as administrators, while the rest of the family members, particularly women and children, became only consumers.

LEGAL CHANGES

Among the legal changes that took place in the first years after independence, there were two that weakened the corporate character of the Brazilian family and strengthened individualism. The first was the affirmation of the equality of all individuals before the law. In the 1831 Penal Code, this legal principle took the form of a declaration that all persons were individually responsible for their crime.[45] No longer was a family—a father or mother, spouse, child, or grandchild—held responsible for a crime committed by one of its members, as had been the case in the seventeenth century. The individual stood alone before the law.

Another legal change that tipped the balance from the patriarchal family to the individual was the lowering of the age of majority to 21, accompanied by automatic emancipation.[46] The age of majority had been 25 during colonial times, but this majority did not mean that at that age a son, much less a daughter, was automatically emancipated. For emancipation to take place, a man or woman either had to marry or had to go through a formal judicial procedure granting that status.

Single men in colonial times therefore continued under their father's authority long into adulthood. For example, when Manoel Pacheco Gato died in 1715, he had four single sons between the ages of 26 and 33 who were still not emancipated; he declared in his will that two of them had gone to the sertão with the obligation of bringing all profit back to their father because they were still filhos-família.[47] After their father's death, all four went through the legal process of emancipation with the consent of their guardian and their mother. (Their mother was careful to remark, however, that she still expected them not to neglect their responsibility to the family, especially their responsibility "as her sons and as brothers of their sisters" to marry off those sisters.)[48]

In colonial times, single sons of whatever age were therefore legally not free and independent agents (though distance could give de facto independence). Single sons were but the workers or, at best, the executives of the family as a productive corporate group. A seventeenth-century Portuguese treatise maintained that filhos-família were like prisoners.[49] Early nineteenth-century regulations in Parnaíba fined anyone who gambled with a slave or a filho-família, seemingly equating their lack of liberty.[50] The issue, however, was probably that neither slaves nor filhos-família were free agents and therefore could not be held responsible for their gambling debts, and that slaveowners and fathers had no wish to assume those debts.

The profit gained through the work of filhos-família went entirely to the family. Of course, the sons' own inheritance came out of that profit, so even though they worked for the family, they were working for their own future as well. However, sons who worked for others were allowed by Portuguese law to retain their wages.[51] Nevertheless, the sons of property owners did not habitually work for others, and it was through marriage—that is, setting up a new productive family—that a man in colonial times automatically became legally and economically independent, despite the expectation that he would still cooperate for the common good of the family.[52]

To become independent of their father's or widowed mother's control, daughters also had to marry or ask judicially for emancipation. In the seventeenth century a woman who never married (and there were very few among Paulista property owners) usually remained under the control of her father or widowed mother until both parents died, but by the middle of the eighteenth century some unmarried women were asking for emancipation after the age of 25 just as many of their brothers did. For example, when the widow Suzanna Rodrigues de Arzão died in 1754, her youngest daughter, Agueda Paes, had been emancipated and administering her property for many years.[53] And four years after Caetano Soares Vianna's death in 1757, his single daughters Mariana, then 40 years old, and Maria, 27, were granted emancipation after witnesses declared that both were extremely capable of administering their property.[54]

Although a woman who married did not become fully emancipated, since she passed from her father's to her husband's control, she had greater status, power, and responsibility than did her unmarried sisters. (Of course, married men in colonial times also had greater status, power, and responsibility than their unmarried brothers.) A woman's parents, however, lost control over her. She gained title to the property she owned jointly with her husband, becoming the mistress of her own house and of numerous Indians or slaves. The words of authority with which propertied colonial women (almost all of whom were married or widowed) dictated their wills indicate the extent to which their position as owner and mistress, or *senhora*, of extensive property reinforced their sense of self-worth. For example, Maria de Lima de Siqueira declared with pride in her will that after her husband's death she supported all her children with great honor, giving them the clothes, pages, and horses their noble condition required, and that she used her own property and not their paternal inheritance for these expenses. If any of her heirs objected to the provisions in her will, she continued, let them first pay back what she had spent on them.[55]

Thus, the weakening of the patriarchal family that started in the eighteenth century affected not only the patriarch but also his representative, his wife and widow. As we saw above, a married woman in colonial São Paulo often played an important role as her husband's representative in business dealings or as administrator of their joint property. And widows became not only the legal head of household, controlling all their property, but many, especially in the seventeenth century, also controlled their unemancipated children, filhos-família, including adult sons.[56]

The nineteenth-century law providing automatic emancipation at majority liberated both children and their parents. On the one hand it meant the legal freedom of the young adult to manage his or her person and property independently from parental authority. On the other, because parents were legally responsible for the repayment of money lent or credit given to sons or daughters who were still filhos-família, children's automatic emancipation at 21 liberated parents from financial responsibility for the debts of their adult children, permitting fathers to allow their sons full independence. This independence made a considerable difference when sons were in business on their own. Under the *Ordenações* a father was *always* responsible for a loan made with his consent to a son who was in business if he was still a filho-família, even if he were of age.[57] Clearly the old law is based on the concept of a corporate family in business. After the law of automatic emancipation, it would take a formal partnership between father and son to make the father as owner of the enterprise, or as senior partner, once again responsible for the business debts of his son. Although fathers and adult sons could and did continue to work together in formal or informal partnerships, patriarchal control as such had been lost. It was replaced by control based on contract or on different hierarchical positions in a business organization.

Early nineteenth-century property owners lived in a different world from that of their colonial predecessors. The majority of estates in the sample were of small landowners, making it a less elitist sample, but one with a greater concentration of wealth as the development of strong export crops increased the avenues for capital accumulation. Land had become a full commodity, and the concept of private property changed from being a conditional right under absolutist rule to being an unconditional right protected from the power of the state. A new middle stratum developed, the middle class, whose relatively high economic and social statuses derived more from a profession, human capital, than from the ownership of land or slaves. The middle-class family was a new kind of family, a unit of consumption instead of a unit of production. And the de facto weakening of parents' power over their adult children that took place in the eighteenth century was legalized in the nineteenth century when the individual (and no longer the family) was made solely responsible for his crime, and sons and daughters were automatically emancipated at 21. Thus, individualism grew and contributed to the loosening of the corporate and patriarchal character of the family.

CHAPTER 8

THE SEPARATION OF BUSINESS FROM FAMILY

ESIDES THE GROWTH of individualism, which weakend the corporate structure of the extended family, another important change was taking place in early nineteenth-century Brazil that would affect the nature of marriage. Business and economic functions were gradually becoming separate from family affairs. Throughout the period, partnerships with persons outside the family were becoming more prevalent and mechanisms were being introduced to differentiate business proceedings from family accounting. Simultaneously, there was a greater specialization of creditors and more efficient collection of debts. It seems clear that these developments and the earlier changes described for eighteenth-century São Paulo were part of the process taking place in the Western world, where the realm of economics was becoming differentiated from other aspects of social life, such as the church and the family, and a full market economy was being created.[1]

SEPARATION OF BUSINESS FROM FAMILY

The process of differentiation of family and business is evident in the inventários themselves. When, as always was the case in the seventeenth century, the family as a productive unit sold its production, the family head became the creditor of the buyer, and such credits were listed in the inventários of husband or wife. When, as became more and more common by the early nineteenth century, it was a partnership or company that was the seller instead of the family even if the company was wholly owned by the deceased, the company was the creditor. Neither its credits nor its debts appeared in the couple's inventários. Instead, their ownership was listed simply as another asset equivalent to the amount invested in the company.

In the eighteenth-century sample, formal partnerships were the exception, whereas in mid-nineteenth-century inventários, there was an increasing number of formal partnerships that coexisted with business situations in which the family functioned informally as a company as in previous centuries, sometimes within the same inventário. In the samples of both centuries, however, formal partnerships only existed in the wealthier estates, in the top 22 percent in the eighteenth century and in the top 25 percent in the nineteenth.

In colonial times, when the family was itself the structure of business, business proceedings were seriously disrupted by the inventário process when the patriarch or his wife died. Since family and business were one, family law applied when the owner died. Because spouses were co-owners of the family enterprise, family inheritance law required that at the death of either spouse an inventory be made of all property, including commercial property such as the goods in a shop, and a division effected among heirs. The heirs of eighteenth-century merchants frequently complained of the losses incurred from holding up business for the completion of an inventory.[2] Going through this elaborate process, in which every bolt of cloth was measured and appraised, may have protected the rights of the heirs of a deceased wife, for instance, but it disrupted the business of the widower.[3] Thus, family inheritance law was a fetter to business efficiency.

Yet it was only in the nineteenth century that formal mechanisms permitting and facilitating a separation of business and family accounting were beginning to be introduced in Brazil. When an inventário included the business debts and credits of a family enterprise that had grown considerably, it became advisable to separate business from family accounting in the inventário, as Marciano Pires de Oliveira explained when his wife died in 1859. He told the juiz dos órfãos that neither the active nor the passive debts of his mule business were liquid nor could they easily be ascertained, partly because his partner, who was also his nephew, owned one-third interest in both the debts and profits and was himself a debtor to the business. De Oliveira added that, to ascertain the exact balance, it would be necessary to liquidate the partnership and adjust all accounts with other businesses.[4] He therefore suggested that all the family's real estate and movables be inventoried, appraised, and divided among the heirs but that the division of the assets, credits, and debits of his business be left for a later date. The judge insisted, however, that he should set a date for the liquidation of the partnership. From a business point of view, this decision could have drastic consequences.

Moreover, the juiz dos órfãos probably should not have made the demand, for under the new Commercial Code passed in 1850, a partnership no longer had to be liquidated at the death of one of the partners' wives, as had been the case under the *Ordenações*.[5] When the partner himself died, the Commercial Code allowed the continuation of a partnership through a new contract with the partner's heirs.[6] Cases like the above, where the juiz dos órfãos protected the interests of minor heirs at the expense of the widower or the business itself, must have prompted the ruling of the 1850 Commercial Code stipulating that only the *juiz de comércio* (judge of commerce) and never the juiz dos órfãos was to have jurisdiction over the liquidation of a partnership.[7] The appointment of different judges for family and commercial law was in itself a part of the process of separating the business enterprise from the family. Marciano Pires de Oliveira's case illustrates the contradiction between the rights of family members as co-owners or heirs of an enterprise and the right of the enterprise to exist and function separately from the family and not be disrupted by deaths or other events within the family.

The Commercial Code of 1850 and later laws contributed to the separation of the family and business in terms of financial responsibility for debts. In silent partnerships (*sociedades em comandita*), the silent partner's liability was limited to the amount he had invested.[8] The law of 1862 permitted the creation of companies of limited liability and joint-stock companies, which limited the responsibility of a family or individual for the debts of such companies. This law protected the family from the reverses a company might experience.[9] Even more significant from the point of view of our analysis is that *no* constituted company or partnership was liable for *any* of the private debts of its partners.[10] These laws liberated business from any family considerations.

As more partnerships were formed, men gradually moved from a primary commitment to the extended patriarchal family or clan to a primary commitment to themselves and their nuclear family. An example of this shift in mentality can be found in the dissolution in 1882 of the partnership of Alfredo Ellis with his uncle and father-in-law, Coronel Chiquinho da Cunha Bueno. Alfredo Ellis broke up the partnership because Coronel Chiquinho allowed his two younger sons to use the partnership's slaves gratuitously.[11] On the one hand, Coronel Chiquinho was acting with the old mentality: his property was the family's property, and his sons' use of the slaves would only increase the family's prosperity; besides, as the patriarch, he could allow his sons to use his property as he wished. On the other hand, Alfredo Ellis, with the new mentality, probably influenced by an English father and an education in the United States, sharply differentiated between the property owned by his father-in-law alone and the property owned by the partnership. By insisting that his brothers-in-law had no right to use the partnership's slaves without paying for their services, he was defending his individual rights, and the rights of the partnership itself, against the old claims of family ties and against the right of the patriarch to do as he wished. Instead of acting as if each individual's property belonged to the entire family—as Paulistas had done in the past—Alfredo, in business dealings at least, did not collaborate with his brothers-in-law (who were not his partners) but instead competed with them. Neither did he submit to the patriarchal power of his father-in-law, as he would if he had been born in the seventeenth or eighteenth century. The partnership itself, moreover, was the mechanism that permitted what would have amounted to insubordination in the past to become principally a question of business differences.

A partnership thus served to define and limit business relations between relatives that in colonial times would have been automatic, lifelong, and somewhat imprecise. For example, when Bento José Martins da Cunha died in 1858, he and his wife owned several houses in São Paulo and Campinas, two slaves, and a fruit farm in the parish of Santa Ephigenia, and Bento had a partnership in a saddlery with their nephew and son-in-law, Cândido José Martins da Cunha.[12] The contract between Bento and Cândido specified that both partners would work full time for the partnership, that it would last only ten years, and that it would not be dissolved if one of the partners died. Despite the fact that Bento contributed two-thirds of the capital, profits were to be divided equally between the two partners. It could be argued that Bento was protecting his daughter's future by contributing so much to the partnership with his son-in-law. Another interpretation, however, is suggested by events after Bento's death. The partnership had eight more years to run and his wife asked that it be adjudicated to her share of the estate so that she could receive an income from the partnership until the date of its dissolution. This outcome may have been precisely what Bento had in mind, namely, that Cândido continue working for the benefit of his mother-in-law until the partnership expired. Another reason to suspect this motive is that the couple's eldest son, who was nineteen when his father died, was studying law, and probably could not have done much to help support the family until he became a lawyer. The formality and limits of this arrangement contrast with colonial practice; in former times the son-in-law would automatically have continued working for the benefit of the larger family during his whole lifetime and would have expected his young brother-in-law to do likewise.

Formal partnership itself was the novelty. Wealthy São Paulo property owners in the middle of the nineteenth century owned much property in formal partnership, even if the partnership was only with family members such as brothers, sisters, or in-laws. For example, when Luis Bernardo Pinto Ferraz died in 1856, he and his wife fully owned a tea plantation on the road to Santo Amaro, but they also owned one-fourth of a plantation in Porto Feliz in formal partnership with his mother-in-law and his sister-in-law (who was both his wife's sister and his brother's widow) and half of another plantation in Araraquara with the heirs of another brother.[13] Another example is the partnership, or *sociedade civil*, that Fernando Pacheco Jordão formed with several of his brothers in 1836 to run the property they had inherited from their father.[14]

These partnerships no longer came about automatically because of birth or marriage as had been the case in colonial times. Men continued to be born into or married into families that could provide capital, connections, or possible partnerships in business, but whether these were in fact provided or not no longer depended on the family relationship itself but instead on individual decisions and voluntary contracts. Joseph Sweigart's study of coffee factors in nineteenth-century Rio de Janeiro describes many examples of family partnerships. A careful examination of these examples provides a clear picture of the way individual members of families dissolved partnerships with relatives and formed new ones with the same or other relatives, or sometimes with nonrelatives, thus changing their business relations with relatives many times over the course of their lives.[15]

In contrast, smaller property owners in early nineteenth-century São Paulo tended to hold property in common with other family members without a formal partnership, functioning more as families had in colonial times. For instance, the eldest son of Antonio Bento de Andrade, who was guardian of his minor brothers and sisters, reported that he and his siblings lived and worked together in great harmony on the family farm, which gave no profit but sustained them.[16] Especially common were cases where heirs owned shares of undivided land; when one of them died, they had no way of knowing which part of the land they had all been cultivating belonged to the deceased.[17]

The introduction of corporations, shares, stocks and bonds, and partnerships with limited liability differentiated the spheres of family and enterprise even further, permitting the easy transmittal of business property, whether by alienation or inheritance, without affecting the progress of business. Shares and stocks and bonds permitted the most extreme separation of family and business. In contrast to the ownership of a farm, for example, the ownership of stocks and bonds required no labor by a family member; no personal administrative abilities were needed for profit to accrue. It is therefore significant that the assets of many wealthy widows in nineteenth-century São Paulo were in the form of stocks and bonds. For example, over 40 percent of the estate of D. Anna Maria de Souza Queiros, worth 82 contos, consisted of bonds, or *apólices* (12 contos), shares, or *acções* (12 contos), and money at interest in the bank (9 contos).[18]

The possibility of converting property to shares, stocks and bonds, or money in the bank liberated widows from the need to take over the administration of the productive property they controlled or to depend on male relatives to do so, as had so often been the case in colonial times. Thus the corporate character of the family was weakened in still another way: widows were now able to be far more independent of their sons, brothers, or fathers, although they might become dependent on strangers (brokers), instead. But the latter dependence was, of course, a market relation, making it different from the former, a family relationship. Conversion to stocks and bonds of a widow's real estate and other property that was complicated to administer also liberated sons, brothers, and fathers from the onus of working to conserve property that was not their own, thereby facilitating greater individualism.

DEBTORS AND CREDITORS

Another sign of the increasing separation of family and business is the diminishing role of the family, as well as the individual, as creditor. In colonial Brazil when family and business were still one, families were almost as frequently creditors as they were debtors. This is in sharp contrast to the situation in twentieth-century industrial nations, where, except for the relatively few individuals who are self-employed or the rare cases where an individual seller of a house assumes the mortgage, most creditors are businesses. As consumers, on the other hand, individuals and families are usually debtors.

In the seventeenth century, outstanding debt was substantial in most estates, usually consisting of unpaid legítimas, dowries, tithes, loans taken from the juizo de órfãos, or commodities bought but not paid for.[19] Such debts were often left unpaid for long periods of time. In one case land was bought but still not paid for 23 years later; in another, the rent for ten years' occupancy of a house was negotiated and paid only after the death of the owner.[20] Dowries sometimes took years to be paid, and the payment or nonpayment of debts was influenced by noneconomic factors, especially family ties.

The seventeenth-century inventários also give evidence of many creditors. Fifty-three percent of the estates in the sample were creditors, the largest proportion of creditors of the three centuries (see Figure 4). Ranking the estates according to size, we find that the wealthiest third included the largest proportion of creditors, yet creditors were quite evenly distributed throughout the sample, since 50 percent of the poorest third were also creditors (see Figure 5).

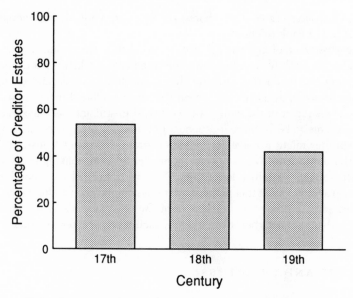

Fig. 4. Percentage of estates that were creditors (seventeenth to nineteenth centuries). Source: sample.

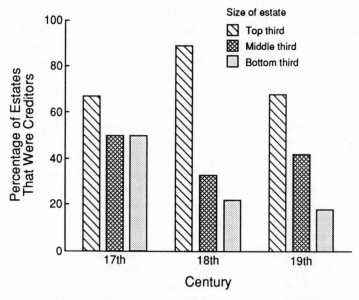

Fig. 5. Estates that were creditors by wealth of estate (seventeenth to nineteenth centuries). Source: sample.

Inasmuch as most credits in the seventeenth-century inventários came from the sale of commodities, the widespread distribution of creditors can be explained as the result of an economy in which families, as productive enterprises, sold commodities but were not paid immediately, and in a similar fashion they themselves postponed payment when buying. Families whose estates were not creditors probably produced mostly for subsistence, or sold surplus commodities rarely.

The distribution of debtors in the seventeenth century reinforces the above conclusions. Eighty-four percent of the lower and middle thirds of the sample had outstanding debts, but *all* the estates in the wealthiest third did.[21] That the wealthiest estates were all debtors suggests not only that they had credit and that, as the most powerful families, they could probably delay payment as long as they chose, but also that they were the most involved in commodity production and distribution, constantly borrowing and trading, while the chronic lack of specie as well as noneconomic factors led to never-ending mutual indebtedness.

The mid-eighteenth century saw fewer creditors than in the seventeenth century, attesting to the development of economic specialization (see Figure 4). And creditors were distinctly more prevalent at the upper levels of wealth, for they were 89 percent of the wealthiest third of the sample, and only 22 percent of the poorest third (see Figure 5). These statistics reflect the eighteenth-century economic scene, in which the wealthiest estates were those of merchants, who were the most likely to make loans and extend credit, while the poorest were subsistence farmers, who sold few if any commodities and were therefore rarely creditors.[22]

Credits were a large percentage of the estates of eighteenth-century merchants, for they made up from 20 to 78 percent of the gross estates of the four wealthiest persons in the sample, all of whom were merchants. In 1769, for example, over three-fourths of José Rodrigues Pereira's estate consisted of promissory notes owed to him, and they came from all over Brazil. Nevertheless, he left a network of partners in Rio de Janeiro, Santos, Minas Gerais, and Mato Grosso who could collect debts, though in many cases they themselves were his debtors. Despite his large network of debt collectors, many of the debts owed José Rodrigues Pereira had already been listed in the inventário of his wife when she died eight or nine years earlier, indicating that debts were carried for a long time.[23]

When such a large part of their estates were credits, eighteenth-century merchants left their children an uncertain inheritance, for the value of most of the estate remained to be collected, a task that could prove difficult, especially if the debtors lived in Cuiabá or Goiás. Merchandise taken there by the river route was usually sold on credit, and on one occasion the successful col-

lection of the debt took 27 years.[24] Other times, debts were never collected.
For example, when Maria de Lima de Siqueira died, almost one-fourth of her
estate consisted of credits that were declared bad loans, as they had not been
paid since her husband's death over 25 years earlier. (These bad loans were
divided equally among the heirs, so that each heir received a fraction of each
loan, spreading the loss equally among them.)[25]

The successful collection of debts owed to an estate depended largely on
the existence of able male relatives willing to devote their efforts to the task.
Sons-in-law or adult sons would be logical persons for this work because it was
in their own interest, but in many instances heirs were small children. In
these cases during the seventeenth and eighteenth centuries, it was fathers,
brothers, or brothers-in-law who worked long hours, months, or years to collect debts for others, their daughters and grandchildren, sisters, nephews and
nieces. A late seventeenth-century example of this lifetime concern with the
extended family and its business is that of Captain Antonio Rodrigues de
Arzão and Bartholomeu Bueno de Siqueira, who were married to two sisters.
After Antonio discovered gold in Minas Gerais in 1696, he died, leaving the
map of his discovery with Bartholomeu, who followed the map and founded
the town of Ouro Preto. He then not only worked his own property in Minas
but also that of Antonio's widow, his sister-in-law.[26] A similar case occurred
one hundred years later, when the second Antonio Prado died in 1793, after
a marriage of only seven years, so that no sons-in-law or adult sons were available to do the job; his three brothers worked for several years to collect the
sums owed.[27] In working for their sister-in-law and her children, instead of
merely for themselves and their own nuclear families, these men demonstrated that the colonial family ethic persisted and that men were still willing
to work for the good of the extended family. This manifestation of the corporate family was to change in the nineteenth century with the further growth
of individualism.

Although eighteenth-century merchants ran great risks in extending
credit, they also earned great profits, virtually becoming bankers.[28] But the
rise in the extension of credit in the eighteenth century and the difficulty in
collecting debts led to a sharp rise in the average percentage of the gross estate that consisted of credits (see Figure 6). By the middle of the nineteenth
century not only were there slightly fewer creditors, but also the average percent of the gross estate represented by credits had declined precipitously from
34 to 15 percent (see Figure 6).

The decline of credits in nineteenth-century estates was probably brought
about by the more efficient collection of debt and the gradual development
of a better system to secure debt. In the seventeenth and eighteenth centuries, a debtor in São Paulo secured loans with his person and all his possessions and in addition provided a guarantor who promised to pay the debt in

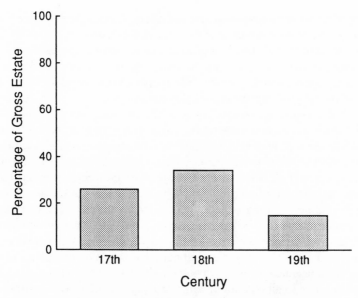

Fig. 6. *Credits as percentage of gross estate (average of estates that were creditors) (seventeenth to nineteenth centuries). Source: sample.*

case of default. To collect a debt when both debtor and guarantor defaulted, a creditor had to go through a lengthy and expensive judicial process of embargo, in which a lien would be placed on all the debtor's possessions, and, if they were not sufficient to pay the debt, the debtor himself could be detained.[29] The problem was that both debtor and guarantor pledged their person and all their present and future property for every debt entered or guarantee given.[30] Since most persons had several debts and could serve as guarantors for the debt of several friends or relatives, they could conceivably owe or guarantee total amounts that were larger than their total property.

Nor did legislation properly protect creditors. When one property had been used to secure several debts, the *Ordenações* decreed that the first creditor to be paid would be the first one to sue, instead of the first creditor to have the debt secured by that particular property, as in modern times.[31]

During the nineteenth century, the law gradually changed to protect the creditor. Local mortgage registers, established in 1843 and implemented in 1846, allowed individual mortgages to be listed. However, there was still no system by which one of several liens on a property was given precedence. The situation remained chaotic until 1864–65, when the Imperial government passed mortgage legislation with more effective protection of creditors through the establishment of a system of mortgage registers that allowed the prioritization and cross-registering of mortgages. With a registered mortgage

giving priority to a specific debt, the creditor could seize the mortgaged property when the debtor defaulted without lengthy litigation.[32]

It was only in the decade following the new mortgage legislation that
mortgage banks became prevalent, but banks did not immediately replace individuals in the granting of credit. The proportion of individual creditors in
the sample was still significant, 42 percent (see Figure 4).[33] The estates of
some of the wealthiest persons in the sample included many loans made to
third parties at interest, showing that they were acting as private bankers.
Although fewer people were acting as bankers than in the eighteenth century, those who did dealt in such large amounts that loans were clearly a significant part of their business. For example, despite owning thirteen houses
and two dry goods stores in the center of São Paulo and a sugar plantation and
a cattle and mule-raising establishment in Mogi-mirim, the largest part of
Antonio de Paiva Azevedo's estate of over 440 contos consisted of letters of
credit and promissory notes worth 340 contos.[34] And Commendador José
Manoel de França was almost exclusively a banker. When he died in 1853,
his gross estate consisted of eight houses in the center of São Paulo, which he
rented out, one small chácara in Santa Efigenia, and over 295 contos of collectable credits at interest (67 percent of his estate), plus 15 contos of bad
loans and 93 contos in cash (coins and gold bars).[35] Meanwhile, mid-nineteenth-century São Paulo was gradually acquiring commercial banks that
were later fully to supplant individual lenders.[36]

Many of the credits throughout the inventários in the nineteenth century
were not loans but business debts. In a small estate with a grocery store, for
example, the credits might be the debts of the store's clients. When Alexandre Antonio dos Reis died in 1867, he left over 2 contos of collectable
credits, *dívidas cobráveis*, from his grocery store.[37] In the case of the many
families who raised mules and ran mule trains, credits came from sales of
cattle or mules or from hiring out mules or mule trains or from transporting
cargo. Promissory notes were used as payment so that they frequently went
through many hands. For example, when young Antonio Prado was conduct-
ing mule trains from São Paulo to Goiás and Bahia in the early nineteenth
century, he sometimes received payments with credits that were several
years old.[38]

The history of the propertied family in Brazil from the seventeenth century
to the middle of the nineteenth is therefore not a history of change in its
members' legal title to property, which remained the same, but of change in
the family's and its individual members' relationship to production and trade.
The seventeenth-century family was a productive group in which family relations themselves constituted the structure for business, conducted under the
direction and control of the patriarch or his representative. As partnerships,

whether with relatives or with outsiders, became more common by the early nineteenth century, they structured business dealings, so that two men, though possibly related, did not necessarily do business with each other as son or son-in-law to father or father-in-law, but as partners whose duties and responsibilities were set forth in contracts and not by consideration of family hierarchy.

As the family ceased to be the structure for business, marriage changed. Although it still could be and frequently was used to further a man's or a family's business prospects by enlarging a network of relations, or by giving a man access to credit, marriage itself no longer defined the business dealings between in-laws as it had in colonial times. And with the rise of professions and the possibilities of entering into partnership with nonrelatives, marriage was no longer the principal way for a man to establish himself; it had become a personal option. Thus, not only the family but also marriage became private.

The individual male had become the intermediary between family and business. Although elite families continued to own the means of production, the administration of partnerships and corporations was separate from the administration of a family, even though the same person might control both. With the development of stocks and bonds, individuals could even own and profit from the means of production without being responsible for their administration. These changes were to transform marriage and diminish the importance of dowry at the same time that they privatized the role of the wife, who had been in colonial times an active partner of the family business.

CHAPTER 9

DECLINE OF THE DOWRY

*A*S INDIVIDUALISM GREW, and as business and family became separate, the practice of dowry diminished. Study of the nineteenth-century sample of São Paulo proprietors demonstrates that most daughters married empty-handed, and the few families who still endowed their daughters gave them relatively smaller dowries and divested themselves of less significant portions of their property for dowries. Moreover, the content of dowries changed, reflecting the transformation of the family from mainly a unit of production to mainly a unit of consumption.

FEWER AND SMALLER DOWRIES

The most striking change in the sample is the small number of families who endowed their daughters. Compared to 91 percent in the seventeenth century and 80 percent in the eighteenth, only 27 percent of the families in the nineteenth-century sample gave dowries to their daughters. In order to learn whether the trend toward a decreasing practice of dowry held true for the wealthier families, I studied those estates in each century that owned four or more Indians or African slaves. In the seventeenth century, 93 percent of

TABLE 17
The Practice of Dowry by Number of Slaves

Dowry practice	Century					
	17th		18th		19th	
ALL FAMILIES						
Gave dowries	43	(91%)	55	(81%)	47	(27%)
Did not give dowries	4	(9%)	13	(19%)	130	(73%)
TOTAL	47	(100%)	68	(100%)	177	(100%)
Missing information	1				1	
SAMPLE	48		68		178	
FAMILIES WITH FOUR OR MORE SLAVES						
Gave dowries	39	(93%)	30	(81%)	23	(38%)
Did not give dowries	3	(7%)	7	(19%)	38	(62%)
TOTAL	42	(100%)	37	(100%)	61	(100%)

SOURCE: Sample.
NOTE: All percentages have been rounded off.

TABLE 18
The Practice of Dowry by Wealth of Estate (Nineteenth Century)

Estates by wealth	Gave dowries		Did not give dowries		Total
Poorest fourth	6.5	(15%)	37	(85%)	43.5
Next fourth	9.5	(22%)	34	(78%)	43.5
Next fourth	9	(21%)	34.5	(79%)	43.5
Wealthiest fourth	22	(51%)	21.5	(49%)	43.5
Missing information			4		4
TOTAL	47	(27%)	131	(73%)	178

SOURCE: Sample.
NOTE: Percentages have been rounded off.

these families gave dowries; in the eighteenth century, 81 percent did so; but only 38 percent of the nineteenth-century families who owned four slaves or more endowed their daughters. Although this decline in the practice of dowry was not as pronounced in the better-off families as in the whole sample, it was still a sharp one (see Table 17). That wealthier families were more likely to give dowries is also demonstrated when we rank the estates in the sample by their size (see Table 18). While only 15 percent of the least wealthy fourth of the sample endowed their daughters, 51 percent of the wealthiest fourth did so. Although the wealthiest families tended to give dowries more frequently than did those of more modest means, it is significant that, even among the wealthiest fourth of the sample, almost half the families did not endow their daughters.

These statistics show that, in contrast to the preceding centuries, most nineteenth-century Paulista property owners were no longer giving dowries. A majority of the families in the sample—73 percent—did not endow their daughters, as compared to only 19 percent who reneged on this duty in the eighteenth century and 9 percent in the seventeenth (see Figure 7).

It is tempting to leap to the conclusion that the families who gave no dowries in the nineteenth century were mostly those of widows or widowers

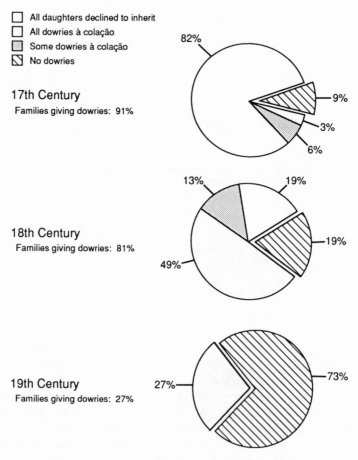

Fig. 7. *Proportion of parents endowing daughters and of dowries coming à colação. Source: sample; all percentages have been rounded off.*

whose daughters married solely with their legítima, as was usually the case in colonial times. But such was not the case here: of the twenty-two families that did not give dowries in the wealthiest fourth of the sample, only seven, or one-third, were those of widows or widowers whose daughters married simply with their inheritance. Moreover, the refusal to endow their daughters was no longer the exception for the widowed, as it had been in the eighteenth century. By the mid-nineteenth century the accepted practice was for widowed parents *not* to give dowries to daughters who married after inheriting from one parent. In the entire sample there was only one case of a widow who gave her daughter a dowry on top of her legítima.[1] The practice of dowry had practically disappeared among the widowed.

It was also disappearing among wealthy two-parent families. In the remaining fifteen families in the wealthiest fourth of the sample who did not endow their daughters, both parents were alive when their daughters married, yet they were allowed to enter marriage without property.

That so many parents allowed their daughters to marry empty-handed suggests that the practice of dowry was no longer perceived as a binding duty, even in the wealthier strata. It also suggests that not all bridegrooms demanded dowries. Whether or not to give a dowry was becoming a matter of choice.

Even among the families who were still endowing their daughters, some trends confirm the observation that dowry was no longer regarded as a duty. In the nineteenth-century sample there was an increase in the proportion of families who endowed some daughters while allowing others to marry empty-handed. Of the eighteenth-century families who endowed their daughters, 87 percent had given a dowry to every married daughter.[2] And of the seven families who endowed only a few of their daughters, merely two allowed their remaining daughters to marry empty-handed. The other five estates were of widows or widowers, some of whose daughters married and were endowed while both parents were alive, whereas the others married after the first parent's death and took their legítima into marriage. In the nineteenth-century sample, in contrast, only 63 percent of the families who endowed their daughters gave every married daughter a dowry.[3] And 70 percent of these families only had one married daughter. Thus, there were only nine families in the whole nineteenth-century sample of 178 inventários who had endowed all of several married daughters.[4]

Nineteenth-century property owners were simply giving fewer dowries. Of the seventeen families who did not endow every married daughter, the majority let some of their daughters marry empty-handed, since only seven were families of widows or widowers whose daughters married with their legítima. The other ten families (over one-fifth of the 47 families in the sample who gave dowries) endowed some daughters and not others. These families were

TABLE 19
*Percentage of Legítima Represented by Largest Dowry
in Family (Nineteenth Century)*

Estates by wealth	Families that gave dowries	Average dowry as percentage of legítima
Poorest fourth	7	159%
Next fourth	9	51
Next fourth	9	25
Wealthiest fourth	21	36
TOTAL	46	56
Missing information	1	
SAMPLE	47	

NOTE: The largest dowry given in each family was used for this
calculation. There were five dowries that were of greater value
than the legítima, from 1.7 to 7.5 times larger.

also swelling the ranks of those who saw dowry no longer as a duty but rather
as a choice.

Another indication of the decline in the practice of dowry is that most of
the families who still endowed their daughters gave much smaller amounts in
relation to a daughter's inheritance than those their ancestors had given in
colonial times. In the eighteenth century the average percentage of the legítima represented by the most valuable dowry given in a family was 147 percent, whereas it was only 56 percent in the nineteenth century.[5] And just as
in the eighteenth century, the largest dowries in relation to the legítima were
those given by small proprietors. Although fewer nineteenth-century small
proprietors than wealthy families endowed their daughters, those who did
gave comparatively larger dowries (see Table 19).

The decline in the size of dowries in wealthy families is exemplified by the
relatively small dowries given by the wealthiest couple in the sample, Captain Manoel José de Moraes and his wife. Their joint estate was worth over
231 contos, and when the wife died, the legítima for each heir amounted to
over 20 contos. Yet the largest dowry received by their daughters was worth
only a little over 3 contos, only half of which came in à colação. That dowry
therefore represented only 8 percent of the daughter's inheritance.[6]

For our study of change in the practice of dowry, the relative value of each
dowry is therefore a more important statistic than its absolute value. The
largest single dowry encountered in the nineteenth-century inventários is the
dowry of over 40 contos given by the Barão de Limeira. We would err if we
concluded that the practice of dowry was strong at the upper levels of wealth
because the Barão gave a dowry larger than the entire estate of 161 of the 178

inventários in the sample. But in fact half of that dowry was less than 20 percent of the legítima of the Barão's daughter, and he and his wife divested themselves of only 5 percent of their property to give all four daughters dowries of approximately the same size.[7]

Those nineteenth-century families who continued the practice of dowry were clearly divesting themselves of smaller portions of their estates for dowries than had colonial families. In the eighteenth century, families had divested themselves of an average of 42 percent of their estate to give their daughters dowries, and in nine of those families the total amount given for dowries was larger than the remaining net estate of the parents. In the nineteenth century, in contrast, the average divestment was only 7 percent, and the largest single total divestment was only worth half the parents' net estate. Parents were no longer making such sacrifices to endow their daughters.[8]

The smaller relative size of dowries is corroborated by the finding that all dowries came in à colação in the nineteenth century (see Figure 7).[9] Endowed married daughters no longer used the legal option of refusing to inherit, since their dowries were never handsome enough to allow them to feel they need not inherit further. And since the dowry was almost never larger than the legítima, in very few cases in the nineteenth century was it necessary to use the terça to equalize heirs.

This complete reversal of practice, from the seventeenth-century custom of rarely coming in à colação to the nineteenth-century usage of never refusing to inherit, demonstrates the decline of the dowry and points to its later disappearance, as does the large proportion of propertied families that did not endow their daughters (see Figure 7).

Since the long-standing rationale for dowry was to help support the new family, giving no dowries or smaller dowries in relation to the daughter's inheritance meant that families were accepting wives' diminished role in the support of a couple. The asymmetry between husband and wife in the propertied classes was becoming more pronounced.

THE COMPOSITION OF DOWRIES

Not only did the amount of support provided by dowries decrease from the seventeenth century to the nineteenth, but the way they provided support also changed. In the seventeenth century, dowries consisted principally of means of production, whereas by the middle of the nineteenth century they consisted primarily of means of consumption. Both means of production and means of consumption provide support, but bringing means of production into a family assumes that the family is a productive unit, whereas means of consumption can be used both by units of production and by those that merely consume. In this way, changes in the content of dowries reflect the transformation in the function of the family, from a unit of production to a unit of consumption.

Paulista dowries contained both means of production and means of consumption.[10] Knowing the productive and commercial activities of Paulistas, we can assume that agricultural land, tools, machinery, cattle, and mules were used as means of production. A house, a trousseau, and jewels were means of consumption, because they were usually used, though they could also be sold for money, and many times were. In those cases, the money could be used to buy means of production (the money is then capital) or further means of consumption. Horses, on the other hand, were means of consumption when they provided transportation for family members, but were means of production when used by those same members to oversee agricultural workers or to accompany mule trains, for instance. Slaves, the most important item in Paulista dowries during the three centuries of our study, can also be classified either as means of production or, when they provided domestic services to their owners, as facilitating their owners' consumption.[11]

Let us start our analysis of the composition of dowries with an item that has traditionally been viewed as one of their most usual components, the trousseau. The articles in a trousseau—clothing, linens, silverware, and furniture—were undoubtedly used by the family itself; they were means of consumption; depending on their relative value, they could also become means of conspicuous consumption. Extremely expensive clothes and silverware in seventeenth-century São Paulo certainly served to increase the status of the newly married couple.

Yet expensive articles in a trousseau could also be sold to provide money when needed, so that they also served as a monetary reserve for the couple or for the surviving widow.[12] For example, in the early nineteenth century, the Visconde de Rio Claro started the business that was to evolve into an enormous fortune with the money that came from selling a piano his wife brought in dowry.[13] In that case, what was donated as means of consumption was converted by the son-in-law into capital. We may therefore reasonably conclude that, when expensive trousseaux were given in dowry, parents were thinking both of their usefulness, their status-enhancing value, and their possible exchange value.

Over three-fourths of the dowries in the seventeenth- and eighteenth-century samples contained a trousseau, but it had practically disappeared from nineteenth-century dowries. (See Figure 8.) In the seventeenth century, the most expensive items in a trousseau were clothes for formal occasions and silverware, usually spoons and tumblers. A few sheets, pillowcases, towels, tablecloths, and maybe some pewter plates completed the seventeenth-century trousseau. By the eighteenth century, personal clothes had become much less important in dowries and had disappeared from many of

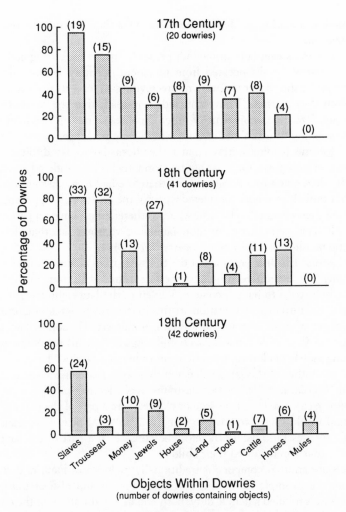

Fig. 8. The composition of dowries: proportion of dowries containing each object (seventeenth to nineteenth centuries). Source: IT, AESP, INP, AMJ 2° O. da F. In seventeenth century, "Slaves" include Indians, and "Money" includes commodities to be sold. "Trousseau" includes clothes, linens, silver, furniture. "Tools" include agricultural tools, machinery, canoes, and stills.

them, probably reflecting the fact that they were no longer as expensive. The trousseau of large eighteenth-century dowries usually consisted of bed, bath, and table linens; a bed itself with its mattress, canopy, and curtains; sometimes bolts of cloth; maybe a chest or some china (imported from India); and always silver spoons and sometimes silver forks.[14] By the nineteenth century, furniture was the principal item in the trousseau of those few dowries that still contained one.

That the trousseau, containing indispensable articles for setting up house-keeping, practically disappeared from nineteenth-century Paulista dowries does not mean that daughters were not receiving such objects from their parents when they married. I have concluded, instead, that the trousseau was being considered the equivalent of other expenses of raising children, such as those relating to a son's education, which were no longer coming from a family's fortune (capital outlays) but rather from day-to-day disbursements (operational expenses). Objects that had formerly been considered an important gift when given to a daughter (and therefore had to be discounted from her inheritance) were now considered a part of the day-to-day support all parents owed their children. The trousseau was therefore no longer a part of the dowry. (It is probable that many more families gave trousseaux than dowries, including families who were not property owners.)

But because the disappearance of the trousseau from dowries did not occur overnight, in a few nineteenth-century estates a trousseau came in à colação or other heirs tried to have it come in.[15] Even in the late eighteenth century there was an instance of litigation in the inventário of Ignacio Correa de Lemos about whether a trousseau was part of a dowry. His son-in-law, Captain Manoel Correa de Lemos, successfully argued that his wife's trousseau, consisting mostly of clothes, was not a part of her dowry, since her two single sisters had clothes of the same value and they were not being asked to bring them in à colação.[16] This case illustrates very clearly that the issue was whether the expense for a trousseau or clothes were a part of the parents' fortune (and would therefore have to come in à colação) or only of their operating expenses (and would therefore be considered a part of the support, *alimentos*, that parents owed their children).

Jewels are another component traditionally included in Paulista dowries. The supreme example of conspicuous consumption and also of moveable wealth, jewels fulfilled a double duty, both enhancing the status of the couple and providing a monetary reserve. Less than a third of the dowries in the seventeenth century contained jewels, whereas two-thirds of the eighteenth-century dowries included them. The discovery of gold and the frequent connections Paulistas had with the mines may help explain why jewels became a much more important item in eighteenth-century dowries than in those of the preceding or subsequent century. By the nineteenth century, less than a fourth of the dowries contained jewels (see Figure 8).

The most striking difference between seventeenth- and eighteenth-century dowries was the importance of means of production in seventeenth-century dowries, and their decline in the eighteenth century, a decline that became even more accentuated in the nineteenth century (see Figure 8).[17] At the

TABLE 20

Number and Sex of Slaves Given in Dowry (Eighteenth and Nineteenth Centuries)

Dowries	Females		Males		Adults		Children, both sexes	Total dowries
18th cent.:								
With one slave	8	(72%)	3	(28%)	11	(100%)	0	11
More than one slave	30	(62%)	18	(38%)	48	(100%)	9	19
TOTAL SLAVES	38	(64%)	21	(36%)	59	(100%)	9	30
19th cent.:								
With one slave	14	(100%)	0		14	(100%)	0	14
More than one slave	12	(75%)	4	(25%)	16	(100%)	3	8
TOTAL SLAVES	26	(87%)	4	(13%)	30	(100%)	3	22

SOURCE: Only dowries in which the adult slave's sex was specified were used (38 out of 41 dowries in which components are known for the eighteenth century and 26 out of 42 in the nineteenth). The nineteenth-century cases in which the only slave given in dowry was a female baby were excluded.

same time, the percentage of dowries that included a trousseau increased slightly in the eighteenth century, those that had jewels doubled, and horses (sometimes for the use of the daughter herself) also increased. Thus, while means of production were decreasingly given in dowry, the giving of means of consumption was increasing. One exception is houses, for they were the only means of consumption that had declined as a component of dowry by the mid-eighteenth century. Seventeenth-century Paulistas had used their numerous Indians to build houses, making them easy to include in dowries, but by the middle of the eighteenth century, houses had become expensive at a time in which dowries were becoming smaller.

The trend that started in the eighteenth century toward giving female rather than male slaves in dowry continued into the nineteenth century and can be viewed as a change in the use of slaves—from production to personal service, thus consumption (see Table 20). Of course, the sex of slaves does not necessarily determine whether they were used for productive work or only to perform personal services. In the seventeenth century both male and female Indians worked in agriculture, and even those Indians destined for the "house" included productive workers, since weaving (performed by both male and female Indians) was usually carried out inside, and cloth, including sail-cloth, was an important commodity in seventeenth-century São Paulo. In the eighteenth and nineteenth centuries not only male but also female slaves worked in the fields. Thus, knowing the sex of slaves does not tell us whether they worked in productive activities or not. Nevertheless, although male slaves could perform personal services, and many times did so, it seems more likely that they were used in productive work, especially when there were few of them. Female slaves, on the other hand, could be used in both ways, depending on the family's needs, with the added advantage that they could have children, an important consideration after the slave trade was cut off in 1850.[18]

Moreover, giving a female slave in dowry meant giving a daughter a slave that she, rather than her husband, would more likely control. In this way, giving a daughter a female slave was similar to giving her jewels. To sell jewels or domestic slaves in order to convert them into capital, or to rent slaves out to provide income, a wife's cooperation was required, since they were assigned to her personal use. Female slaves, trousseau, and jewels were therefore components of dowry that were meant more for the bride than for the groom, though he would benefit from the slaves' services, from the use of the trousseau, and from all three as symbols of conspicuous consumption.

This pattern of change in the composition of dowries from means of production to means of consumption indicates a decrease in the say of the bride's family about the productive activities of the groom. In the seventeenth century a young man's father-in-law, and sometimes even his brothers-in-law, had direct authority over him, and the components of his wife's dowry determined what production he would oversee. If a field of sugar cane and a still were included in the dowry, he would be likely to manufacture rum. If a field of wheat and a mill were included, he would probably sell flour. Not only did a seventeenth-century dowry give a married couple most of what they needed to set up a productive establishment, but it also determined where the couple would live (if a house and/or land were included) and what they would produce.

Seventeenth-century Paulista dowries were therefore both enabling and limiting to the groom. By the eighteenth century dowries became both less enabling, because they were comparatively smaller, and less limiting, because they included fewer specific means of production. This change in the composition of dowries took place during the period when there was a slight lessening of patriarchal power over adult sons, which undoubtedly corresponded to significantly less power of fathers-in-law over their sons-in-law. This trend intensified in the nineteenth century.

From the point of view of the groom, money was the one component of dowry to which no strings were attached. Money (or, in the seventeenth century, commodities to be sold) was completely enabling without being limiting. Money received in dowry was undoubtedly used to buy means of production and labor during the seventeenth and eighteenth centuries. Whether money received in dowry in the nineteenth century served to buy means of production or whether it was used to support the couple's standard of living for the first few years of their marriage remains to be studied.

The proportion of dowries containing commodities to be sold or money

TABLE 21

Components of Dowries by Size of Dowry (Nineteenth Century)

| | Number of dowries with each component | | | | | | |
Dowries by size	Slaves	Jewels	Money	House	Land	Tools	Livestock
Smallest (13)	1	3			1	1	8
Middle (14)	10	2		1	1		
Largest (13)	13	3	10	1	1		

SOURCE: Forty dowries in which components of dowry are known.

declined consistently during the three centuries, from 45 percent in the seventeenth century to 32 percent in the eighteenth and 24 percent in the nineteenth (see Figure 8). The picture we find when we consider only those dowries that contained money is different, however. By the nineteenth century, dowries that contained money contained a larger percentage of money than before. In the eighteenth century, the average percentage of the dowry represented by money was 37 percent; by the nineteenth century, it had risen to 56 percent.[19] Thus, though fewer dowries in the nineteenth century contained money, in those instances where it was included, it was a significant component of the dowry.

In fact, one of the striking characteristics of the sample of nineteenth-century dowries is that the components of dowries varied according to the size of the dowry (see Table 21). The smaller dowries were the only ones that included cattle, horses, mules, and tools. They were most like those of the seventeenth century, composed predominantly of means of production that the groom would use. Such dowries were given by the families of small proprietors, who, as we saw in the preceding chapter, were still productive units without formal partnerships, also most like families in colonial times. At the same time, however, small landowners gave the fewest dowries, suggesting that though they were the most traditional group, the market economy placed constraints on their capacity to divest themselves of property.

The principal component of the middle-sized dowries was a domestic slave, indicating a shift toward a dowry strictly for the bride, and reflecting parents' desire to ensure that their daughters did not have to do housework (see Table 21). Giving only a slave also suggests that parents of the middle strata were allowing the groom to provide the principal support for the couple.

The largest dowries all included slaves, too, but the principal component of most of these was money. Thus, the larger dowries included both slaves to serve the bride and money for the groom, which he could use either to invest in his business or to help pay the couple's initial expenses. The larger dowries were traditional in the sense that, because of the husband's legal and customary right to administer the couple's property, the decision of how to use the largest component of the dowry, namely money, was probably made solely by the groom. Yet money was the one element a groom could receive that gave him the greatest individual freedom in its use. It was the component that liberated the groom the most from his father-in-law's control. Thus, the larger dowries, despite their conformity to tradition, were greater conduits of individualism and separation between the generations.

The changes that took place between 1600 and 1870 in the content of Paulista dowries illuminate changes taking place in the family and its relation to property. The change from giving mostly means of production to giving mostly means of consumption accompanied the change from the family's being *the* unit of production to the family's separation from production. This process of separation was not complete in the mid-nineteenth century; small proprietor families were still units of production, while large *fazendeiros* (plantation owners or ranchers), though owning productive enterprises, usually received from them sufficient income to obviate the need to carry out their administration themselves. Fazendeiro families therefore functioned as units of consumption. At the same time a growing number of proprietors owned no productive enterprises at all, living off professional fees or the income from stocks and bonds or rents. Their families were definitely just units of consumption.

OTHER HELP TO CHILDREN

Nineteenth-century parents were not only giving fewer dowries to their daughters but also giving fewer gifts to sons. The proportion of families who gave gifts to their sons decreased from a high of 17 percent in the eighteenth century to a low of 8 percent in the nineteenth (see Table 22). There were therefore fewer pre-mortem gifts of property to adult children of both sexes in the nineteenth century than in colonial times. This shows a great change in what parents considered to be their responsibility toward their children, and it is probably connected to the rising opportunities for young men of the propertied classes to make their way in life without the initial ownership of property, but instead through the professions, the army, or the state bureaucracy.

Parents, however, continued helping their adult children in other ways, such as loans of money or of land and slaves. This procedure had the advantage for parents that, unlike dowries, such contributions were entirely voluntary and could be temporary; repayment could be demanded before death. Were parents compensating daughters and sons-in-law for the lack of dowries by providing greater numbers of loans?

TABLE 22
Material Assistance to Children (Seventeenth to Nineteenth Centuries)

	Number and percentage		
Assistance	17th cent.	18th cent.	19th cent.
Dowries	43 (91%)	55 (81%)	47 (27%)
Gifts to sons	3 (9%)	10 (17%)	12 (8%)
Loans to married daughters	4 (9%)	11 (16%)	28 (16%)
Loans to sons	4 (11%)	14 (23%)	38 (26%)
Debts owed to married daughters	2 (5%)	7 (11%)	12 (7%)
Debts owed to sons	4 (11%)	4 (7%)	10 (7%)
Use of land/slaves by married daughters	4 (8%)	7 (10%)	48 (27%)
Use of land/slaves by sons	7 (20%)	12 (20%)	40 (27%)

SOURCES: For statistics on married daughters: sample. For statistics on sons: number of cases as percentage of families studied in which there were either married sons or sons who had reached the age of majority (35 in the seventeenth century, 61 in the eighteenth, and 147 in the nineteenth). (All percentages have been rounded off.)

NOTE: The statistics for "Use of land/slaves" is, if anything, too low, for this is the only information of the above that was not required in an inventário, so that its inclusion is fortuitous, such as cases claiming that an heir has in his possession a slave belonging to the estate, or others stating that a certain heir received the land on which his house was built, thereby confirming usufruct. There were undoubtedly unreported cases.

Table 22 shows that the percentage of families giving loans to their married daughters did not increase in the nineteenth century. Moreover, the number of families making loans to married daughters and their husbands were even fewer than the number of those who gave dowries. However, the proportion of families who granted loans to sons increased slightly, from 23 percent in the eighteenth century to 26 percent. That loans were given to sons more frequently than to married daughters may mean that parents in the nineteenth century felt less responsible for married daughters and sons-in-law than for sons (as the decrease in dowries also shows).

Certainly brothers-in-law no longer felt as much solidarity as they had in colonial times. For example, there was extensive litigation between Antonio Barboza Machado and his brother-in-law, Izaias Antonio de Godoy, over who would receive a certain piece of property, and in his defense, Antonio's lawyer said that Izaias was after all "a stranger except for the fact that he had married into the family." [20] No brother-in-law would have been described in this way in colonial times! Thus, relatives by marriage were not as important in the nineteenth century as in previous centuries and the larger kin were becoming less cohesive. Interestingly enough, both Antonio and Izaias were working and living on the land of their respective fathers-in-law, indicating that matrilocality was still prevalent in São Paulo. That both were living on their fathers-in-law's land may also mean that parents who no longer gave their daughters dowries instead allowed them to settle on their land.

In fact, quite a few families allowed their children to build a house on parental land or to cultivate the soil without receiving title (see Table 22). An example of this practice is found in the inventário of Maria Francisca do Rosario of Santo Amaro, in which the widower listed their real estate in these terms: 1 farm in the neighborhood of Tupara with a house, 330$000; 1 small plot united to the farm where the heir (son), Antonio Floriano de Andrade, lives, 25$000; 1 small plot with a small house where the co-heir (son-in-law), Antonio de Souza, lives, 40$000; 1 plot in the neighborhood called Santa Ritta where the co-heir (son-in-law), José Pires de Albuquerque, lives, 100$000. The widower then declared that he had given no dowries or gifts to any of his children, suggesting that he viewed allowing his children to settle on his land as a substitute for dowries or gifts.[21]

The practice of allowing daughters and their husbands to use land or, occasionally, slaves, grew in the nineteenth century. The proportion of parents giving such permission almost tripled from the eighteenth to the nineteenth centuries. (See Table 22.) And four-fifths of the parents who allowed their married daughters to use their land had not given them dowries. Clearly, allowing married daughters to settle on family land did in fact compensate daughters for not giving them dowries. Not only had most of the families who allowed their daughters the use of the land not given dowries, but two-thirds were also small proprietors, families who owned no more than two slaves. Thus, it was precisely the families that gave fewer dowries who allowed their daughters to settle on family land. However, they were also allowing their sons the use of the land, and in approximately the same proportion. Thus, small rural proprietors showed a tendency to equalize the treatment of sons and daughters; they gave practically no dowries and allowed both sons and daughters the use of the land.

Although there appears to have been a general tendency toward equalizing the treatment of sons and daughters in terms of dowries and gifts and the use of land, at the level of education parents were spending much more for sons than for daughters. In the eighteenth century some educational expenses were considered an advance on the legítima. For example, the eighteenth-century merchant Caetano Soares Viana declared in his will that his son, the Reverend Father Francisco Manoel Caetano, owed him 618$000, which he had spent to get him into the Carmelite monastery, including the money spent on his studies of philosophy and his vestments and other necessities prescribed by religion. So as not to wrong his other heirs, Caetano Soares Viana stated that the whole amount had been given to his son as an advance on his inheritance.[22] Yet the Ordenações decreed that money spent on education should not be brought back into the estate unless it were excessive, thereby allowing parents to decide whether such expenses should come in à colação or not.[23]

Most nineteenth-century Paulistas did not have educational expenses brought back into the estate, so that the expenditure on children that was rising the most, the education of sons, did not appear in inventários. The only case in the sample where educational expenses came à colação was that of Bento José Martins da Cunha's son, who was studying at the school of law when his father died. The son had recently received 413$404 worth of books for his studies, and his widowed mother had this amount discounted from his legítima of 702$890, indicating how expensive education was.[24] Yet an education was most important in nineteenth-century São Paulo because a profession was practically a requirement for elite men and served as a path for upward mobility for medium-sized property owners. The will of José Mathias Ferreira de Abreu also illustrates how expensive the education of sons was becoming, for he stated in his will that he wanted to leave the remainder of his terça to his two daughters "because I have spent so much money on my sons' education while I have spent nothing on my daughters."[25]

Sons' educational expenses reversed the advantage daughters had had in colonial times. Yet the favoring of daughters with dowry had come from capital outlays that could be equalized when parents died by the process of colação. Although nineteenth-century parents were treating their sons and daughters equally regarding capital outlays, they were strongly favoring sons over daughters with educational expenses. Because these expenditures were no longer counted as an advance on sons' inheritance, they could affect the size of the estate and diminish a daughter's inheritance.

By mid-nineteenth century, dowry was clearly on its way out. Most property owners no longer endowed their daughters at marriage, and the minority who did frequently gave dowries to only one or two of their daughters, dowries that were relatively smaller than those in colonial times and for which parents divested themselves of only a small part of their estate. The composition of dowries had also changed, from mostly means of production to mostly means of consumption. The large number of even wealthy proprietors who allowed daughters to marry empty-handed suggests that dowry was no longer of vital importance to the marriage bargain.

CHAPTER 10

A NEW MARRIAGE BARGAIN

B Y THE MIDDLE of the nineteenth century the marriage bargain had altered. Since the bride brought no dowry or only a small one to marriage, the support of the newlyweds came to depend increasingly on her husband's contribution, whether in property or employment, and his negotiating position was strengthened. At the same time, marriage came to be viewed much less as a matter of property and much more as a personal tie between individuals, with love as the paramount motive for marriage. With property no longer the *sine qua non* of marriage, young people in Brazil were allowed to choose their own spouses more frequently. In this process the authority of parents over adult children diminished while the power of the husband over his wife may have increased.

CHANGES IN PORTUGAL

These changes appear to have been taking place in Europe already in the eighteenth century, for the Iberian states passed several new laws reflecting their concern with young people's independence in choosing their marriage partners. The *Ordenações*, issued in 1603, had allowed parents to disown and disinherit a daughter who married without their consent. In its laws of 1772 and 1775, the Portuguese government extended the old ruling to sons, so that now they too could be disinherited if they married without their parents' consent.[1] The Spanish Royal Pragmatic of 1776 did likewise, adding that the measure was necessary to prevent unequal marriages, thereby implying that they were taking place.[2]

The Portuguese law of 1775 was decreed after much public controversy over the matter, for the church had long upheld young people's right to freely choose their spouses, even when they were still under their parents' legal authority. The church principle regarding marriage and betrothal was rebutted in Portugal in a 1773 treatise that expostulated on the lack of utility for the state of betrothals celebrated without parents' consent and attacked the church for teaching young people to disobey their parents on the question of marriage, "one of the most important acts of civil life." In Lisbon, meanwhile, the church itself was ambiguous in its defense of the freedom to marry; parish priests were instructed to be sure of parents' consent before publishing the banns.[3]

One of the main concerns of the 1775 law was preventing the "alienation, seduction and corruption of filhos-família of both sexes" that led to unequal marriages without the consent of parents, relatives, or guardians who, in "all civilized nations, regulate the civil effects of such contracts."[4] The law's text decried the number of cases where heiresses or women with large dowries had been seduced in order to force their marriage, or cases where a young man was invited into a home with a marriageable daughter whereupon the family complained that he had compromised their daughter, thereby obliging him to marry her.

The seeming prevalence of such stratagems, aimed at forcing unequal marriages, and the resulting concern of the state to prevent them by reinforcing the power of the *pater familia* with the 1775 law, leads to the conclusion that young people in Portugal in the eighteenth century were behaving in a new way. New patterns of sociability permitted young people to meet and fall in love. The consequence, as one scholar has pointed out, was that the Portugese nobility, "that had married off its daughters without their even knowing the man they were to marry, had from then on to count on something new. The noble young girl . . . sequestered, courted, sought after, could now love and choose."[5]

Furthermore, what the Portugese laws of 1772 and 1775 and the Spanish Royal Pragmatic show is that the state was especially concerned about the unequal marriage of sons, not daughters. Yet why would the state suddenly be concerned with sons marrying beneath them? The *Ordenações* had only been concerned with daughters who married without their parents' consent, not with sons. What is more, the *Ordenações* did not permit parents to disinherit a daughter who, though marrying without their consent, managed to marry up.[6] In the 1772 Assento, in contrast, sons were to be disinherited if they married without parental permission, whether they married their equals or not.[7]

The new concern with sons suggests that sons, and not daughters, were innovating by not following their parents' wishes regarding marriage. Interestingly enough, this was happening during the period in which a Portuguese law decreed in 1761 was in effect. The 1761 law prohibited dowry and female inheritance to the nobility and the very wealthy, and it was precisely they who were a part of the court and whose actions were therefore most evident to the state.[8] Thus it is probable that men from aristocratic families, who would no longer receive a dowry or even the expectation of an inheritance from women who were their equals, felt free to marry for love, and many married beneath them. Their families, who had formerly relied on a son's self-interest to accept an arranged marriage or at least to make an equal marriage, now cried out at the seduction of their sons by less wealthy families with marriageable daughters (ergo the 1775 law's concern about the seduction of children of *both* sexes).

CHANGE IN BRAZIL

Similar currents were present in Brazil, both the state restriction on the right of minors to choose their marriage partners and the growing independence of those same young men and women. Brazil followed the 1775 laws and later incorporated them into the Empire's Criminal Code of 1831, which made it unlawful for clerics to celebrate the marriage of minors without their parents' consent.[9] Since the age of majority had been lowered from 25 to 21, the restriction on minors marrying without their parents' consent probably applied more frequently to women than to men, who more rarely married before reaching 21. Lowering the age of majority was probably not sufficient to immediately stop parents from arranging the marriages of both men and women.[10] Yet even minors were now being asked at the judicial level whether they were marrying freely, something that only the church had asked previously.[11]

Families, for their part, changed their strategies. Instead of arranging the marriage of a man and a woman who had not even met, as had often been done in colonial times, families planned frequent meetings of the young people they hoped would marry, leaving the outcome to the natural process of love and sexual attraction.[12]

This strategy was used by Antonio Prado, the future Barão de Iguape, to marry off his half-sister, Maria Marcolina, to Rodrigo Antonio Monteiro de Barros in 1827. Rodrigo, 22 or 23 years old, had just received his degree at the University of Coimbra in Portugal when he moved to São Paulo with a letter of introduction from his father to Antonio Prado, asking him to introduce the young man to the best Paulista families. As family tradition has it, Antonio Prado invited the young man to stay in his own house and virtually kept him hostage there, while Rodrigo dreamed of the pleasures of Coimbra and Rio. Antonio then introduced Rodrigo to Maria Marcolina, 23 years old and "beautiful, well-mannered, intelligent, and educated." By the following year Rodrigo and Maria Marcolina were married, to the great delight of both families (suggesting some connivance on the part of Rodrigo's father), and Antonio was credited with the happy result.[13]

Dowry was not at issue in that marriage bargain. Although Maria Marcolina undoubtedly received a dowry when she married, as did all the Prado women in the early nineteenth century, it is not mentioned in the family story, suggesting that Maria Marcolina's dowry did not play any part in Rodrigo's decision. Tradition lists her personal qualities instead as the paramount factor, though the wealth and status of her family must certainly have influenced the outcome.

Tradition does, however, retain a clear picture of what Rodrigo Monteiro de Barros contributed to the bargain. Besides belonging to one of the most important and wealthy families of the Empire, Rodrigo was a lawyer, and the Prado family had few lawyers. Rodrigo was thus to represent the family politically.[14] The marriage of Rodrigo to Maria Marcolina therefore followed traditional usage in that the family of the bride benefited from the incorporation of the groom into the family. What differed was the inducement given him. However, the general replacement of love for dowry as an inducement to marry did not occur overnight in São Paulo, for, as we saw above, some families continued giving dowries throughout the nineteenth century.

Neither was the material advantage of the instant acquisition of property at marriage to cease as an important consideration in a man's decision to marry. Alfredo Ellis, whom we studied above as an example of modern thinking in the separation of business and family, acted very traditionally when it came to marriage. In 1874 he married his cousin, soon after her mother died leaving her a fortune of 30 contos. Although Alfredo Ellis was at the time a doctor of medicine who had practiced with his father for four years and had inherited his father's clinic when his father died, at marriage he gave up his medical practice, ceding the clinic to his brother, and invested his bride's fortune in a new coffee plantation in partnership with his father-in-law.[15] He followed the old Paulista custom, becoming incorporated into his wife's and maternal uncle's family and tradition and abandoning that of his father, but in a new way, via a partnership. From the point of view of his uncle, moreover, his daugher's marriage had secured an active collaborator for an expanding coffee business, though that collaboration was based on a contract and not exclusively on kinship ties as would have been the case in colonial times.

FEWER ARRANGED MARRIAGES

Although change was taking place gradually, an analysis of the information on single daughters in inventários indicates that nineteenth-century parents were no longer arranging their daughters' marriages as frequently as they had in previous centuries. We can assume that a family would want every daughter to marry, and that when the family controlled the marriage decision, the eldest daughers would be married off before the younger ones. An increase in the number of families with single daughters who were older than their married sisters therefore points to a decrease in the family's ability to control its daughters' marriages.

The seventeenth-century sample shows no single daughters who were older than their married sisters. Only two families in the sample had single daughters over 25, the age of majority, and in both cases the single daughters were the youngest. That their sisters had been married off first confirms the family's role in arranging marriage. Nevertheless, it is possible that daughters exercised the right to veto a proposed marriage and that some parents consulted their daughters in the choice of a husband. When Gaspar Cubas o velho declared in his will that he did not want anyone to force his youngest daughter to marry, he shows that it was not unknown for a parent to consider a daughter's wishes.[16] On the other hand, that he had to put such a request in his will indicates that forcing daughters to marry was a common practice.

In the eighteenth century most parents still appear to have arranged their daughters' marriage; it was the youngest girls who were single in eight of the thirteen families in the sample that had single daughters over age 25 (see Table 23). Nevertheless, in the other five families, single daughters were older than their married sisters, showing that those daughters had not married in the order of their birth. If we assume that the giving of a dowry helped parents control their daughters' marriages, it seems significant to find that in three of these five families no dowry had been given to any of the married daughters. (All five families were in the less wealthy half of the sample.)

The picture had changed considerably by the nineteenth century; more and more families were clearly not controlling their daughters' marriages. Single daughters were older than their married sisters in more than half the families with single daughters 21 or over (see Table 23). In at least 20 percent of the entire sample, therefore, daughters did not marry in the order of their birth. The proportion of families whose daughters did not marry in order was probably much higher, since we have no way of knowing in what order

TABLE 23
Order of Marriage of Daughters (Eighteenth and Nineteenth Centuries)

Families	18th cent.		19th cent.	
Where only the youngest daughters were unmarried	8	(62%)	29	(45%)
With single daughters who were older than their married sisters	5	(38%)	35	(55%)
Total with single daughters over 25 in 18th cent., over 21 in 19th cent.	13	(100%)	64	(100%)
Where all adult daughters were married	48		110	
Whose daughters' ages are unknown	7		4	
SAMPLE	68		178	

TABLE 24
Families Where Heirs Married Immediately After Inheriting

Families	17th cent.		18th cent.		19th cent.	
Where single heirs married immediately	2	(5%)	5	(11%)	20	(15%)
Other families with single adult heirs	35	(95%)	39	(89%)	112	(85%)
Total with single adult heirs	37	(100%)	44	(100%)	132	(100%)
With only married adult heirs	5		14		42	
Missing information	6		10		2	
SAMPLE	48		68		178	

daughters married in those families where all adult daughters were married at the time of inventário.

In all these cases it appears that families were not having their way. For example, Candida Maria Miquelina de Oliveira's youngest daughter was the only one of her six daughters who was married at the time the inventário was processed. Although this daughter had received a dowry, the dowry was certainly not the decisive element in that marriage; otherwise the parents would have favored their eldest daughter who was already 32. Nevertheless, after Candida Maria died, her third daughter married immediately, indicating that though the family had not arranged the marriage (for she had two older, single sisters), money, in the form of an inheritance, remained an important element in the possibility of marriage.[17] In fact, some heirs, both women and men, married immediately after inheriting, and the proportion of families where this occurred rose slightly from 11 percent of the sample in the eighteenth century to 15 percent in the nineteenth (see Table 24). Property was therefore still many times a part of the marriage bargain.

CHANGES IN THE HUSBAND'S ROLE

Besides the growth of love as an inducement to marriage and the diminishing control by parents of their children's marriages, there also were transformations of the *mentalité* regarding the husband's proper role in marriage. These changes can be studied in petitions by minors for a license to marry. After the 1831 Criminal Code made it unlawful for clerics to marry minors without their fathers' consents, children whose father was deceased were required to get a license to marry from a judge, usually the juiz dos órfãos, and present it to the priest before the wedding.[18] By studying the petitions, the concerns of the judges, and the reasons given by mother or guardians when they approved a marriage, we can detect some interesting trends in the nineteenth century.

To best understand these trends, we must first return to the practice of earlier centuries. Marriages were usually arranged for both sons and daughters in colonial times. In the seventeenth century, for example, José de Góis e Morais had his son come from Portugal to marry a certain girl "because he had so contracted with her parents."[19] Angela de o Campo declared in her will that her parents "married her to Diogo Guilhermo."[20] And when the eighteenth-century historian Pedro Taques recounts the life of seventeenth-century Ignacio Dias da Silva, he tells us that "his parents married him . . . to D. Anna Maria do Amaral Gurgel."[21] Taques's frequent approving phrases describing such arrangements in the previous century show that he considered them still the normal procedure.

Nevertheless, the eighteenth-century sample has a few signs of rebellion, for some children refused marriages arranged for them, and others married without their parents' consent. In 1752 Caetano Soares Viana, for example, was very upset because his son had married without his permission a woman who was not his equal.[22] And in the extensive litigation in Francisco de Godoy Preto's inventário, one son-in-law's claim that his wife was the first endowed daughter was contested with the words, "They were not endowed at all, for his wife married against her father's wishes."[23] Whether this was true or not, it shows that it was not unknown for a daughter to marry without her father's consent. Ignes Dultra, studied above, who was not endowed by her parents while all her sisters were, must have married without their approval. These and other cases demonstrate not only that some children did not go along with their parents' plans, but also that the church willingly married people who did not have their parents' consent. The 1831 Criminal Code stopped the church from doing this in an attempt to stem the growing number of marriages made without parental approval.[24]

Inventários frequently included the proceedings through which the judge decided whether the proposed or (in the eighteenth century) already effected marriage of a minor heir was a good one. The juizo de órfãos was involved because marriage meant instant emancipation for a man who was a minor and the instant possession of his inheritance if he had lost at least one parent, or his bride's inheritance if she had lost a parent. In cases of minors who still had a living father, the juiz dos órfãos was only minimally involved, just to witness and register the transference of the inheritance to the married son or son-in-law. But when the minor son or daughter had lost both parents or the father, even if the mother was the children's guardian, the juiz dos órfãos had to be shown that the marriage was a good one before handing over the property to the young couple.

In the eighteenth century, judges were especially concerned with the equality of the marriage partners. Their concern followed a Portuguese tradition; learned treatises on marriage from earlier centuries advocated equality as did countless popular sayings. A seventeenth-century saying was "If you want to marry well, marry your equal." A Portuguese priest in the same century described marriage as a yoke, adding, "for the yoke to be borne easily, it is necessary to have similar oxen." [25] A book written in the seventeenth century by Francisco Manoel de Mello to advise a male friend who was getting married described the ideal marriage as one in which the spouses were equal in their blood, their property, and their ages; equality of blood was important for the satisfaction of the spouses' parents, equality of property was important for their children's satisfaction, and equality of ages was important for their own satisfaction. [26]

This plethora of sources in early seventeenth-century Portugal advising the equality of spouses most likely indicates a struggle against an inequality in which the wife was the superior. This seems evident in Francisco de Mello's treatise, for on the same page as the advice above, it says that it is dangerous for a man to marry a woman who is his superior in "who she is, what she knows, and what she owns." Wives' perceived superiority to their husbands probably arose because of the dowry system.

The practice of dowry may also have contributed to men marrying women who were older than they were. In colonial Brazil, where many women married very young and frequently to men who were much older, it is surprising to find how many marriages were between younger men and older women. In eighteenth-century Guaratinguetá, a town in the captaincy of São Paulo, fully 14 percent of the marriages were between older women and younger men, and in two cases the wives were over twenty years older. [27] A study of the 1765 census in the city of São Paulo also found that in 7 percent of the marriages the wife was older than her husband. [28] It is possible that there were even more cases in the eighteenth century in which the wife was older than her husband, or in which there was less difference in ages between an older husband and a younger wife than reported, for I found several cases in which the wife's age in the 1765 census does not correspond to information gleaned from inventários or even to the age of the eldest child, suggesting that sometimes wives were declared younger to the census taker than they really were.

Of course, when eighteenth-century Paulista judges inquired whether a prospective bride or groom was equal to the minor who sought permission to marry, they were not concerned with equality of ages between prospective spouses, but with equality of status and property.[29] Yet for the payment of the minor's legítima, the required testimony was whether the groom was capable of administering the property. For example, when Roza Ortiz de Camargo petitioned to marry José Franco do Prado, her guardians were first asked whether José was equal to Roza; the answer was that he was, for he was the son of a good family, though his property was still in his father's hands because he was a filho-família. With this information, the judge gave the necessary license for Roza to marry, yet when José came to collect Roza's inheritance he still had to provide three witnesses to his ability to administer property.[30]

The eighteenth-century concern with the groom's ability to administer property depicts the husband's role in marriage as an administrator and indicates that one of the purposes of marriage itself in that century was the administration and development of property. People were well aware of this aspect of marriage. One man wrote that his wife, who had been a widow, married him because she needed someone to administer her property. And when Policarpio Joaquim de Oliveira married at age sixteen, his widowed mother did not object to his choice of a bride but thought rather that he was much too young to be free of her tutelage and to administer his legítima.[31] Her opposition, therefore, did not center on the personal (private) aspect of marriage, but on the public functions he would assume with marriage.

The concern for both the equality between spouses and the husband's ability to administer property was expressed in every eighteenth-century petition. In a few, there was also another concern, that the orphan daughter needed protection. Thus the argument for Anna de Lima to marry a man of unknown parentage was that it was a good marriage because she was poor and unprotected. When her sister petitioned to marry a man whose parents also were unknown, the same argument was used, that he would protect her because he was "a good man, very enterprising, very capable of administering a house, and with good principles."[32] That these girls with an impeccable lineage had to marry men of unknown parentage because they had little property shows the consequence of not having a good dowry in eighteenth-century society. It also shows that a woman's good lineage did not necessarily compensate for her lack of property. Nevertheless, the resulting marriage bargain maintained a certain balance; lineage and a small amount of property were traded for protection. The argument that the bride was unprotected was even

TABLE 25
Reasons for Granting Minors Permission to Marry
(Nineteenth Century)

Reasons	Number of petitions	
Equality between spouses	7	(18%)
Groom is a good administrator	0	
Groom is wealthy	8	(20%)
Groom is hard working	12	(30%)
Groom can protect bride	4	(10%)
Bride consents or so wishes	18	(40%)
Granted only because mother or guardian approves (no reasons)	7	(18%)

NOTE: There were 40 petitions. Some give several reasons, so percentages add to more than 100.

used in a case where the bride was wealthy. The groom, however, was going to contribute four times as much property as the bride to the pool of community property, so that the concept of protection can still be viewed as meaningful.[33]

Nineteenth-century petitions for minors to marry, in contrast, show increasing concern for the husband's competence in supporting his wife. Sixty percent of the petitions included the husband's wealth, hard work, or "protection" in their concerns—all proof of a husband's ability to support his bride (see Table 25). The equality of the spouses, on the other hand, was no longer the universal concern it had been in the preceding century; it was included in only 18 percent of the petitions. The concern about the groom's ability as an administrator had practically disappeared, for it shows up only negatively: two petitions were denied because the intended groom was too young to know how to administer his bride's property. For example, when Gertrudes de Araujo Ribeiro, granddaughter of the very wealthy Paulista Brigadeiro Manoel Rodrigues Jordão, petitioned to marry in 1876, the judge responded, "I would not scrupulously defend the person and property of the orphan, D. Gertrudes de Araujo Ribeiro, if I agreed to her marriage to João Baptista Bueno Netto. Since I do not know the gentleman personally, I asked the opinion of several circumspect persons and I have learned that he is not yet capable of shouldering the grave responsibility of marriage, especially with this orphan who has a considerable fortune to be administered by her husband. The gentleman is still an orphan [a minor] and has not yet acquired a profession." Although Gertrudes's eldest brother, who was her guardian, had agreed to the marriage, adding that both families were happy with it, he was overruled; two weeks later Gertrudes was in the home of the parents of another young man, Silverio Rodrigues Jordão, telling the notary that "she wanted to marry [him] very much of her own free will."[34] Gertrudes, who was twenty, was obviously being pressured to conform to what others wanted for her.

The fact that Gertrudes was asked for her consent, which was duly recorded by the notary, was in itself a big innovation in nineteenth-century petitions. Despite the 1831 Criminal Code, there was growing judicial emphasis on the free consent of both parties, especially on ascertaining the wishes of the bride, even though in cases such as that of Gertrudes, it appears to have been only perfunctory. In 40 percent of the petitions the bride was specifically asked whether she agreed to the marriage, and many times the principal reason given by mothers or guardians for their approval of the marriage was that the groom was the bride's choice, and that they felt he would make her happy (see Table 25).[35] For example, there is a petition in 1863 presented by Gertrudes Angelica do Espirito Santo who said that she "has in her company a granddaughter called Benedicta . . . eighteen years old, and wishing to marry her off, she has contracted to marry her to Bras de Souza e Mello of the same parish, a young man of good manners and good behavior, who is to her granddaugher's liking." The girl's tutor and uncle added that he judged "that her marriage to Mr. Bras de Souza e Mello is advantageous because he is a young man of excellent behavior who will protect my niece." To add further confirmation, the prospective bride and groom signed a joint declaration: "We declare to your Lordship that we have contracted this marriage of our own free will."[36] Thus, despite the greater emphasis of the law on parental consent, legal usage gave increasing importance to individual choice.

ASYMMETRIES IN THE MARRIAGE RELATIONSHIP

The changing concerns in the petitions to marry show a change in the marriage bargain. The eighteenth-century marriage bargain stressed equality of property and family, and the main concern was in the groom's ability to administer property. The marriage bargain in the nineteenth century was more concerned with the personal and emotional aspects of marriage, such as the happiness of the bride, and stressed the groom's ability to protect (support) the bride. The concept of protection or support of the bride implies, moreover, an asymmetrical relationship within the marriage, with the husband the stronger partner and the wife the dependent.

This transformation, from an equal partnership based on both spouses' contribution of property to an asymmetrical relationship, is reflected in changes in the surnames of married women. In the seventeenth- and eighteenth-century samples, all wives used only their maiden names (see Table 26). In the nineteenth century, the majority of wives either used their maiden

TABLE 26
Surnames of Married Women (Seventeenth to Nineteenth Centuries)

Name	17th cent.		18th cent.		19th cent.	
Only maiden name	99	(98%)	94	(94%)	84	(40.8%)
No surname	2	(2%)	6	(6%)	77	(37.4%)
Husband's surname only	0		0		26	(12.6%)
Maiden and husband's name	0		0		19	(9.2%)
TOTAL	101	(100%)	100	(100%)	206	(100%)
Missing information	5		10		13	
TOTAL INVENTÁRIOS	106		110		219	

NOTE: Names used for this table are those of the deceased herself, or of the widow or predeceased wife of the male deceased.

name (in wealthier or well-established families) or had no surname at all (usually small proprietors), showing a class difference among proprietors that roughly correlates with our findings on literacy. Nevertheless, among the higher strata there was a growing number of married women, over 20 percent of the entire sample, who carried their husband's surname either in place of or in addition to their maiden names (see Table 26).

There was also a significant increase in the proportion of children who bore their father's surname. As we saw above, Portuguese custom did not require all siblings to bear the same surname. In the seventeenth-century sample only 60 percent of the children of the decreased bore their father's name. The rest used their mother's or one of their grandmothers' surnames. In the eighteenth century the proportion of children who bore their father's name had increased slightly to 66 percent, but in the nineteenth-century sample it rose to 82 percent.[37] The greater proportion of children with their father's surname in the nineteenth century suggests that the power of status of fathers was gaining vis-à-vis that of mothers.

Even at the judicial level it appears that the power of the husband was increasing in relation to his wife's. This can be seen in the question of permission for children to marry. It is not clear whether a wife's assent was necessary for a child's marriage in colonial times, but it was required to give dowries that included real estate. The Portuguese law of 1775 decreed that to be able to marry, children must have the consent of both their father and mother. Yet in the Brazilian 1870 edition of the Ordenações, a jurist stated that despite the law, the practice was to consider the father's consent sufficient.[38]

The growing number of children with their father's name and the increasing emphasis on the husband's support of his wife were all novel tendencies undoubtedly related to the decline in the importance of the institution of dowry. The Ordenações had nothing to say about a wife's adopting her husband's name, and regarding her support it allowed a man to stop providing his wife the "necessaries" for her support if her dowry had not been paid.[39] Hence, during the period in which the marriage bargain required a dowry, the wife's support had been contingent on the payment of that dowry. But in the nineteenth century, as the use of the dowry declined, the husband's ability to support a family became the principal requirement for marriage.

As professions and employment grew, more people in the general population entered legal marriages.[40] This trend confirms further that marriage had changed from being principally a property arrangement to being primarily a personal relationship. In colonial times, legal marriage had been limited principally to the upper classes, while the rest of the population entered consensual unions.[41] As the nineteenth century progressed, more and more people married. This is demonstrated by the sharp decline between 1798 and 1828 in the proportion of free persons over 50 who had never married in the captaincy of São Paulo. In 1798, 29.8 percent of the men and 38.3 percent of the women over 50 had never married, whereas by 1828 only 8.8 percent of the men and 20.3 percent of the women over 50 had never married.[42] We must await further studies of the 1872 census to know whether, as is likely, the trend toward more people marrying continued throughout the nineteenth century.[43] Statistics for Rio de Janeiro, however, confirm that more people were marrying. In 1872 only 23 percent of the population of marriageable age was married, but the percentage increased to 31 percent by 1890 and to 40 percent by 1906.[44]

More people of all classes now married. But these more numerous marriages, based on love and mostly supported by the husband's work, were more unequal between spouses than were those fewer marriages made in colonial times in which both partners contributed to the support of the family.

MARRIAGE CONTRACTS

A study of the few marriage contracts found in the samples corroborates the tendency toward more asymmetrical marriages. As we saw above, the Portuguese marriage system established complete community property unless a prenuptial contract was signed, and the latter were usually only entered into by noble families or those who were very wealthy. It is possible that during colonial times the wealthy of the Brazilian northeast or Rio de Janeiro used prenuptial contracts, but this does not seem to be the case in São Paulo for I found reference to only one marriage contract in the seventeenth-century sample (which did not hold up before the juiz dos órfãos), three in the eighteenth century, and eleven in the nineteenth.[45]

Marriage contracts were entered into to establish a different system of property ownership within the marriage. Thus, even though they were rare in São Paulo, their study can give us clues to what rights each spouse or each family joined by the marriage alliance wanted to defend. The *Ordenações* allowed future spouses to make a prenuptial contract for any kind of property regime in marriage, so long as it did not violate the rights of necessary heirs— that is, children, grandchildren or, in their absence, parents.[46]

The most common arrangements were either a complete separation of property or a *contrato de dote e arras*. Both optional systems of marriage property continued to be lawful in Brazil in the twentieth century, for they were incorporated into the 1917 Civil Code.[47] With a contrato de dote e arras, the dowry remained separate from the pool of community property and had to be restituted intact to the widow after her husband died. The marriage system that resulted was called *regime dotal*, and the property the wife brought to the marriage, whether given as dowry, inherited, or received in some other way, could not be seized by the husband's creditors in cases of default. With a regime dotal, if the wife predeceased her husband, her dowry was the only part of the couple's property that her heirs inherited. If the husband predeceased the wife, the part of their property she received was the dowry plus the arras, a gift promised by the husband in the contract to help in her support, and which was not supposed to be more than a third the size of the dowry. If they had so contracted, she could also receive half of all profits accrued from her husband's administration of both her dowry and his property.[48] Prenuptial marriage contracts were clearly intended to protect each spouse's property from the other spouse's rights within the community property system. Thus the contracts probably reflect initial economic inequality between the spouses.

The system of community property, however, encouraged people to try to make equal marriages, for if one spouse contributed all or most of the property, he or she would only retain half when the spouse died, losing half of it to the spouse's necessary heirs, children or parents (if the spouse died before the couple had children). If it was the wife who contributed the greater amount she also risked losing it during the course of the marriage if her husband were a bad administrator. But if the wife brought nothing to the marriage, the system of community property was advantageous to her, for when her husband had property or they built up an estate after marrying, she was an equal partner and received half their assets when her husband died.

Only one of all the São Paulo marriage contracts I found had to do with the dowry received by the bride from her parents, that of João Correa de Lemos in the eighteenth century. He declared in his will that he and his wife had married with a contrato de dote e arras and listed the dowry his wife had brought, jewels and a large sum of money. His will specified no arras, and the juiz dos órfãos did not even consider the contrato de dote e arras in the division of property, probably because the will also said they had married under the regime of community property.[49] In this particular case, if the contrato de dote e arras had been followed, the wife would have kept the whole estate, as it was smaller than her dowry, and their children would have inherited nothing until she died. The decision the judge made to ignore the testator's reference to a contract is just another demonstration that for Paulistas in colonial times, as in the nineteenth century, the most common practice was not to make marriage contracts, but instead to allow the dowry to disappear into the pool of community property.

The other two eighteenth-century marriage contracts involve people who remarried after their first spouse's death and wanted to protect their estates for the children of their first marriage. When Francisco de Godoy Preto married his second wife, he and his father-in-law, Captain Lourenço de Camargo Pires, signed a marriage contract in which Lourenço renounced the inheritance that would be his if his daughter predeceased her husband before having children, saying that he would not even demand restitution of her maternal legítima, which she was taking to the marriage. The bridegroom was clearly protecting his property from division in case his bride died without children. His father-in-law, however, must have been a wily man because Francisco died thinking that, since they had had no children, his widow might not be *meeira*, that is, she might not have the right to half the community property. But the contract specified that Maria Pires de Camargo's father would not inherit from her, not that she would not be meeira. What actually transpired after her husband died was not only that she was meeira, but that she delayed the process of inventário for twenty years, retaining *all* their property during that time and not allowing the division and payment to her adult stepchildren. That she was able to do this might have been because she had strong support from her family, or it might have been due to her own character, since her father said in the contract that she had been hard to marry off. The latter interpretation seems more likely, for she was also a highly educated woman for the time. She wrote very well, and her husband's inventário included a large library that he did not have when his first wife died, so it probably belonged to Maria.[50]

The second eighteenth-century marriage contract that intended to protect the rights of the children of a first marriage was that which Joanna Soares de Siqueira signed when she married her second husband, Captain Manoel Lopes Viana. She had clearly married with much more property than her husband possessed, and though she considered him in her will, she shows that the contract was meant to protect her heirs' rights to her estate. In her will she carefully repeated the terms of the marriage contract and even named the notarial office where it was kept. She stated that they had married with complete separation of property, but the income derived from her property would be shared half and half, including the income from almost 400$000 in cash that she had given her husband to administer. In her will she left him the use of the house they were living in and a slave, but these were to revert to her heirs at his death.[51]

Of the eleven nineteenth-century contracts, only one, the marriage contract of Second Lieutenant João Carlos da Silva Rangel and D. Anna Maria de Moura, had the purpose of protecting the property the wife brought to the marriage from the possibility that her husband would dissipate it.[52] Anna's guardian objected to the marriage because, though bride and groom were socially equal (they were cousins through their mothers and both were illegitimate), Anna had already inherited a sizable fortune from her father, who had been a priest, while it was not sure whether the groom would ever inherit from his father. The solution proposed by the bride's guardian, which was finally accepted, was to have the principal part of Anna's property, sixteen bonds and the part of a house she had inherited, go into the marriage as her dowry, a dowry that could not be alienated nor be made liable for debts contracted by her husband. He would have the right to administer her dowry, and all income derived from it was to be community property, as was all other property held by the couple.

The foregoing is an excellent example of the marriage system described above, called regime dotal, in which the bride's dowry remains separate from the other conjugal property and cannot be alienated, and, more important, it cannot be seized by her husband's creditors. The example of João Carlos da Silva Rangel shows how there can be a regime dotal though the bride had *not* been given a dowry, but instead had inherited property, which became the "dowry" within the marriage property system. I have found so few instances of the use of regime dotal in São Paulo (none of the deceased in the sample had used it) that it appears to have been an exception.

A similar case, in which a part of the wife's property was protected from the vagaries of the husband's business, was that of Elvyra de Souza Queiroz. One-third of her property was kept out of the community property by a marriage contract arranged because that part of her fortune had been bequeathed to her by her grandmother on condition that she and her husband have only its usufruct, as it was to go to their children if they had them, or to a specific charity if they did not.[53]

The other nine nineteenth-century marriage contracts appear not to have been intended to protect the wife or her property so much as to exclude her from the community property. An example is the marriage contract between Brigadeiro Manoel Rodrigues Jordão and his future wife, Gertrudes Galvão de Lacerda.[54] Although she came from a well-established and wealthy family, she took no dowry to marriage, though she undoubtedly expected to receive an inheritance. Their contract stipulated complete separation of their property, and the groom endowed the bride with six contos that she could freely use and dispose of when widowed, and that her forced heirs could inherit when she died, even if she predeceased her husband.[55] In the marriage contract, the brigadier stipulated that the contract itself could not be used to invalidate or impede his receiving from the crown the entail (*morgado*) he had solicited (the marriage contract was signed in 1820, before independence and before morgados were prohibited in 1835).[56] It seems reasonable to conclude that this particular marriage contract was made precisely because the husband was soliciting an entail. With the contract, the property his wife later inherited would not go into the entail and would serve as an inheritance for the younger children who would be excluded from the entail.

Another example of a contract with complete separation of property is that of Dr. William Ellis (the father of Alfredo Ellis) who, when he married the young widow Maria do Carmo da Cunha Bueno, signed a marriage contract stipulating complete separation of property.[57] Since Maria do Carmo belonged to one of the very old, important families of São Paulo, which was also wealthy, and as a widow had independent means, it could be that her English husband insisted on a marriage contract separating their property because he did not wish to be seen as having married her for her money. On the other hand, she or her family may have insisted on the contract. Besides, Maria do Carmo had two children with her first husband, and William might not have wanted those children to inherit through their mother any part of the money he was working so hard to acquire. On his part, he had two filhas naturais, daughters born while he was still single, whom he recognized and named as heirs on a par with any children he and Maria do Carmo might have. Besides complete separation of property, William promised Maria do Carmo in the contract a dower of three contos that she would receive if she survived him, having lived with him in harmony. If she predeceased him, the dower was to remain his.[58] This marriage contract was clearly intended to establish a marriage regime such as the spouses could have established in a marriage settlement if they had married in England.

Two of the other marriage contracts were also of foreigners, who, like Dr. Ellis, were not used to community property or to the system of inheritance that made one's children necessary heirs who could not be disinherited. In neither of these cases did the marriage contract hold up before the juiz dos órfãos, because both would have deprived the necessary heirs of their legal right to inherit from each spouse.[59] The first contract did so by saying that husband and wife would inherit from each other, and the second by specifying that if the wife predeceased the husband, he would retain all property except for a small amount to go to her mother.[60]

The other five marriage contracts, that is, almost half the contracts I found among the nineteenth-century documents, were ones in which the future husband had much property and clearly did not want his future wife to receive half of it when he died, as would have been the case under the system of community property. All the contracts provided for separation of property, and most settled some relatively small amount on the wife for her support in widowhood. In these marriages the wife clearly appears to have been socially or economically inferior to her husband. For example, Luis Manoel da Paixão Branco married his black cook right before his death with a marriage contract of complete separation of property. He then made a will in which he left her only a small part of his estate, the grocery store, leaving the rest to their children whom he had duly recognized.[61]

Demetrio da Costa Nascimento married his wife a month before her death with a marriage contract with complete separation of property. At her death only her small amount of property went to her children, the eldest of whom, a married daughter, was not his; thus, he may not only have attempted by means of the contract to preserve in his own hands as much property as possible but also to avoid having his wife's daughter by another man inherit any of his possessions.[62]

Joaquim Elias da Silva, who had had ten children with three different women, married the mother of his last seven children a year before he died with a marriage contract stipulating separation of property and leaving to her only the usufruct during her lifetime of two contos out of his estate of 33 contos.[63]

When Antonio Francisco Baruel died in 1859, his widow frankly stated that the reason they had made a marriage contract with complete separation of property was because she was poor. Furthermore, in the contract her husband endowed her with only 800$000, whereas if she had married him without a contract, she would have been to entitled to 11:500$000 when he died.[64] The contract called it a dowry (dote), but it was not a dowry as we have defined it, but was instead an amount settled on the wife by her husband for her support in widowhood. Its use appears to have increased in nineteenth-century São Paulo.[65] Sometimes it was inaccurately called arras, which was legally intended to complement the dowry, not substitute for it.[66] This was the case of Bento Joaquim de Souza e Castro, a pharmacist and capitalista, who married D. Henriqueta Viana Pereira Lima with a marriage contract that stipulated separation of their property. To help support her in widowhood, his will left her the usufruct of the remainder of his terça, which he called arras.[67]

The greater frequency of marriage contracts, especially those of separation of property in which the husband endowed his wife, must have had some relation to the decline of the practice of dowry. Most of these men married women with little or no property, and either tacitly or explicitly (as in the case of Antonio Francisco Baruel) they supported the family without their wives bringing dowries or inherited property to the marriage.

These marriage contracts were therefore examples of a new kind of marriage, no longer a marriage to which the wife immediately contributed substantial amounts of property, but a marriage in which initially the husband alone (whether with property or only with his work) supported his wife and children. This was as true of marriages with women from families with modest means as of those with women from wealthy families. The daughter of a wealthy couple, however, brought the expectation of a good inheritance to her marriage, plus the possibilities of partnership for her husband in her family's enterprise or at least family connections that might further his own business.

The rise of love as the principal reason for marriage came about as the family changed from being primarily a unit of production to being a unit of consumption, facilitated by the existence of professions or other careers that allowed men to support wives without inheriting property or receiving large dowries and gave them the viable option of marrying girls with no expectations at all. This possibility increased the negotiating power of the husband-to-be vis-à-vis the bride, even if she belonged to a wealthy family, because it meant he did not *need* a dowry to marry. Such male independence undoubtedly contributed to the decline in the practice of dowry.

The decreasing use of dowry with the resulting loss of negotiating power by the bride and her family and the increased negotiating power of the future bridegroom showed up in the nineteenth-century sample in the greater number of women who married before their older sisters, and in the rising number of marriage contracts that excluded the future wife from community property. And when brides no longer contributed large dowries to marriage, a more asymmetrical marriage was created that lasted until the wife from a wealthy family inherited or for the duration of the marriage when the wife came from a propertyless family. Nineteenth-century petitions to marry indicate that the ability of the husband to support a family was now viewed as the essential condition for marriage, instead of the colonial emphasis on the equality of spouses and the husband's ability to administer property, which had depended on the bride's contribution of a large dowry. These transformations gave the husband greater weight within the marriage vis-à-vis the wife and her family of origin, clearly demonstrated by the increasing number of wives who adopted their husband's surname and of children with their father's surname.

CHAPTER 11

PROBLEMS WITH THE DOWRY

WE HAVE TRACED the declining practice of dowry. To be able to explain why the dowry finally disappeared we must also examine what problems developed with the dowry and how Brazilians changed their opinions about it. This chapter will commence by studying evidence of eighteenth-century Portuguese concerns with the adverse effects of dowry on modernization, followed by an examination of actual problems Brazilians experienced with the dowry system and a description of the strong ideological change against dowry that came about in Brazil in the second half of the nineteenth century.

PROBLEMS IN PORTUGAL

A law was passed in Portugal in the middle of the eighteenth century that suggests that the government of Pombal saw problems in the practice of dowry. After the Treaty of Methuen in 1703, Portugal had close ties with Great Britain, and under the enlightened despotism of Pombal, many measures were taken to strengthen and modernize the Portuguese empire.[1] Among these was the law of August 17, 1761, that completely eliminated female inheritance and dowry in noble or very wealthy families.[2] This law had no relevence for Paulistas, for it applied only to persons with the rank of fidalgo or higher whose property produced an income of over three contos a year; no one in eighteenth-century São Paulo fit that description. Even though the law was revoked seventeen years later, when Pombal was no longer in power, it points to new state concerns.[3] It is likely that the 1761 law reflects English influence, since it brought Portuguese inheritance laws, though only for the very wealthy and the nobility, closer to the English model, in which sons were favored and daughters had few inheritance rights.

Because it was contrary to previous Portuguese law and practice, the 1761 law indicates that Pombal's govenment saw problems in the institutions of dowry and female inheritance. The new law stipulated that daughters were to receive no inheritance and no dowry, and, if they were still single when their parents died, they were to live with their brothers, who had an obligation to support them. When a woman wanted to marry, her parents or, in their absence, her brothers should help her, but only to give her a trousseau of linen worth up to one and a half contos but no real estate, money, or jewels. Neither should her family buy her wedding clothes and jewels; these should come from her husband or his parents or guardian. Since the nobility and the very wealthy usually married with a contrato de dote e arras, under the new law widows would no longer have dowries to support them in widowhood; the law therefore decreed they should remain in possession of all the couple's property and receive for their exclusive use one-tenth of its income until they died or remarried. When a man died who still had not inherited, his parents or brothers had to give his widow a monthly allowance until she died or remarried.[4] The only exceptions to this law among the great nobility would be for the queen's ladies-in-waiting and for women who had no male siblings.[5]

By abolishing female dowry and inheritance rights, the new law channeled all property solely through men and postponed the dismemberment of the parents' estate until their death. The rationale for the 1761 law is very clear in its defense of sons as opposed to daughters. The crown stated that it was concerned with the rights of sons and the welfare of families, arguing that when daughters inherited, their brothers were deprived of sufficient means to serve the crown and augment the splendor of their families, and that families were ruined by giving many large dowries.[6] Although the crown differentiated between the suppression of dowry and the suppression of female inheritance, it seems clear that the prohibitions on female inheritance and on dowry were intimately connected. Since dowry was an advance on a daughter's inheritance, eliminating her inheritance rights without eliminating all or most of her dowry would have resulted in practically no change; she would still have received a share of the family's estate. For the law to channel all property through male heirs therefore required the abolition of both female inheritance and dowry.

The advantage the new law gave to sons changed the marriage bargain. Under the old laws the dowry had worked to induce a man to marry to establish himself and increase his property; the dowry also led him to marry his equal, a woman who would bring to marriage a dowry at least as large as the one his sister received. The 1761 law, in contrast, liberated noble men from the constraints of the earlier marriage system; they could now marry whomever they chose, even women who were not their equals, and they could just as easily choose to remain single, for marriage no longer meant an instant acquisition of property; it was an immediate cost instead.

The law had its disadvantages for men as well. Whereas under the earlier law they could marry a wife with a dowry and control that property long before their parents died, they now had to wait until their parents died to receive property they could control, or else court their parents' favor in order to receive property *inter vivos*. The new law was therefore only advantageous to men who had ways to acquire property on their own. Men increasingly did have such chances through the growth of commerce, professions, and the state bureaucracy.

For the women of the noble and wealthy families affected by the 1761 law, it had disastrous consequences, for it eliminated both the equality of brothers and sisters and the equality of man and wife. It was a harbinger of the new kind of marriage, in which the wife was totally dependent on her husband's support. By eliminating the responsibility of the bride's family for most of the expenses associated with marriage, the new law gave the husband or his family full control of the marriage transaction and full responsibility for the support of the marriage. From a practice in which the bride entered marriage as her husband's economic equal or even superior, or at least with a substantial contribution, this law created a nobility in which all support and property came from the husband, and the bride contributed only her person, entering and remaining in marriage and widowhood exclusively as a dependent.[7] The 1761 law was such a revolutionary change in the long-standing customs of Portugal that it is not suprising that it was subsequently revoked. Interestingly, though the law of 1778 brought back female inheritance (for wealthy and noble families, since it had never been lost for families of more modest means), a prohibition on excessively large dowries remained, suggesting that wealthy Portuguese society had accepted the prohibition on dowries more easily than women's complete exclusion from inheritance, and were therefore moving toward the disappearance of the dowry.

PROBLEMS IN BRAZIL

Some of the problems dowry presented in Brazil, and which undoubtedly contributed to its demise, are further illustrated in the crown's rationale for the 1761 law. In the first place, the crown argued, giving very large dowries ruined the families that gave them, especially if they had many daughters.

Second, dowries placed constraints on the families receiving them, for within the contrato de dote e arras, dowries had to be secured because they were to be returned intact or for equivalent value either to the widow or her heirs. This was problematic when the dowry included movables that depreciated but had to be compensated for at current prices or with equivalent goods. Third, the crown argued that dowries were disadvantageous to the women who received them, for they did not accomplish their purpose of supporting a widow as they should. Under the system of contrato de dote e arras, a widow had to sue her husband's heirs to receive the dowry back, resulting in long and expensive litigation.[8]

Despite the fact that the crown was referring to the system of contrato de dote e arras, which was used very rarely in São Paulo, the first two of its arguments are relevant to the more common system in which the dowry was lost within the community property. In either system families could be ruined if they had many daughters and gave them large dowries. That families did so in colonial São Paulo, despite depleting their estates considerably, can be explained by the greater value they placed on the extended family vis-à-vis the individual family of the parents. But by the nineteenth century Paulistas were no longer reducing their property for the sake of their daughters; most families gave no dowries at all and those who did only divested themselves of an average of 7 percent of their estate.[9] With the rise of individualism, families had reversed their priorities.

The second argument the crown used in defending the 1761 law, that dowries brought problems to the receiving families, was also appropriate to the dowry system in which the dowry was pooled within the community property. Although under that system the dowry did not have to be returned intact to the widow or her heirs, it did have to come in à colação when the wife's parents died, creating considerable litigation and similar problems of appraisal.

In fact, questions of appraisal were central to what was problematic in the institution of dowry. The system of colação set out in the *Ordenações* had been equitable in times when property maintained the same value throughout a lifetime, but it was not seen as fair in the booming nineteenth-century economy of São Paulo.

This was especially the case because dowry or a gift given on occasion of an heir's marriage had an important advantage for the recipient over other gifts to heirs. According to the *Ordenações*, the heir who had received a dowry or other gift given at marriage had the option of bringing it back à colação at either the price it had when it was given or at the price at the parent's death. In the case of gifts to heirs that were not given at marriage, the value to be used when brought back à colação was always the value at the moment of the donor's death.[10]

The possibility of choosing between one or the other value could make a big difference to an inheritance in mid-nineteenth-century São Paulo, since the region was experiencing inflation concomitantly with land valorization and the rise in the price of slaves due to the suppression of the slave traffic.[11] The average appraised value of slaves in the sample went from 495$000 in 1850–1854 to 1:006$000 in 1860–1864, and the appraised value of one house in São Paulo went from five contos in 1854 to eight contos in 1865.[12] Clearly the siblings of a daughter who had received land, a house, or slaves in dowry would not think it fair if she were permitted to bring them back à colação at their original price, thereby increasing her actual inheritance.

All kinds of ruses were undoubtedly used to not permit the law to be applied. Francisco Vieira de Paula and his wife, for example, probably gave their daughter a dowry, though the inventário itself treated the transfer of land to the daughter at marriage as a loan. It is likely that the family realized that if the land was considered a dowry, she would be able to bring back into the estate only the original value of the land, which was much lower than its value at the time of inventário, and would therefore receive a larger inheritance to the detriment of other heirs. The parents themselves or the heirs in agreement probably decided to consider it a debt so as to prevent litigation and injustice to the remaining heirs.[13]

In that period of land valorization, having received a dowry might also work against the interests of the daughter and her husband. Floriano Antonio de Lima found this to be the case with the dowry of 600$000 his wife had received. At the time of his father-in-law's death, an outsider was interested in buying one of the estate's properties. Floriano asked the judge for time to raise the money to pay back the dowry to his mother-in-law in order for his wife to inherit a full share of that piece of property. The judge agreed to the postponement, the mother-in-law agreed to receive the dowry back, and the daughter and son-in-law made a good profit when the land was subsequently sold.[14]

Because of their increasing value, slaves were a frequent cause for litigation, and the cases in which a dowry consisted of a small slave child were especially problematic.[15] Francisco Carlos de Camargo and his wife, Umbelina, had serious problems when the inventário was made at his mother-in-law's death. Umbelina's dowry had been a two-year-old female slave worth 51$000. By the time Umbelina's mother died, the slave was 32, in her prime, and worth 1:000$000, so Francisco and Umbelina tried to bring her back à colação for the original price but they were not successful.[16]

A similar case, that of a baby slave girl given to Josefa Joaquina Bueno at marriage, would have presented a serious problem to the rest of the family when Josefa Joaquina's father died eighteen years later if she had insisted on using the slave's original price, since the estate was very small and only owned one other slave, a thirteen-year-old male. Josefa Joaquina did not attempt to have her slave come in à colação at the original price, but accepted the current price of 500$000. Her legítima, however, amounted to only 66$000, and Josefa Joaquina was supposed to return the difference to her widowed mother and brothers and sisters. Since Josefa Joaquina was by then a widow herself, she could not be expected to return this large amount of money, so that the family divided the ownership of the slave among all the heirs (though it is unclear who retained usufruct of the slave).[17]

There seems to have been a growing consensus among nineteenth-century Paulistas that giving heirs the choice of which price to bring property received in dowry à colação was not just. In most inventários where slaves were brought à colação, there was no litigation since the endowed heirs accepted the use of the current price. For example, when the wife of Captain Manoel José de Moraes died in 1860, their six children, both sons and daughters, brought slaves à colação at their current prices (though their prices at the time they were given were duly registered). Two of the slaves received 27 years before in dowry by the eldest daughter had died, and since she was no longer enjoying their services, those were the only ones to come in à colação with their original price.[18]

Nineteenth-century property owners also perceived a problem in another privilege that Portuguese inheritance law gave dowry and other gifts to heirs in comparison with loans made to heirs. These problems become evident in cases like that of Francisco Vieira de Paula above, where Paulista families gave their daughters property at marriage, but in the process of inventário, instead of calling it dowry, it was considered a loan.[19] For the recipient, dowries and gifts had one great advantage over loans. According to the inheritance law in *Ordenações*, which still applied in nineteenth-century Imperial Brazil, a loan given to a son or daughter had to be brought back into the estate in its entirety at the death of the first parent. In contrast, since a dowry or a gift to a son was considered given by both parents, only half was subtracted from the heir's legítima at the death of each parent.[20] This meant that an heir who had received a loan equal to a sister's dowry had to bring the whole amount back into the estate and deduct it from his or her inheritance, receiving therefore a smaller inheritance than the sister, who only had to bring back and deduct half the dowry. (However, the heir who received a loan would not have to deduct anything at the death of their second parent, inheriting then much more than his sister.) Such heirs would seek to equalize the inheritance of all siblings by having their sister's dowry considered a loan. This may be another reason the heirs of Francisco Vieira de Paula chose to have the land given to their sister considered a loan instead of a dowry.

The case of José Manoel Godinho's family illustrates the difference be-

TABLE 27
Division of an Estate with a Dowry or a Loan

Actual division (dowry)		Hypothetical division (loan)	
Net estate to be divided	1:318$260	Net estate to be divided	1:318$260
Plus Rita's half-dowry	125$000	Plus Rita's debt (full dowry)	250$000
Plus sister's half-dowry	75$000	Plus sister's half-dowry	75$000
TOTAL	1:578$260	TOTAL	1:643$260
Divided among eight heirs, each legítima	197$282	Divided among eight heirs, each legítima	205$407
Rita's half dowry	−125$000	Rita's debt	−250$000
SHE RECEIVES	72$282	SHE MUST RETURN	44$592

SOURCE: José Manoel Godinho, 1863, 2° Of. da F., no. 441.

tween a loan and a dowry. After José's widow declared that Rita, one of their married daughters, had received a gift of some land, her son declared that that land had not been given at his sister's marriage (as a dowry) but as a loan. Later Rita herself appeared with her lawyer to show a deed of donation made by both her parents, successfully arguing that whether it was called a dowry or not, since both parents had given her the land, she had to bring in only half its value à colação because only one of her parents had died.[21] The value of the land given to her was 250$000, and Table 27 compares the way the division of property was actually effected with the way it would have been had the dowry been considered a loan. Having the dowry declared a loan would have benefited all other heirs to Rita's detriment. The litigation or pressure by unendowed heirs to have a dowry considered a loan was therefore clearly an attempt to eliminate the benefit received with a dowry.

A slightly different conflict also demonstrated the importance of the amount to be brought in à colação, though in this case it was the son-in-law who tried to get the advantage. When the inventário of his father-in-law was made, Francisco Carlos de Camargo claimed that since the slave his wife received in dowry was given by his mother-in-law after her husband's death, the value of the slave did not have to come in à colação at all. The inventário, however, was only carried out 30 years after the father's death, so the judge ruled that the slave had been given from the undivided estate of husband and wife, and half its value must come in à colação.[22]

It seems clear that inflation and the process of valorization of land and slaves brought about by the strong new market economy and the end of the slave traffic made the dowry system, as set down in the *Ordenações*, no longer equitable.

IDEOLOGICAL CHANGE

At the same time that the practice of dowry declined sharply and the equity of the dowry system was being contested in the courts, the ideas held about dowry experienced a change. Throughout the nineteenth century there were manifestations of opposition to the dowry system in Brazil, though its practice probably continued to some extent through the end of the century and was even mentioned in the Civil Code that went into effect in 1917.[23]

A proponent of the new ideas was José de Alencar, one of the best-known Brazilian romantic novelists, who published a novel in 1875 that can best be described as a treatise against the dowry. It is called *Senhora*, the title itself being a play on the two meanings of the word in Portuguese: a married woman or housewife, and an owner and mistress of property. The story is of a poor girl whose lover could not marry her because she had no dowry. While he was away on a trip, she inherited an unexpected fortune and had her revenge when he returned by using an intermediary to "buy" him with a large dowry while keeping her identity a secret, the better to humiliate him after the wedding. Alencar describes how the girl felt when she became rich, courted assiduously by young men who were only after her wealth and who cared nothing about her as a person, and how she turned things around by evaluating each man in monetary terms. Of one suitor she said, "He is a distinguished young man and well worth one hundred contos as a bridegroom, but I have the money to pay for a more expensive husband, so that I need not settle for him."[24] Alencar was providing two arguments against the dowry: one was addressed to women, asking them whether they wanted to be loved for themselves or for their dowry; the other, to men, suggesting that they had no pride if they sold themselves for a dowry.

Like other romantic novelists, in other novels Alencar stressed the value of marriage through love, but he also emphasized the need for men to cease being profligate, to stop womanizing and gambling, and to assume the responsibilities of a family through the work ethic. For example, in *A viuvinha*, Alencar tells the story of a young man who received a large fortune when his father died. After a few years, tired of gambling, drink, and women, he met an innocent young girl in church, and they fell in love and planned to marry. The day before the wedding, he learned that he had dissipated all his father's fortune and that because of his neglect, the company he owned was bankrupt. Immediately after going through with the wedding (to protect his bride's reputation), he ran away simulating suicide. After three years in the United States, where he earned his own living for the first time in his life, he returned to Rio de Janeiro, and with his new commercial abilities, hard work, and a spartan livestyle, slowly remade his fortune, finally returning to his bride, who had faithfully remained a widow.[25] Alencar was spreading the gospel of the hard-working bourgeois man and of the beautiful, innocent, lov-ing, and dependent wife.

Early Brazilian feminists also condemned the dowry. Francisca Senhorinha da Motta Diniz, in an article published in 1873, wrote:

How many parents labor unceasingly under the harshest conditions to amass a dowry for their daughter and then deliver her body and soul to a *son-in-law* who will soon squander this dowry? After all, he secured the dowry through a marriage which he viewed not as an *end* in itself but just as a means of obtaining a fortune *without work-ing*. Although the true purpose of marriage has always been the legitimization of the *union of man and woman* so that they will live together as one and love each other as Christ loved his church, in this corrupt, immoral, and irreligious society, *marriage is a means of making one's fortune*. Marriage is the goal of the rascal who does not want to work and who acts like some strange kind of acrobat turning somersaults to snare a dowry, no matter if the woman attached to it is pretty or ugly, young or old—all will do.[26]

This article makes some of the same arguments reflected in Alencar's novels. It sees dowry as an impediment to marriage as it should be, made only for love. It also sees dowry as a corrupting influence on men who are transformed into dowry-hunters seeking to live off an easy fortune, instead of marrying for love and working hard to support their families.

Another voice against the dowry was that of Zaira Americana, who pub-lished a book in São Paulo in 1853 with the intention of showing "the im-mense advantage for the whole of society of the perfect education, virtue and illustration of women as mothers and wives of men."[27] Her book encouraged the education of women, criticizing Brazilian women's love of luxury and os-tentation, saying that it was only because of that weakness that many women did not marry, since prudent men considered it a defect in a wife.[28] She ex-tolled marriages made for love, adding that daughters should be taught not only to direct servants and slaves, but also to do their own housekeeping if the man they married could not afford servants or slaves.[29] Americana espe-cially praised the example of the women in Montevideo and Buenos Aires who did not give their daughters a dowry, but instead said to their future son-in-law, "my daughter does not have a dowry of money, instead she takes vir-tues and a thousand precious moral qualities. She knows how to be a perfect housekeeper and is an excellent daughter and therefore will be a good wife and gentle mother." She added that so many marriages took place in Mon-tevideo and Buenos Aires because men did not have to worry about their wives' love of luxury, laziness, or indolence. Said Americana, "the husband works, but his wife helps him greatly."[30]

Like Alencar and da Motta Diniz, Americana was calling for a bourgeois family, one in which the husband worked at his business and the wife administered the home. This was a revolutionary call, for early nineteenth-century Brazilian women of the upper classes had the reputation of leaving all household matters to their servants and slaves. For example, when John Mawe had dinner in a Brazilian home in the early nineteenth century, he complimented his hostess for the dessert they had just eaten, but realized she felt offended by his remark. He had supposed she had at least directed the cooking, but she told him that her slaves took care of everything.[31] Within Americana's call for a formal education for women, she condemns the vices of the aristocratic wife who loves parties, luxury, and ostentation and leaves the administration of the household to underlings. She extols the virtues of the bourgeois housewife, who is frugal and carefully supervises servants and slaves, if they are a part of the household, or has the ability to do her own housework when she has no help. Thus, while she was condemning dowries and calling for a prudent bourgeois housewife, Americana was exhorting mothers to educate their daughters to marry either up or down, that is, either to know how to manage servants or slaves as they did in their parents' house or to do their own housework.

Her exhortation to mothers to prepare their daughters to marry down may have reflected the decline of the practice of dowry. One of the more insightful general explanations of the aim of the dowry is that it is not "merely to help the married couple to get a living, but to enable them to keep on the same social level as that of their families—to avoid being outclassed."[32] If a dowry ensured that daughters remained in their parents' class, the lack of a dowry would mean they could as easily marry down as up.

This situation contrasted greatly with that of the preceding centuries. The great dowries that daughters received in the seventeenth century meant they continued to enjoy their parents' status and standard of living even if they married men with little or no property. In the eighteenth century, in contrast, when men started to contribute more property to the marriage than their wives, dowries ensured that women raised their economic status.

In the nineteenth century, the decline in the size and frequency of dowries meant that families lost (or relinquished) control over the fate of their daughters. What the status or standard of living of a daughter would be when she married depended increasingly on whom she married, and whom she married depended increasingly on her personal qualities (including her education) and less on whether she contributed a dowry to the marriage. Since her parents no longer ensured with a dowry that their daughters would marry their equals or their betters, they also had to prepare them to marry down, as Americana recommended. Francisca Senhorinha da Motta Diniz also maintained that "girls must be prepared for *reverses of fortune.*"[33]

The new interest in the education of women was therefore a kind of protection from the uncertain consequences of marriage without a dowry. The principal emphasis of Americana's tract is that educated women would help educate their children, making them more attractive as brides. This idea became quite prevalent. For example, Senator José Joaquim Fernandes Torres suggested that girls be educated so that when they became mothers they could teach their children to read and write and help solve the problem of illiteracy. [34]

Thus a woman's education became a substitute for the dowry, enhancing her value in the marriage bargain. In my sample there are many signs of the growing concern for the education of girls. For example, judges began to ask guardians whether not only sons but also daughters had learned to read and write. [35] There is also evidence that female literacy (and therefore education) had increased substantially among property owners. In 40 percent of the families of the nineteenth-century sample, all women could read and write, while in another 10 percent, some of the women in the family (usually daughters) could read and write. The women who knew how to read and write, however, tended to be in the wealthiest families. [36] Only 25 percent of the women in the bottom two-thirds of the sample were literate, whereas in 66 percent of the wealthiest third of the sample all the women were literate. [37] As parents gave fewer dowires, they substituted for them by increasingly educating their daughters, and thereby made them more attractive as future wives.

THE CHANGING MARRIAGE TRANSACTION

What reality do these changing practices and perceptions reflect? For clarification on the meaning of dowry and therefore on the significance of its decline, let us first turn to the opinions of the late nineteenth-century Brazilian jurist Clovis Bevilaqua. Describing the history of the dowry, he wrote that, in primitive societies, women were first captured and later bought. A Kafir male, he explained, bought a wife as a worker, a servant. Later on in history wives stopped being prized for their qualities as servants and came instead to be valued for their moral and physical beauty. Then, "women lost their venal value . . . [and] instead of being bought, they became the buyers of husbands." [38]

Bevilaqua's words describing husbands as commodities go against the conventional wisdom that it was women with dowries who were commodities. [39] Yet the issue is not a simple one to unravel, because in São Paulo, as elsewhere, women with or without dowries were "given" in marriage by their fathers, becoming a part of what has been termed the "traffic in women." [40] And, as we saw above, many times in seventeenth-century São Paulo the bride herself, dressed in luxurious clothes, was actually listed as the first item in the dowry promised by her parents to her and her husband. [41] But a case can well be made that a bride given with a dowry within a system of reciprocity required something in return. If we consider the great numbers of substantial dowries given to colonial women who married Portuguese men without possessions or nearby kin, what was received in return could only have been the groom himself.

Although his wording was strong, Bevilaqua was therefore probably right when he said that men had been acquired through dowries. We have seen that in seventeenth- and eighteenth-century São Paulo men would not marry without a dowry. This means they needed an inducement to marry—in modern terms, a material incentive.[42] The process by which men were being bought with a dowry was similiar to the way employees in the modern world sell their work and time for the promise of a salary, fringe benefits, and bonuses. That men themselves in colonial times had this view is plainly shown in a letter written in late sixteenth-century Mexico by a cloth trader to his nephew in Spain. He wrote:

You reported that you had married, much to your liking, with Catalina, youngest daughter of Mr. Alonso Gil, and that they gave you about 300 ducats with her. . . . If only you would have come at that time, either I am a man of little account, or with the aid of God I could have arranged a marriage for you worth at least 15,000 pesos or more. Here men of your parts are not held in such small esteem as you have held yourself.[43]

The Spanish cloth trader said it plainly; the size of the dowry a man could receive with his bride had to do with his worth. A seventeenth-century Portuguese writer plainly enumerates the qualities that permit a man to marry into a family that is better than his own, allowing that family to wish to become his relative. His worth was measured by his untainted blood, valor in arms, distinction in letters, or wealth.[44] In colonial São Paulo a husband's worth had to do with his lineage, his race, his claim to nobility, his wealth, or his ability as a warrior, lawyer, or merchant. In the early seventeenth century, race and lineage were undoubtedly most important, with ability as a warrior (or, as we saw in one case, metallurgical expertise) running close behind. Although race and lineage continued to be important determinants of worth in the eighteenth century, the importance of wealth and entrepreneurial ability grew.

As in colonial Spanish America, individual men in colonial São Paulo frequently had marriages with dowries arranged for them. The negotiation and contracting for marriage were sometimes carried out directly with the groom (especially when he was an older man or was a newcomer to São Paulo), but in cases where the groom was a young man and it was the alliance of two families that was looked for, the contracting and negotiating went on principally between the patriarchs, the heads of the two families, and neither the bride nor the groom was an explicit part of the process.[45] By the eighteenth century, men, and sometimes women, began to be more independent of their families in the arrangement of marriage.

But whether men were selling themselves for a dowry, or whether it was their fathers who did it on their behalf, it was commonly not the bride herself who did the buying, but her family. Nevertheless, there were exceptions. For example, in one 1685 title deed, Maria Antunes, the daughter of the deceased Francisco da Cunha Vaz, seemed to be actually "buying" a husband herself, for she promised all her inheritance, two Indians, to a certain man "if he would marry her."[46] So it is possible that a woman had some influence, or at least veto power, with those who negotiated and contracted her marriage. The only brides who probably negotiated their own marriages were widows, but certainly not all of them, for young widows were frequently married off by their fathers. Older widows, however, probably did much of their own negotiating, as we saw in the case of the eighteenth-century widow Joanna Soares de Siqueira, who clearly married a man she wanted, signing a marriage contract to protect her property for her children while also helping and protecting her new husband. Thus, Bevilaqua was only partially correct when he said that women became buyers of men. In colonial São Paulo at least, it had been mostly families who used dowries to acquire men, and only occasionally individual women.

Nevertheless, a wife whose husband had been "bought" did not come to marriage as her husband's dependent; she came as his superior, or at least his equal. Bevilaqua's wording, "buyers of husbands," was strong, moreover, and though he placed these words within the context of an explanation of the continued relevance of old dowry laws in the new Brazilian Republic, they are forceful enough to indicate that he was actually expressing condemnation of the practice, by which he was following the currents of ideological change described above.

Thus dowry came to be frowned upon, not only for substantive reasons but also due to a change in people's perceptions of marriage itself and of men's and women's roles within it. By giving fewer or smaller dowries, parents were objecting to being deprived of the lifetime use of their property. Heirs protested the inequities of dowry in an inflationary economy by carrying out expensive litigation against their endowed sisters. In the meantime, there were intellectuals who explicitly condemned the dowry and censured men who married for money, while encouraging women to feel they should be loved for themselves alone. Romantic novels spread the message of marriage for love while stressing a bourgeois work ethic for men. As men and women absorbed the message, the stage was set for the disappearance of the dowry.

CONCLUSION

DISAPPEARANCE OF THE DOWRY

BY THE SECOND HALF of the nineteenth century, when an ideological repudiation of the dowry occurred, the practice of dowry had declined sharply in São Paulo, pointing to its eventual disappearance. In the early seventeenth century no daughter of property owners entered marriage without a contribution of property for the couple's support. Most daughters received a dowry. The few who married without a dowry had already lost a parent and therefore took their inheritance into marriage. By the middle of the eighteenth century, 9 percent of property-owning families, mostly small proprietors, allowed their daughters to marry empty-handed; they received no dowry although they had not yet inherited. One century later almost three-fourths of the women of the propertied class entered marriage with no property of their own. Although they would later inherit, they no longer contributed with a dowry to the initial support of their new family.

The decrease in the practice of dowry by the middle of the nineteenth century was evident among all classes, for nearly half the families in the wealthiest fourth of the sample had not endowed their daughters. Of those families who still gave dowries, most endowed only one or two of several married daughters, and the size of those dowries was much smaller in relation to the daughters' inheritance than in colonial times.

The decline in the practice of dowry was accompanied by a reversal of parents' priorities. In the early seventeenth century daughters were favored over sons, receiving greater amounts of property in their dowries than what their brothers inherited subsequently, or else receiving such large bequests that they also inherited much more than their brothers. By the mid-nineteenth century parents were treating sons and daughters more equally with regard to inheritance, while they favored their sons in pre-mortem family expenses such as education.

These transformations in the practice of dowry took place as the marriage bargain changed, affecting the equality of brothers and sisters. Despite parents' favoring of daughters over sons in the seventeenth century, married brothers and married sisters ended up owning similar amounts of property, for it was customary for men to marry women who brought much more property than they did to marriage. By the mid-eighteenth century the approximate equality between married brothers and sisters no longer existed because husbands were now contributing much more to marriage than their wives. Thus, endowed women married men with large fortunes and remained permanently in a better situation than their brothers who could only marry women with dowries much smaller than their sisters'.

This transformation in the marriage bargain was probably related to the rise of commerce in the eighteenth century, which permitted individual men with entrepreneurial skills to accumulate large fortunes unrelated to the initial size of their capital. Thus a merchant did not need a wife's contribution of property as much as a planter or cattle raiser did, though he benefited immensely from the connections he acquired when he married the daughter of another merchant. Since a merchant was more interested in his bride's family than in her dowry, he could accept a dowry that contained fewer assets than those he contributed to the marriage. A merchant's readiness to accept a smaller dowry made it difficult for other men to continue as in the past marrying women with more property than their own.

The resulting inequality between married brothers and married sisters must have troubled parents, so that they gave fewer or smaller dowries. By the mid-nineteenth century the marriage bargain had altered even further, for the husband now provided practically all the support of the new family. Unless they had already inherited, most daughters of property owners took no property to marriage, and the few who had been endowed took relatively small dowries that did not contribute substantially to the couple's support. As for the equality of married brothers and married sisters, the situation was fluid, for a woman with no dowry or only a small one could marry either up or down, whereas her brother's immediate economic future was based principally on his education and ability. He no longer depended on the property he received from his wife in marriage as in former centuries, although obviously the political, business, and family connections the new wife provided would still be of importance.

Besides the change in the marriage bargain, other transformations in the family and in marriage contributed to the decline and disappearance of the dowry. In the first place, the great patriarchal power over adult offspring that was the rule in seventeenth-century São Paulo gradually diminished. In the eighteenth century sons migrated, transported mules and oxen to the mines, or plied long-distance trade, making it more difficult for their fathers to control them. With the growth of individualism in the nineteenth century, sons became even more independent of their fathers in their business lives, and both sons and daughters were acquiring freedom in the selection of a marriage partner. Such freedom was itself a consequence of the decline of the practice of dowry.

In the second place, the family changed from being the structure itself of a productive enterprise to being an entity that was separate from the family business, and from being a unit of production to being a unit of consumption. This reality was mirrored by the change in the composition of dowries, which was now similarly mostly means of consumption rather than means of production as in the past.

Although property could still play an important part in the marriage of individuals, it no longer was the *sine qua non* for marriage to take place. In the seventeenth century, marriage had been one of the principal ways to establish a new productive enterprise, for which the property was contributed by both spouses. And that enterprise was of vital importance not only to the married couple but to their families as well, so that families encouraged such marriages by giving substantial dowries. But as more formal ways to start businesses and form partnerships were introduced, and business and family became separate, marriage ceased to be the main way a new productive enterprise was formed. Men, even at an elite level, developed other ways, whether as merchants or through professions or army careers, for example, to maintain their families, and the wife's contribution of a dowry stopped being essential to the support of the new couple. Responding to the newlyweds' lesser need for a dowry, parents started giving comparatively smaller dowries whose value was mostly symbolic, or no dowry at all. For a man, marriage changed from being the way to establish himself independently, by the acquisition of property through his wife's dowry, as in the seventeenth century, to an immediate cost in the nineteenth.

Dowry had been an important vehicle for patriarchal control, and as parents' power over their adult offspring lessened, its practice declined. Moreover, adult children's growing autonomy undoubtedly contributed toward lessening parents' obligation to provide a dowry, while the more individualistic ways of doing business and the new ways men could earn their living helped to free men from the need for a dowry in order to marry.

At a more general level, the decline and disappearance of the dowry could also be due to its being a fetter on the free use of property, hindering the rapid circulation of capital that is necessary in market economies. Morgado, or entail, which was abolished in Brazil soon after independence, was a similar fetter, for it preserved property undivided and protected it from creditors.[1] Dowry as practiced in the regime dotal was also protected from creditors, and the husband remained responsible for its preservation because it had to be returned in full to his widow, thereby limiting his use of this property. The regime dotal was little used in São Paulo, but dowry that went into the pool of community property also served as a fetter inasmuch as there was always the possibility that at least some part of the dowry might have to be returned to siblings when parents died. At the same time, a father with daughters to marry and dowries to think of was clearly restricted in the free use of his property. Furthermore, dowry made the inheritance process longer, more complicated, and, if there were extensive litigation, much more expensive, thereby diminishing the availability of capital. In the change from a family-based economy to the individualistic market economy of industrial capitalism, dowry had become a hindrance.

For the daughter of property owners, the disappearance of the dowry transformed her position within marriage for the worse. A bride with a dowry contributed immediately to the couple's support, and her husband was therefore beholden to her. The idea that dowry gives a wife power in marriage is very old, for Cato advised men to "flee the wife who seeks to rule by virtue of her dowry."[2] When the practice of dowry disappeared, unless she had already inherited, the daughter of a propertied family brought only the expectation of an inheritance to the marriage. The change in the source of the couple's initial support undoubtedly altered the balance of power within the marriage to the husband's advantage.[3] Scholars have claimed that when production left the home during the process of industrialization in Europe and the United States, there was a shift in marital power. Women were relegated to the domestic sphere, where they became economically dependent on their husbands and lost the status and bargaining power in marriage that their role as producers had assured them.[4] The disappearance of the dowry had the same effect for women of property. Confirmation of this effect can be seen in the opinion of the nineteenth-century Brazilian jurist who stated that, so long as the father approved a child's marriage, it was no longer necessary to follow the law strictly and obtain the mother's consent. This was the exact reverse of the seventeenth-century legal concern that the wife must always explicitly agree to the giving of a dowry that included real estate (thereby showing her consent to the marriage).

Marriage, which had always been an institution to support children (with the income derived from the property contributed by both parents), also became an institution for the support of wives.[5] One nineteenth-century Brazilian jurist wrote that in Roman times the dowry had been the principal difference between a kept woman and a wife.[6] The disappearance of the dowry therefore converted marriage into something similar to concubinage, transforming it into a relation in which the wife, instead of making a substantial initial contribution to the marriage, was wholly dependent on her husband. At the same time, the decline in patriarchal power of father over son and son-in-law and the trend toward greater independence of the conjugal pair left the bride without as much close support and protection by the members of her family as she had received in colonial times.

From the seventeenth to the nineteenth century the terms of the marriage bargain had changed from a situation in which the bride and her family were in the stronger position to one in which it was the bridegroom who held the best cards. Since men in the nineteenth century, even elite men, were capable of earning their living without owning the means of production and therefore no longer needed to marry to receive such means through their wives' dowries, men were no longer automatically up for acquisition. Dowries became irrelevant. On the other hand, there were few ways for women (especially middle- or upper-class women) to maintain themselves, so that unless they were to continue depending on their families, women who had not inherited property still needed marriage for their support. It was women, therefore, not men, who were now available for acquisition, no longer for a bride-price paid to their families, as in primitive societies, but for the promise of support.

However, though this change may have been for the worse for the daughters of property owners, it increased the possibility of legal marriage for propertyless women. In consequence, a growing proportion of the population now married.

If dowry had been a way to ensure that a daughter stayed in her parents' social class, the decline of the dowry signified a shift from a woman's retaining her family's status to a woman's adopting the status of her husband. This shift was visible in Brazil in the change in practice for married women's surnames. Colonial married women took a substantial dowry to marriage and retained their maiden names, remaining members of their family of origin and retaining their family's status. In the nineteenth century, in contrast, when wives took no dowry or only a small dowry to marriage, they increasingly adopted their husband's surname, becoming more independent from their family of origin and more dependent on their husband.

Although we found an increase by 1870 in married women's use of their husband's surname and a growing emphasis on the husband's ability to support his family, these changes would only later become incorporated into law. The new marriage law, passed in 1890 after the proclamation of the Brazilian Republic, allowed a wife to use her husband's family surname and obliged the husband to support his children.[7]

By requiring only the husband to support the couple's children, the new marriage law eliminated the wife's legal responsibility for their support. The *Ordenações* had established that "when a child is born of a legitimate marriage, so long as the marriage lasts between husband and wife, they both must raise him at their expense and give him the things he needs according to their status and condition."[8] This duty of both parents to support their children was replaced in the new law by the husband's sole responsibility.

The 1917 Civil Code went even further. It made the wife's assumption of her husband's surname at marriage automatic and required the husband to support not only his children but also his wife, whether she had brought property to marriage or not.[9] In this way the Brazilian Civil Code fully legalized the change from an institution of marriage that was principally a property relation between equals to an institution of marriage based on the personal relationship of the spouses, in which wives were usually economically dependent on their husbands. In the process the practice of dowry disappeared.

Appendixes

APPENDIXES

A. CONTENT OF DOWRIES IN SEVENTEENTH CENTURY SÃO PAULO

I. Maria de Proença, daughter of Baltazar Fernandes and Izabel de Proença, married to João Borralho Dalmada (AESP, Livro de Notas ord. 6074, no. 26, Liv. 1640–1642).

Means of Consumption	Means of Production
3 dresses	1 farm in São Sebastião with a field of
Gold earrings	manioc and a field of cotton
Gold necklace	20 agricultural tools
1 bed and its linens	2 African slaves
1 table and 6 chairs	30 Indians
1 buffet	1 boat or canoe with oars
Tablecloths and towels	500 alqueires of flour placed in Santos
30 china dishes	
2 chests with locks	
1 large pot	
1 small pot	
1 house in town	
1 house on the farm	

II. Francisca de Siqueira, daughter of João Baruel and Izabel de Siqueira, married to Manoel Rodrigues de Morais (João Baruel, 1665, AESP, INP, #ord. 485, c. 8).

Means of Consumption	Means of Production
2 dresses (3$200)	Cash (350$000)
1 gold necklace (10$000)	1 African male slave (45$000)
Gold earrings, 4 rings (6$400)	2 female Indians (no value)
6 silver spoons (3$960)	
2 silver tumblers (55$060)	
24 dishes, 2 platters (1$440)	
1 hammock ($480)	
Bed hangings (2$000)	
1 wool blanket (3$000)	
6 sheets (6$000)	
2 pillows ($800)	
4 throw pillows (2$400)	
2 tablecloths (2$000)	
30 napkins ($600)	
10 towels (1$000)	
2———— ($800)	
1 house in town (60$000)	

Total dowry: 521$040

III. Antonia Dias, daughter of Gonsallo Ferreira and Izabel Fernandes, married to Pero de Gomes (Izabel Fernandes, 1641, IT, vol. 28).

Means of Consumption	Means of Production
1 dress (16$000)	4 Indians

IV. Maria Vidal, daughter of Pedro Vidal and Mecia de Siqueira, married to Francisco Baldaia (Mecia de Siqueira, 1648, IT, vol. 37).

Means of Consumption	Means of Production
1 dress	1 cow
	2 sheets of silver
	2 Indians

Total dowry: 3$440

V. Elvira Rodrigues, daughter of Martim Rodrigues and Suzanna Rodrigues, married to Cornelio de Arzão (Martim Rodrigues, 1612, IT, vol. 12, p. 13. Suzanna Rodrigues promised the dowry while Martim was away).

Means of Consumption	Means of Production
1 mattress	4 adult Indians, 2 children
2 cotton sheets	24 head of cattle
1 blanket	Half the pigs her parents owned
Pillows	1 year-old field of ———
2 cotton tablecloths	1 field of cotton
12 napkins	1 horse
3 towels	1 colt
2 good chairs	
1 dress	

VI. Beatriz Rodrigues, illegitimate daughter of Pedro de Moraes Dantas (Pedro de Moraes Dantas, 1644, *IT*, vol. 14, p. 289).

Means of Production

9 Indians

VII. Izabel Bicudo, daughter of Manoel Pires and Maria Bicudo, married to Bartholomeu de Quadros (Maria Bicudo, 1660, *IT*, vol. 16, p. 97).

Means of Consumption	Means of Production
Half her dowry:	100 braças of land
2 skirts (2$300)	12 Indians (no value)
1 cloak and a vest (3$640)	Flour (8$000)
1 mattress, bedspread (4$000)	50 alqueires of wheat (4$000)
3 towels, 1 sheet,	A promissory note (15$000)
1 tablecloth, 3 napkins (2$400)	

Value of half her dowry: 40$020 (without land or Indians)

VIII. Catarina de Sampayo, daughter of Gonçalo Lopes, married to Antonio Nunes, his second wife (Antonio Nunes, 1643, *IT*, vol. 38).

Means of Production

Delivered:
2 hoes
1 scythe
2 pigs
Promissory note for 4$000
Still owed:
Half the cattle which . . .
Half a field of manioc
Half another field
1 colt

B. KINDS OF REAL ESTATE IN
THE EIGHTEENTH-CENTURY SAMPLE

See Marcílio, A cidade, p. 43, for a map of the region considered the district (termo) of the city of São Paulo in 1750. Parnaíba had been created as a separate town in 1625, yet it is closer to the center of São Paulo than Jaguarí, which was within its termo.

Fifty-five inventários gave property information, as specified below.

Owners with both urban and rural property: 26 (47.2 percent). Location of urban houses: 19 in the different parishes of the city of São Paulo, 2 in the town of Parnaíba, 1 in the town of Mogy das Cruzes, 2 in Guaratinguetá, and 2 in São Sebastião. The rural estates of the 19 families with houses in the center of São Paulo and other urban centers of the city were spread throughout the district of the city, in the parishes of Nossa Senhora do O, São Bernardo, Guarulhos, Santo Amaro, Cotia, Atibaia, Tremembé, Juquerí, and Santana, and in the bairros of Bras, São Miguel, Pinheiros, Penha, and Piratininga. Sometimes houses were owned in more than one town. For example, Balthazar Rodrigues Fam, whose inventário was presented to the juizo de órfãos in Parnaíba, owned a farm and four town houses in Parnaíba but also two houses in the center of São Paulo.

Owners with only rural property: 24 (44.4 percent). The whereabouts of 16 of these are known: 2 in Parnaíba, 1 in Sorocaba, 1 in Tabuaté, and the rest in the parishes and bairros of São Paulo: 1 in Bras, 2 in Santo Amaro, 2 in Atibaia, 1 in Nossa S. do O, 1 in Guarulhos, 1 in Penha, 1 in Cotia, 1 in Juquerí, 1 in São Bernardo, and 1 in Nazaré.

Rural families who did not own the land they lived on: 3 (5.5 percent). All did own property that required an inventário such as slaves, cattle, or improvements. In all three cases, the deceased was a widow, suggesting that when the husband died, the land was adjudicated to the children while the widow retained the movable property.

Owners of only urban property: 2 (3.7 percent). These were also widows.

C. PROPERTY OWNERS' CONNECTIONS WITH
THE GOLD MINES

Within the richest 25%	Evidence in inventários
José Rodrigues Pereira (net estate 14:632$500)	11 gold bars and cash totaling 2:169$400; a brother in Cuiabá
Manoel Velozo (net estate 10:875$300)	Two married daughters in Cuiabá
Manoel Soares de Carvalho (net estate 4:925$500)	Traded extensively in Cuiabá and had partners there

Caetano Soares Viana (net estate 4:593$000)

Many debtors in Cuiabá and Goiás

Balthazar Rodrigues Fam (net estate 8:313$900)

Gold bars in the inventory and many uncollectable debts in the mines

Maria de Lima de Siqueira (net estate 4:070$700)

Three gold bars in her inventory

Francisco de Godoy Preto (net estate 7:402$000)

A remittance of gold dust from the mines was expected. *

Escolastica Velozo (net estate 6:633$700)

Three gold bars, the proceeds of the sale of slaves in Cuiabá

Maria Leite de Barros (net estate 1:895$300)

An endowed married daughter in Minas Gerais

Maria Bueno de Araujo (net estate 2:663$500)

A son, a priest, in Minas Gerais

Within the Poorest 25%

Silvestre da Silva Carneiro (net estate 205$600)

A son in Goiás

Catarina Pires Ribeiro (net estate 61$500)

A widowed daughter in Minas Gerais

Source: 69 estates with known net value of the estate, listed in decreasing value of the estate.
* Francisco de Godoy Preto was the discoverer and *guardamor* of the mines of Papuá (Silva Leme, *Genealogia*, vol. 6, p. 44).

D. INFORMATION IN INVENTÁRIOS

I. A typical seventeenth-century division of property: Catharina do Prado, widow, 1649 (*IT*, vol. 15, pp. 103–4). (She had 11 children but her 8 married daughters refused to inherit so only 3 heirs remained.)

Total estate	290$400
Subtract debts and costs	55$920
Net estate	234$480
Terça (one-third)	78$160
Subtract bequests	24$040
Remainder of the terça for Joanna da Cunha (only single daughter)	54$120
The rest, to be divided among the 3 heirs (Joanna da Cunha, João Gago da Cunha, and João do Prado da Cunha)	156$320
Legítima for each heir	52$106

Note: Joanna da Cunha, the minor single daughter, received a total of 106$226, the sum of her legítima and remainder of the terça.

II. Division of the estate of Manoel João Branco, 1641 (IT, vol. 13).

The net estate was divided in half because Manoel João was married, and half the property belonged to his widow. Although they had three children, there were only two heirs because Anna Leme, the wife of David Ventura, refused to inherit. The other daughter came in à colação.

Debts that the estate owed David Ventura from the dowry:

A gold chain	50$000
A saddled horse and three mares	10$000
Six chairs	6$000
A house for the mill (minus the millstones received)	16$000
One African slave	25$000

Division of the estate:

Gross estate	1:190$568
Debts to David Ventura and inventory costs	382$640
Net estate	897$928
Half for the widow	403$964
Terça (from husband's half)	134$308
Two-thirds for heirs	269$308
Plus half a dowry (second daughter)	88$250
Plus half the son's gift	30$000
Total to be divided	387$558
Legítima (2 heirs)	193$779

Each heir was paid the difference between the legítima and the half dowry or gift brought à colação.

III. A typical eighteenth-century division of property: Maria Bueno de Araujo, married, died 1766, bairro of Penha (AESP, INP, #ord. 544, c. 67).

Her 6 heirs: 2 sons (1 a priest absent in Minas Gerais), 2 married daughters, and 2 single daughters over 25. She was 61 when she died, and her husband was 71, according to the 1765 census. The capital they reported to the census was 500$000 (DI, vol. 62, p. 236).

Total net estate	2:663$594
Half for the widower	1:338$792
Tercinha*	147$976
To be divided among heirs	1:180$870
Plus half the priest's patrimony	200$000
Plus half the first dowry	209$240
Plus half the second dowry	255$511
Total to be divided	1:848$537
Legítima (above total divided by 6)	308$089

Each endowed heir was paid with the half dowry or patrimony in his or her possession plus the difference between the legítima and half dowry or patrimony.

* The tercinha was one-third of the terça, to be used for masses for the soul of the deceased, taken out of the estate by law in the early eighteenth century when a person died intestate. By the late eighteenth century the law had been abolished.

IV. Less typical division of property: Maria de Lima de Siqueira, widow, 1769, bairro of Cotia (AESP, INP, #ord. 545, c. 68).

This example has two *dotes levantados*, that is, refusals to inherit because of large dowries, which were therefore subtracted from the terça.

Her 11 heirs: 5 sons (including 1 priest with a patrimony, and 2 Franciscan friars) and 6 married daughters (2 married before their father died, and 4 married afterwards).

Her gross estate	5:727$511
Uncollectable credits	1:524$306
Real gross estate	4:203$205
Debts and inventory costs	132$422
Net estate	4:070$781
Terça (she had made a will)	1:356$227
Two-thirds, for her heirs	2:713$852
Plus dowries à colação (*conferidos*) (from mother only):	
D. Monica M. de Camargo	591$560
Martha Maria de Camargo	492$340
Catharina da Silva de Camargo	844$253
Ignacia M. de Camargo	613$120
Plus half the patrimony of P. Salvador (given by both parents)	140$000
Plus half the dowries levantados (given by both parents):	
Deceased Manoel Jose da Cunha	1:109$320
Deceased Thome João de Souza	1:028$340
Amount to be divided among 9 heirs (the 2 Franciscans did not inherit)	7:848$827
Legítima:	872$022
Disposition of the terça	1:356$227
Difference between the first half-dowry levantado and the legítima	237$248
Difference between the second half-dowry levantado and the legítima	156$248
Bequests	340$360
Remainder of the terça	623$071

V. The dowries and inheritance of Maria de Lima de Siqueira's children (1769, AESP, INP #ord. 545, c. 68).

Daughters endowed by both parents while father lived:

#1	2:218$640
#2	2:056$640

Daughters endowed by mother after father died: they each received their paternal legítima (884$254) plus their share of the remainder of their father's terça, which he left to his four single daughters (605$585), totaling 1:489$835. To this amount their mother added a dowry:

#3	1:489$835 +	591$560 (dowry)	= 2:081$395
#4	" +	492$340	= 1:982$175
#5	" +	844$253	= 2:334$088
#6	" +	613$120	= 2:102$955

The sons each received the two legítimas amounting to a total of 1:756$276. The priest had also received a patrimony of 280$000, half of which was discounted from each legítima.

VI. Fernando Lopes de Camargo and Maria de Lima de Siqueira's divestment for dowries (Maria de Lima de Siqueira, 1769, AESP, INP, #ord. 545, c. 68).

Couple's net estate when husband died	17:041$878
Wife's half	8:520$939
Fernando's half	8:520$939
Plus first half-dowry	1:109$320
Plus second half-dowry	1:028$340
Plus priest's half-patrimony	140$000
His estate plus his total divestment	10:798$599

He divested himself of 2:277$660 (21 percent) of his estate.

Maria's net estate	4:070$781
Plus total donations given during husband's lifetime (1/2 of each)	2:277$660
Plus total of 4 dowries given after he died	2:541$273
Her estate plus her total divestment	8:889$714

She divested herself of 4:818$933 (54 percent) of her estate.

Note: I calculated Fernando Lopes de Camargo's net estate from the information given in his wife's inventário that the paternal legítima had been 884$254. To do this I followed the *partilha*, or division, process in reverse, deducting only the two eldest daughters' half-dowries and the priest's half-patrimony, given during their father's lifetime.

VII. Dowry of Martha de Camargo Lima, wife of Ignacio Soares de Barros (Maria de Lima de Siqueira, 1769, AESP, INP, #ord. 545, c. 68).

"Rol do que prometo ao Cap^{tão} Ignacio Soares de Barros por me fazer m^c de cazar com minha filha Martha de Camargo Lima, o que lhe pertence da folha de partilhas e remanescente da terça de seu pay Fernando Lopes de Camargo que importa de legítima e terça 1:489$835. Mais de minha parte . . ." (List of what I promise Captain Ignacio Soares de Barros for doing me the favor of marrying my daughter Martha de Camargo Lima, that which belongs to her in the division of her father's property and *remanescente da terça* 1:489$835. Plus on my part . . .):

1 male slave, João, with his Creole wife, Maria
1 Creole female slave named ———
Plus cash (300$000)
Plus a gold cross
Plus gold earrings
Plus ten ——— buttons
Plus a necklace (12$000)
Plus eight silver spoons (5$360)
Plus a dozen pewter plates (2$000)
Plus a bed with cotton bedspread and curtains and 4 linen sheets (10$000)
Plus a good suit of clothes (vestido de praça) (30$000)
Plus a horse and saddle (16$000)
Plus a large pot and a chamber pot
Plus two tablecloths and napkins
Plus 4 linen towels and others of cotton
Plus 2 towels with lace
Plus a hammock
Plus a large chest
Plus a debt for ——— in hands of her brother-in-law João
Plus a debt for ——— in hands of her brother, P. Francisco de Jesus Camargo
    Signed at the request of my mother
    Joseph Ortiz de Camargo Lima (1748)

"At the request of" was used when a woman did not know how to sign her name, and Maria de Lima de Siqueira, like most but not all eighteenth-century women, did not. Monica, one of her six daughters, did.

This dowry was appraised for the inventory at 492$340.

Reference Matter

GLOSSARY

Acções: Shares.

Agregado: Nonrelative living in the household or on the estate.

Aldeias: Indian villages; in particular, mission settlements.

Alqueire: In colonial times, a grain measure that varied from place to place. Also a measure of land that varies regionally.

Alvará: Decree.

Apólices: Bonds.

Arras: *See Contrato de dote e arras.*

Arroba: A measure of weight equal to 14.688 kilos.

Bairro: Neighborhood.

Bandeira: Paulista quasi-military expedition to search for gold or other minerals and to capture Indians.

Bandeirante: Leader, or white or mestizo expeditionary on a *bandeira*.

Braças: Old measurement, equivalent to 2.2 meters.

Cabeça de casal: Head of the marriage partnership (the husband), or his widow, or a son or daughter who administered the estate after both parents' death.

Carijó: Member of an Indian tribe.

Carta de data de terra: Land grant given by the municipal council.

Chácara: A small suburban farm with a country house, frequently with fruit orchards and vegetable gardens.

Colação: Judicial process by which half the dowry or other gift given by parents to their children (whole dowry when given by a widow or widower) came back into the estate for accounting purposes at the death of each parent; the heir/recipient of the dowry or gift received the difference between his or her inheritance and the dowry or gift.

Conto: Unit of currency worth one thousand mil-réis, written 1:000$000.

Contrato de dote e arras: A prenuptial contract that established a marital property arrangement in which the wife's dowry remained separate from the husband's property, though administered by him, and could not be alienated or mortgaged because it had to be returned intact to the widow. *Arras* was an amount a husband added to this dowry for his wife's support in widowhood.

Covado: Measurement of length, equivalent to 66 centimeters, used in colonial times to measure fabrics.

Cruzado: Monetary unit used especially in sixteenth- and seventeenth-century Brazil, worth 400 réis.

Desembargador: Magistrate of the High Court.

Dívida malparada: Bad loan or uncollectable debt.

Dívidas cobráveis: Good loans.

Dízimos: Tithes paid to the crown for the support of the church.

Donatário: Donatary captain, who received from the Portuguese crown the ownership and judicial, administrative, and political control of a large region of Brazil. São Paulo belonged to the donatary captain of São Vicente until the early eighteenth century.

Dote: Dowry.

Dote conferido: A dowry brought in à colação (eighteenth-century usage).

Dote levantado: A dowry whose recipient refuses to come in à colação, probably because the dowry is larger than the legítima (eighteenth-century usage).

Esmola: A charitable gift.

Expostos: Abandoned infants.

Fidalgo: The lowest rank of the nobility, as in Spanish, hidalgo.

Filho-família: Unemancipated single son, still under his father's or widowed mother's legal authority.

Filho natural: Child born out of wedlock to two single persons, between whom there was no religious impediment to marriage.

Guarda Nacional: National Guard.

Inventário: The entire judicial process of settling an estate, thereby including other documents besides the inventory proper, such as the will, when there was one, claims of creditors, receipts of payment, reports of the guardians of minors, all litigation, and the final division of the estate.

Juiz de comércio: Judge of Commerce.

Juiz dos órfãos: A special judge to guard the interests of orphans, defined as minor heirs of a deceased, whether the other parent survived or not.

Juizo de órfãos: Court to protect the rights of minor heirs.

Juiz ordinário: Elected magistrate or justice of the peace.

Legítima: Inheritance, each necessary heir's share of the estate. Two-thirds or all (in the case of someone who died intestate) of the net estate of a deceased was allocated to the necessary heirs and divided by the number of those heirs to give the value of each individual legítima. During colonial times, all legitimate children were necessary heirs, as were all *filhos naturais*. In the nineteenth century, new laws made it progressively harder for natural and other illegitimate children to inherit when there were legitimate heirs. In the event the deceased was childless, his or her parents were the necessary heirs.

Mameluco: Of mixed blood, with a white father and an Indian mother.

Matrona: Matriarch.

Meeiro or meeira: Owner of half the conjugal (community) property.

Mesada: Monthly allowance.

Monções: Flotillas of large cargo-carrying canoes that left São Paulo seasonally for the gold mines in Goiás and Cuiabá (eighteenth century).

Montepio: Annuity fund.

Morgado: Entailed estate. Also, the owner of such an estate.

Ordenações: The Portuguese Code of Law passed in 1603 under Philip II of Portugal (Philip III of Spain).

Ouvidor: Royal judge.

Parentela: Extended family or kinship group.

Paulista: An inhabitant of the province of São Paulo.

Pedreiro: Stonecutter.

Quartos: Rooms.

Quinto: The royal fifth, a tax on gold and other precious metals.

Recolhida: A member of a *recolhimento*.

Recolhimento: A religious home for women, similar to a convent, but in which women were not permitted to solemnly profess.

Regime dotal: A marriage system in which the wife's dowry remained separate from the husband's property and could not be alienated or seized by creditors.

Remanescente da terça: A bequest of the remainder of a testator's terça after the funeral, masses, and other legacies had been deducted.

Senhora: Mistress or owner of property. Also housewife or married woman.

Sertão: Wilderness, bush, or hinterland.

Sesmaria: Land grant given in the seventeenth century by the *donatário*, lord proprietor of the region, and in the eighteenth by the crown.

Sitio: Farm.

Sociedade em comandita: A silent partnership.

Terça: A third of a testator's net estate, the only portion that could legally be bequeathed in a will.

Terras devolutas: Land given in a grant but which had reverted to the municipal council, *donatário*, or crown because it had been abandoned or had never been cultivated.

Trapiche: Small sugarmill run by animal traction.

Vaqueiro: Cattleman.

Visitador: Ecclesiastic inspector.

NOTES

Complete references for the works cited in short form are given in the Bibliography, pp. 225–39.

ABBREVIATIONS

AESP:	Arquivo do Estado de São Paulo.
AMJ:	Arquivo do Ministério de Justiça.
DI:	*Documentos Interessantes para a História e Costumes de São Paulo.* 93 vols. São Paulo: Arquivo do Estado de São Paulo, 1897–1980.
INP:	"Inventários Não Publicados." Archival Collection at the Arquivo do Estado de São Paulo.
IT:	*Inventários e Testamentos, Documentos da Secção de Estudos Históricos.* 44 vols. São Paulo: Arquivo do Estado de São Paulo, 1921–1975.
Ordenações:	Cándido Mendes de Almeida, ed., *Código Philippino ou Ordenações do Reino de Portugal.* 14th ed. Rio de Janeiro: Typographia do Instituto Philomático, 1870.
1° Of.:	Primeiro Ofício da Família. Archival Collection in the Arquivo do Estado de São Paulo and the Arquivo do Ministério de Justiça.
2° O. da F.:	"Segundo Ofício da Família." Archival Collection in the Arquivo do Ministério de Justiça.

INTRODUCTION

1. This book also responds to the call for further longitudinal studies of the family and dowry in Latin America made by Cancian, Goodman, and Smith in "Capitalism, Industrialization."

2. In her excellent study "From Brideprice to Dowry," p. 42, Diana Owen Hughes maintains that the practice of dowry rose with the strengthening of the larger kin group vis-à-vis the conjugal pair. My study will show that its demise occurred with the *weakening* of the larger kin group vis-à-vis the conjugal pair.

In *Brideprice and Dowry*, Goody concludes that dowry is part of "diverging devolution"—that is, a system of inheritance where both sons and daughters inherit. In the Portuguese system, whether a daughter received a dowry or not, she always inherited.

3. For England see Goody, *Development of the Family*, p. 241. For Germany see Kaplan, "For Love."

4. For example, see Dimaki, "Dowry in Modern Greece," p. 175.

5. Harrell and Dickey, "Dowry Systems."

6. Lavrin and Couturier, "Dowries and Wills"; Arrom, *The Women*, chap. 3. For other studies of dowry in Latin America, see Couturier, "Women and the Family"; Socolow, *The Merchants*, chap. 2; Bossen, "Theory of Marriage"; Chowning, "A Mexican Provincial Elite"; and Korth and Fleuche, "Dowry and Inheritance." For studies on dowries given by charitable institutions in Brazil, see Russell-Wood, *Fidalgos*, chap. 8, and Mesgravis, "A Santa Casa da Misericórdia," who shows that the last dowry was given by that institution in 1836 (pp. 190–91). See Soeiro, "The Feminine Orders," for dowries to convents.

7. Pero Nunes, 1623, *IT*, vol. 6, p. 59.

8. Federal Deputy German Hasslocher, speaking on the floor of Congress on December 12, 1907 (see *Congresso Nacional*).

9. See, for example, Amaral, "Como se constitue," and Hermenegildo Almeida, "Direito romano."

10. *Ordenações*, Liv. 4, Tit. 96, par. 12, and Tit. 97. During colonial times, law in Brazil was based on the *Ordenações*, a Portuguese code of laws passed in 1603. Its family law remained largely in effect under the independent Brazilian Empire, that is, from 1822 to 1889, and parts of it until 1917.

11. According to Portuguese law, depending on the circumstances of his or her birth, an illegitimate child could also inherit. Throughout most of our period, the *filho natural* was a legal heir. To inherit from his or her father, however, a *filho* or *filha natural* required the father's explicit recognition; in his will or merely behaving as a father might be sufficient in the seventeenth century, but by the mid-nineteenth century, it was necessary to register paternal recognition in a notary's office. See *Ordenações*, Liv. 4, Tit. 82, n. 5, and Lewin, "Natural and Illegitimate Children."

12. See *Ordenações*, Liv. 4, Tit. 96, par. 12, and Tit. 97, and Silva, "Sistema" and *Sistema*, pp. 97–110. See also Samara, "O dote" and *As Mulheres*, p. 148.

13. See *Ordenações*, Liv. 4, Tit. 47; for the second meaning, see n. 4 by Teixeira de Freitas.

14. *Ordenações*, Liv. 4, Tit. 46, par. 1. A prenuptial agreement, however, could

change the marriage regime and establish complete separation of the spouses' property, or a *contrato de dote e arras*, or a mixed system. When there was a *contrato de dote e arras*, the word dowry meant the property brought by the wife to the marriage and which, though administered by her husband, was kept separate from his property and could not be alienated nor have a lien put on it. See Samara, "O dote," and Silva, *Sistema*, pp. 97–101.

15. See Lavrin and Couturier, "Dowries and Wills," and Arrom, *The Women*, chap. 3.

16. When there was a valid ecclesiastic separation, called a divorce, and the wife was the innocent party or the couple separated under mutual consent, the wife also received her half of the community property in the settlement. For the colonial period, see Silva, *Sistema*, pp. 240–43.

When a married woman or man died, the community property was first divided in half, and the surviving spouse kept his or her half. The other half was considered the estate of the deceased. The law required that two-thirds of the estate of the deceased be divided equally among the necessary heirs of the deceased, his or her children (or grandchildren, *per stirpes*, in the case of children's having predeceased the parent), or, in the absence of children, to the parents of the deceased. (If the deceased had no children or parents, his or her share of the estate passed to collateral heirs if he or she died intestate. Since collaterals were not necessary heirs, a person without children or parents could will his or her entire estate to anybody.) Spouses did not inherit from each other, they just kept their half of the property, though they could receive bequests. Testators who had necessary heirs were allowed to freely dispose of only one-third of their estate (in the case of married testators, one-sixth of the community property). See *Ordenações*, Liv. 4, Tit. 96.

At a wife's death, an inventário was usually made, listing and dividing the property, thereby protecting her children's rights versus those of later children born to her husband. In practice, when children were minors, the father retained the property and administered it until the children came of age. When a husband predeceased his wife, an inventário was also made, except that it was not automatic that the widow would continue administering her minor children's inheritance; sometimes in colonial Brazil she did, but more frequently a male guardian was named. In the nineteenth century a trend is visible toward not making an inventário at all until the second spouse died (whether male or female), thereby in practice allowing the widower or widow to continue administering the whole community property. This sometimes occurred even if their children were adults.

17. Assuming that the particular town or neighborhood a family lived in would not influence the practice of dowry, I accepted all inventários with married daughters in each archival collection. The published inventários for the seventeenth century include those of the *juizes dos órfãos* of both São Paulo and Parnaíba, two contiguous *municípios* (municipalities that are almost like counties because they include not only the town for which they are named but also considerable rural areas). The sample for the eighteenth century, from INP, has 51 estates under the jurisdiction of the juiz dos órfãos in São Paulo, 9 in Parnaíba, 3 in São Sebastião, 2 in Guaratinguetá, 2 in Mogy das Cruzes, and 2 in Sorocaba. The inventários of the nineteenth-century sample

were all of families with homes in the city of São Paulo and its immediate surroundings, although wealthy families owned much property in other parts of the state, and in one case the judge wondered about his right to jurisdiction since most of that family's property was in Minas Gerais. There were 45 families with homes in the parish of Sé, with the only street addresses in the sample (though numbers were not used). Otherwise there were 36 families in Santo Amaro, 17 in Itapuerica, 16 in Cotia, 12 in Juquerí, 8 each in São Bernardo and Parnaíba, 7 in Nossa Senhora do O, 6 each in Guarulhos and Santa Ephigenia, plus 9 more in various neighborhoods or parishes such as Santana, Penha, Bexiga, Pinheiros, Estrada de Santos, da Conceição, and aldeia São Miguel.

18. I further reduced the number of inventários studied by using only the published inventários for the seventeenth century and one out of two possible collections of documents for each succeeding century.

I elected to study the decades of the fifties and sixties so that I could compare information in the censuses of 1765 and 1767 with information in inventários. I changed the dates to be studied for the seventeenth century when I learned that the Arquivo do Estado has published *all* extant "Inventários Não Publicados" only through 1651. Those of later dates were chosen by the archive personnel from the larger number that await funds for publication, and they are skewed toward male, wealthy, well-known personalities and well-preserved manuscripts.

19. The published inventários for the period 1640–1651 are *all* the surviving inventários in the Arquivo do Estado de São Paulo.

20. I excluded from the sample three inventários (with married daughters) that had been damaged by water and were unreadable. The inventários in INP for 1750–1769 at the Arquivo do Estado are approximately half those surviving; the rest are in the collection of documents labeled "Inventários do Primeiro Ofício." I chose to study mainly INP because they are the same collection as the published inventários and because they are cataloged chronologically, whereas the "Inventários do Primeiro Ofício" are cataloged alphabetically by the name of the deceased.

The inventários that are most plentiful in São Paulo archives for the seventeenth and eighteenth centuries are inventários with minor heirs carried out judicially by the juiz dos órfãos, whose role was to protect the rights of orphans (defined as minors whose father or mother had died, even though the other parent still lived). Therefore they are by definition skewed against the existence of adults as heirs to the estate. This was borne out by the examination of the documents. There were married daughters or their heirs in only 32.8 percent (48 out of 147) of the published inventários for the period 1640–1651, and in 28.5 percent (71 of 249) of the inventários for the period 1750–1769 in INP.

21. The inventários in 2° O. da F. for 1850–1869, at the Ministério de Justiça, cataloged chronologically, are approximately half those surviving; the others are in 1° Of. There does not appear to be any jurisdictional difference between the two ofícios in the nineteenth century, for both have documents for people living in the parish of Sé and other central parishes.

All inventários were carried out judicially in the nineteenth century, so the proportion of inventários with married daughters is greater than in previous centuries, 45.5 percent (178 out of a total of 392).

I did not limit my study to the 294 inventários of the sample. I also studied inventários with married daughters outside the chosen time periods and others that had no married daughters but were of interest because they included references to dowry or marriage contracts or because they were of relatives of the families studied in the sample, making a total of 435 (see accompanying table).

Inventários Studied Extensively

Inventários	17th cent.	18th cent.	19th cent.	Total
Sample	48	68	178	294
	(1640–1651)	(1750–1769)	(1850–1869)	
Others with married	28	18	5	51
daughters	(1599–1674)	(1721–1790)	(1826–1877)	
With no married	30	24	36	90
daughters	(1600–1674)	(1721–1790)	(1826–1877)	
TOTAL	106	110	219	435

22. See Costa, *The Brazilian Empire*, and my Chapter 7 below. For Latin America, see Chevalier, "New Perspectives." For the development of individualism, see Dumont, "The Modern Conception" and *Homo Hierarchicus*. The nineteenth-century English scholar who best described the change between status and contract is Sir Henry Maine.

23. Kuznesof, "From Family Clans."

24. See Faoro, *Os Donos do poder*, vol. 1, p. 162.

25. For São Paulo, see Chapter 7 below. For a general analysis of the evolution of private property and the bourgeois family, see Engels, *The Origin of the Family*, esp. pp. 137 and 234–35.

26. Weber, *The Protestant Ethic*, pp. 21–22. For the Brazilian case, see Chapter 8 below. For the separation of the family, especially the conjugal family, from general social life, and the formation of a "private" part of life as opposed to a "public" part of life in Europe, see Ariès, *Centuries of Childhood*.

27. For this change in Brazil, see Candido, "The Brazilian Family," and Lewin, *Politics*, esp. pp. 188–200. For the change in Europe, see Stone, "The Rise of the Nuclear Family," and Flandrin, *Families in Former Times*. For the argument that romantic love is related to greater individualism, see Lantz, "Romantic Love." For the importance of the larger kin group in Brazil, see Wagley, *An Introduction to Brazil*, pp. 184–204, and Lewin, "Some Historical Implications." For an "ideal" conceptualization of the elite extended Brazilian family, see Freyre, "The Patriarchal Basis." For a critique of the assumption that descriptions of the structure and behavior of elite families of very specific regions could be applied to the enormously varied structures and experiences of Brazilian families of different classes, regions, and periods, see Corrêa, "Repensando a família patriarcal."

28. For the change from a strongly patriarchal family to the greater independence of adult children in Brazil, see Candido, "The Brazilian Family," and Lewin, *Politics*, pp. 190–98.

29. By documenting these changes in the Brazilian family, I do not mean that the

family has necessarily become better. See Laslett's introduction to *Household and Family* for a criticism of the nineteenth-century view that change in the family was an "advance."

CHAPTER I

1. For the founding of São Paulo, see Morse, *From Community to Metropolis*; Deus, *Memorias*, p. 122; Taunay, *São Paulo* and *História da cidade* (1953); Machado d'Oliveira, "Quadro historico"; Sampaio, "A fundação da cidade de S. Paulo," in Sampaio, ed., *São Paulo*.

2. The crown, for example, was unable to stop their expeditions to capture Indians. See Schwartz, *Sovereignty and Society*, pp. 165–67.

3. For the clan as organizing principle of other societies with weak governments, see Goody, *Development of the Family*, p. 31.

4. Four villages were established near São Paulo under the direction and administration of the Jesuits, and they depended directly on the governor general of Brazil. See Serafim Leite, *História*, vol. 6, pp. 228–29.

5. Taunay, *História da cidade* (1953), p. 15.

6. Serafim Leite, *História*, vol. 6, p. 290.

7. See Buarque de Holanda, "Movimentos," p. 66, n. 20.

8. The same use of the blood-feud in sixteenth- and seventeenth-century Scotland is shown by Wormald, "The Blood Feud."

9. Taunay, *História da cidade* (1953), chaps. 3, 4, and 5; Costa Pinto, *Lutas de famílias*, esp. chap. 4; Francisco Carvalho Franco, *Os Camargo*, esp. chap. 6; Monsenhor Camargo, *A Igreja*, pt. 2, chaps. 2 and 3; and Taques, *Nobiliarquia*, vol. 2, pp. 80–83. Serafim Leite, *História*, vol. 6, p. 300, argues that the feud occurred between the Garcias (instead of the Pires) and Camargos.

10. See Costa Pinto, *Lutas de famílias*, pp. 37–85. The pardon is described on pp. 51–52.

11. This sense of collective responsibility was also common in Scotland. See Wormald, "The Blood Feud."

12. Monteiro, "São Paulo," p. 237.

13. Quoted by Costa Pinto, *Lutas de famílias*, p. 79.

14. Anna Luiz, 1644, *IT*, vol. 29, p. 122.

15. Monteiro, "São Paulo," p. 100.

16. *IT*, vol. 13, p. 247.

17. João da Cunha Lobo, 1681, *IT*, vol. 20, pp. 423–24; Anna de Alvarenga, 1648, *IT*, vol. 29; João Tenorio, 1634, *IT*, vol. 9. In other cases, debtors to an estate were identified with their in-laws, such as in a 1613 estate: "Antônio da Silva, son-in-law of Maria Rodrigues, declared that he owes the deceased 16$000"; or in a 1663 estate: "João Tavares, son-in-law of Gouvêa" (see Antônio da Silveira, 1613, *IT*, vol. 30, p. 103, and Antônio Raposo da Silveira, 1663, *IT*, vol. 16).

18. Francisco Carvalho Franco, *Dicionário de bandeirantes*, p. 71.

19. Alcântara Machado, *Vida e morte*, p. 103, found only two women in over four hundred published *inventários* dated from 1578 to 1738 who knew how to sign their

names: a Flemish widow in 1626 and a woman in the early eighteenth century. Although women did not know how to sign, their presence was required at any official transaction for which their consent was necessary, such as the sale of community property real estate or the contracting of a daughter's dowry, and they would request that an independent witness sign for them.

20. For example, Francisco Pinheiro's wife (see the will of João da Cunha Lobo, 1681, IT, vol. 20, p. 425), and Dona Lucresia Borges, the wife of Antônio Raposo Tavares (see Ana Luis Grou, 1644, IT, vol. 29, p. 133).

21. Marrying off a daughter and endowing her was as much a business transaction as a family affair, since the marriage established a new branch of both the family and its business. See Pedro Fernandes, 1653, and Anna Tenoria, 1659, IT, vol. 12.

22. IT, vol. 26, p. 179.

23. Henrique da Cunha Machado, 1680, IT, vol. 21.

24. "Inventário dos documentos do Arquivo Ultramarino," Anais da Biblioteca Nacional do Rio de Janeiro, vol. 39, 1921, p. 199, as quoted in Dias, Quotidiano, p. 34. For widows as head of household, see Ordenações, Liv. 4, Tit. 91.

25. Miguel Garcia Velho, 1653, IT, vol. 15.

26. Buarque de Holanda, "Movimentos," p. 66.

27. Ferreira, História do direito, pp. 37–46; Alcântara Machado, Vida e morte, pp. 235–37.

28. Luis Dias, 1641, IT, vol. 13. These declarations in wills defended the rights of heirs, because most agreements made regarding a bandeira were oral ones based on trust. Without the declarations in a will, lengthy litigation could ensue.

29. Oliveira Viana, Populações meridionais, vol. 1, p. 64. Monteiro, in "São Paulo," tells us that the expedition consisted of 140 Portuguese men and 1,500 Tupi Indians.

30. Paulo Prado, Paulística, p. 191.

31. Costa Pinto, Lutas de famílias, pp. 40–41. Inventários are full of such examples. For example, when Paula Fernandes died in 1648, two of her sons and two of her sons-in-law were on a bandeira together (Paula Fernandes, 1648, IT, vol. 35), and when Maria Pedrosa died in childbirth in 1645, both her husband and her brothers were away in the wilderness (Maria Pedrosa, 1645, IT, vol. 33).

32. Fernão Dias Borges e Izabel de Almeida, 1643, IT, vol. 14, p. 273.

33. Maria Vitoria, 1657, IT, vol. 34.

34. Francisco Borges, 1649, IT, vol. 39.

35. Catharina do Prado, 1649, IT, vol. 15, p. 162.

36. Raphael de Oliveira, 1648, IT, vol. 3, p. 312.

37. Clemente Alveres, 1641, IT, vol. 14.

38. Yet the first interest of the Portuguese was not to have to use the labor of their own hands. See Gandavo, História da província Santa Cruz, pp. 93–94 (written in the sixteenth century). For evidence of commercialization to other parts of Brazil and even Angola, see Serafim Leite, História, vol. 6, p. 265, and Taunay, História da cidade (1953), p. 111. For tithes see Caio Prado, Jr., The Colonial Background, p. 375, and Dom Oscar de Oliveira, Os dízimos.

39. For example, when Pedro de Araujo's inventory was made, cotton worth 2$400 was found that his widow had their Indians spin and weave, selling the cloth for

10$000. Pedro's stepfather had the six pigs worth 2$000 killed and processed, and he sold the pork, sausage, and lard in Santos for 11$430, using the money to pay one of Pedro's outstanding debts. See Pedro de Araujo, 1638, *IT*, vol. 29, pp. 227 and 251.

40. For an example of how Indians were used to take commodities and even people back and forth from Santos, see Pero Nunes, 1623, *IT*, vol. 6, p. 58.

41. Alcântara Machado, *Vida e morte*, p. 40. On p. 45, he agrees with Oliveira Viana's conclusion that it was land that was central to power in colonial Brazil, despite the fact that on p. 44 he had said that land was worth nothing without people to work it. A contemporary reported that the source of Amador Bueno's wealth was the Indians he brought back from the wilderness. See Fonseca, *Vida do venerável Padre Belchior*, p. 106.

42. See Alden, "Black Robes," pp. 19–46; Ferreira, *História do direito*, pp. 88–100; and Schwartz, *Sovereignty and Society*, pp. 129–39.

43. Belchior Carneiro, 1607, *IT*, vol. 2, pp. 163–65.

44. For example, Francisco Baldaia's will of 1648 mentions that, in partial payment of a money loan, he had received a young Indian, worth ten *cruzados* (*IT*, vol. 38/39). In Luis Alveres Correa's 1658 inventário, his Indians' "services" were appraised as worth 11$000, and a third party who paid the amount received the Indians (*IT*, vol. 43, p. 254). In 1662 the widow of Luis Pedrozo frankly reported that she had sold 60 Indians, giving as her justification that they had mutinied and were a danger, and also because the sale would benefit the estate and her orphaned children (*IT*, vol. 43, p. 289).

45. Simonsen, *História econômica*, pp. 215–19.

46. Ibid., pp. 214–22.

47. The source is my sample. One cruzado was 400 réis. Total assets for 41 estates: 6:331$200 = 15,820 cruzados (not correcting for marital status). Further confirmation of this relative poverty can be found in Taunay, *História da cidade* (1953), p. 57: a 1664 report to the municipal council of São Paulo stated that the funds belonging to minors and placed with the juiz dos órfãos, which acted like a bank lending out at interest, had a total of between 16,000 and 20,000 cruzados. Also, an administrator in a sugarmill in the northeast earned in one year more than what 40 Paulistas accumulated in their lifetimes (see French, "Riqueza").

48. Alcântara Machado, *Vida e morte*, pp. 38–39.

49. Dariz Abreu, "A terra e a lei," p. 53.

50. Ursulo Colaço, 1649, *IT*, vol. 39.

51. Fernão Dias Borges e Isabel de Almeida, 1643, *IT*, vol. 14, pp. 274–76.

52. Simonsen, *História econômica*, p. 221, mentions that Alcântara Machado found only some 20 wealthy estates out of 400 he examined, that is, only 5 percent. Monteiro, in "São Paulo," pp. 346–59, makes a thorough analysis of stratification among property owners of Parnaíba in 1680.

53. Luzia Leme (widow of Cap. Pedro Vaz de Barros), 1655, *IT*, vol. 15. See Taunay, *História da cidade* (1953), p. 62, for the number belonging to Antônio Pedroso de Barros and Manoel Prêto.

54. These two were those of Anna Luiz, 1643, *IT*, vol. 29, and Catharina do Prado, 1649, *IT*, vol. 15. Anna Luiz owned 89 Indians with her husband, and Catharina do Prado owned 45 Indians as a widow. Because of the community property

law, the widower of Anna Luiz kept half the couple's Indians (the rest went to their children), so he and the widow Catharina do Prado each had about the same number of Indians.

55. Cristovão Diniz, 1650, *IT*, vol. 41.

CHAPTER 2

1. My emphasis. Angela de Campos e Medina, 1641, *IT*, vol. 13, p. 99.

2. The sample comprised 48 families with married daughters between 1640 and 1651. Four of these had not given dowries, plus there was a bankrupt estate in which it is unclear whether a dowry was given.

3. Anna Cabral, 1643, *IT*, vol. 29, widow of Alvaro Rabello, 1639, vol. 12. Maria inherited fifteen Indians and 9$562 in assets from her father, and five Indians and 26$039 from her mother.

4. The source is my sample. Besides Anna Cabral, the other estates with married daughters where there were no dowries are those of Domingos Simões, 1649, *IT*, vol. 39; Gaspar Barreiros, 1646, *IT*, vol. 33; and Manoel de Massedo, 1650, *IT*, vol. 41.

5. Martim Rodrigues, 1603–1612, *IT*, vol. 2, p. 30. The dowry also contained six Indians, twelve cows, one bull, one colt, a tablecloth, six napkins, towels, a table, and a dress.

6. Maria Gonçalves, 1599, *IT*, vol. 1; Clemente Alveres, 1641, *IT*, vol. 14.

7. See Introduction for explanation of the process of colação.

8. Catharina do Prado, 1649, *IT*, vol. 15.

9. Suzanna Dias, 1628, *IT*, vol. 33, p. 13.

10. See Yver, *Egalité entre héritiers.*

11. João Baruel, 1665, AESP, INP, #ord. 485, c. 8. Married daughters and their husbands were usually asked before the inventory of the estate was completed whether they wanted to inherit, so that their decision was based on a very approximate estimation of the size of the estate. João's net estate, with the addition of the three dowries and two gifts to his sons, was worth 4:151$668. His three daughters' dowries, worth 521$040, 426$170, and 545$240, respectively, were all smaller than the legítima of 618$517. (The amount of the legítima was copied from the manuscript, but it is in error.) The dowries João Baruel gave were unusual for the seventeenth century because they all included large amounts of cash.

12. His gift was worth 59$200, whereas the largest dowry was 718$000. Messia Rodrigues, 1665, *IT*, vol. 17.

13. 60$000 versus 170$500. We know the value only of the smallest dowry, for it was the one to come back into the estate. Manoel João Branco, 1641, *IT*, vol. 13.

14. See Dom Oscar de Oliveira, *Os dízimos*, p. 149.

15. Francisco's patrimony was worth 277$000. João Baruel also paid 32$000 for expenses necessary for his son Salvador to become a Franciscan novice.

16. Maria Leite da Silva, 1670, *IT*, vol. 17.

17. Pedro de Oliveira, 1643, *IT*, vol. 14. When her husband died five years later, Antonia's half of the estate was worth 61$310. (Affonso Dias, 1648, *IT*, vol. 15.)

18. Pedro Dias, 1633, *IT*, vol. 9, pp. 56, 65–67.

19. Also see Russell-Wood, *Fidalgos*, pp. 173–76. Chojnacki, "Dowries and Kinsmen," p. 593, shows that in Venice brothers also bore the brunt of sisters' dowries.

20. Estevão Furquim, *IT*, vol. 16, p. 301; vol. 17, p. 55.

21. For example, Luis Castanho de Almeida chose the husbands of his sisters. (Taques, *Nobiliarquia*, vol. 1, p. 266.)

22. *IT*, vol. 33, pp. 37–39; *IT*, vol. 14, p. 137. Because of the two meanings of the word dowry, care must be taken when analyzing what people said. If, when he said "dowry," he meant the property she took to marriage, he might have meant only her inheritance or else her inheritance plus what he gave her in addition—a frequent usage in the seventeenth century.

23. *IT*, vol. 3, pp. 264–65.

24. Anna de Moraes, 1616, *IT*, vol. 25, pp. 99–100.

25. Ursulo Colaço, 1641, *IT*, vol. 39, pp. 21–22.

26. Constantino Coelho Leite, 1693, *IT*, vol. 25, pp. 141–42. A married daughter could be obliged to bring her dowry à colação if the dowry exceeded the legítima plus the *terça*—the third of his estate that he could legally bestow. See *Ordenações*, Liv. 4, Tit. 97, par. 3.

27. Lourenço Castanho Taques (o velho), 1671, *IT*, vol. 16, p. 73.

28. Maria Leite da Silva, 1667, *IT*, vol. 17, p. 419.

29. Pedro Fernandes, 1648–1653, *IT*, vol. 12, p. 405. Anna Tenoria, 1664, *IT*, vol. 12, p. 447.

30. Izabel de Proença, 1648, *IT*, vol. 37, p. 113.

31. Russell-Wood, "Women and Society," p. 15.

32. Since he was a married man (not a widower), his terça or third was in fact only one-sixth of the estate he held jointly with his wife, since half of their estate belonged to her and remained with her. For a more complete explanation of the inheritance system see Note 16 in the Introduction.

33. Pedro de Araujo, 1638, *IT*, vol. 29.

34. Ignes Dias de Alvarenga, 1641, *IT*, vol. 28.

35. Suzanna Dias, 1628, *IT*, vol. 33, p. 15.

36. Catharina do Prado, 1649, *IT*, vol. 15, p. 104.

37. Estevão Furquim, 1660, *IT*, vol. 16. His mother-in-law, Maria Vitoria, also favored her daughters over her sons, leaving her remainder to her two single daughters. Each of her six sons received an inheritance of 9$240 plus three Indians, whereas the two single daughters received more than twice that amount, 21$500 plus seven Indians each. (Bernardo da Motta e sua molher, 1646, *IT*, vol. 34.)

38. The source is 58 inventários where the number of single adult and minor daughters are known. Because these are by definition all families with married daughters, this statistic should be treated with caution. It is my impression, however, from studying other seventeenth-century São Paulo inventories, that a single daughter over 25 was exceptional.

39. Gaspar Cubas o Velho, 1646, *IT*, vol. 37.

40. Manoel Rodrigues, 1646, *IT*, vol. 33.

41. It would appear that the daughter herself is listed as a part of the dowry, but since she is one of its recipients, I would argue that the emphasis is on the extremely

expensive clothes, the idea being that the bride went to marriage dressed as befitted her station. There are more examples of this wording in other seventeenth-century dowries.

42. Baltazar Fernandes signed the document and a male witness signed for his wife (whose presence and consent were legally required), using the customary seventeenth-century formula in these cases, "because she is a woman and does not know how to read and write." See AESP, Livro de Notas Ord. 6074, no. 26, Liv. 1640–1642. I thank John Monteiro for bringing this dowry to my attention.

43. Izabel Fernandes, 1641, IT, vol. 28; Pedro de Moraes Dantas, 1644, IT, vol. 14, p. 289.

44. Mecia de Siqueira, 1648, IT, vol. 37.

45. Alcântara Machado, Vida e Morte, pp. 156–58, first showed that seventeenth-century São Paulo dowries always contained Indians.

46. Pero Nunes, 1623, IT, vol. 6, p. 59.

47. Manoel José da Cunha, 1746, AESP, 1° Of., no. 14.123.

48. Estevão Furquim, 1660, IT, vol. 16.

49. Manoel João Branco, for example, says "I gave" while his wife says "we gave" when speaking of the same dowries (Manoel João Branco, 1641, IT, vol. 13). Other examples of married male testators saying "I gave": Ursulo Colaço, 1649, IT, vol. 39, and Domingos Fernandes, 1653, IT, vol. 27.

50. See Ordenações, Liv. 4, Tit. 48.

51. Izabel Fernandes, 1641, IT, vol. 28, p. 152.

52. Catharina Diniz, 1674, AESP, INP, #ord. 490, c. 13.

53. Maria Rodrigues, 1648, IT, vol. 37, p. 143.

54. Manoel João Branco, 1641, IT, vol. 13, p. 283.

55. Neither could a husband refuse an inheritance or bequest of real estate without his wife's consent. See Ordenações, Liv. 4, Tit. 48, including n. 4.

56. João Baruel, 1665, AESP, INP, #ord. 485, c. 8.

57. Gaspar Cubas, 1648, IT, vol. 37, p. 50.

58. An elderly widow, in contrast, was usually represented by a son or sons or by a son-in-law.

CHAPTER 3

1. Raphael de Oliveira, 1648, IT, vol. 3, pp. 309–10. For another such marriage see Silva Leme, Genealogia, vol. 4, p. 429, n. 1.

2. Fidalguia, or nobility, could be transmitted to children by mothers if the father was not a fidalgo, or nobleman. See Villasboas, Nobiliaria portuguesa, p. 164.

3. Pedro de Oliveira, 1643, IT, vol. 14.

4. Bernardo da Motta e sua molher Mª Vitoria, 1646, IT, vol. 34.

5. A total of 44 whole or partial dowries are listed, of which 18 contained land and 15 did not (information is missing for 11). Houses were included in 17 dowries but not in 14 (information is missing for 13).

6. Pedro de Araujo, 1638, IT, vol. 29, p. 254.

7. I thank Roberta Delson for suggesting this point. For the requirement that land be cultivated, see Dariz Abreu, "A terra e a lei," and Guimarães, *Quatro séculos*, p. 43.

8. Braz Rodrigues de Arzão, 1695, *IT*, vol. 23, p. 159.

9. Maria Bicudo, 1659, *IT*, vol. 16, p. 76.

10. Cristovão Diniz, 1650, *IT*, vol. 41, p. 132.

11. Deus, *Memorias*, pp. 83–84.

12. Taques, *Nobiliarquia*, vol. 2, p. 251.

13. Dona Maria Bueno, 1646, *IT*, vol. 14.

14. Valentim de Barros, 1651, *IT*, vol. 15, p. 224. His wife's share of the estate was 340$065 (p. 210) plus 57 Indians (p. 214).

15. Taques, *Nobiliarquia*, vol. 3, p. 53.

16. Simão Borges Cerqueira (husband of Leonor Leme), 1633, *IT*, vol. 9. Their estate amounted to 62$920. Luzia Leme (Leonor's sister), 1656, *IT*, vol. 15. The estate she owned with her husband, Captain Pedro Vaz de Barros, amounted to 1:329$550. Manoel João Branco (husband of Maria Leme, another sister), 1641, *IT*, vol. 13. Their net estate amounted to 807$000.

17. Messia Rodrigues, 1665, *IT*, vol. 17, pp. 140–47. The monetary value of Margarida's dowry was 718$000, compared to those of her three sisters who brought their dowries à colação, worth 149$444, 140$020, and 180$160, respectively.

18. Taques, *Nobiliarquia*, vol. 2, pp. 90–107. Two of Catharina's sons were the first Paulistas to go to the University of Coimbra in Portugal, becoming priests and remaining in Portugal in important positions. We do not know the size of Catharina's dowry, since it did not come in à colação.

19. Taques, *Nobiliarquia*, vol. 2, p. 73.

20. Quoted in Silva, *Sistema*, p. 17.

21. Caio Prado, Jr., in *The Colonial Background*, pp. 123–24, tells how European travelers commented even in the nineteenth century about the good life of Europeans who married in Brazil into families who wanted to "purify their blood." For works that analyze the importance of race in marriage, see Martinez-Alier, *Marriage, Class and Colour*, and McCaa, "*Calidad, Clase*, and Marriage."

22. Silva, *Sistema*, p. 18. The crown was interested in seeing that white women went to Brazil and did not return (see Russell-Wood, "Female and Family," pp. 62–64).

23. Silva, *Sistema*, p. 18.

24. Russell-Wood, in "Female and Family," p. 90, shows how several Bahian bachelor testators (who as such had no forced heirs) left their fortunes exclusively to their female collaterals, such as their sisters (expressly excluding male relatives), to be transmitted only to those sisters' daughters. He explains this as being due to their fear that male relatives would taint the family succession by their relations with non-whites. See also Boxer, *Mary and Misogyny*, p. 61.

25. This is my conclusion after studying Silva Leme, *Genealogia*.

26. Cited by Dias, *Quotidiano*, p. 75. Throughout the eighteenth century, Paulistas probably continued to be ashamed of their Indian ancestry. This is certainly the impression one gets when comparing the eighteenth-century Paulista genealogy prepared by Pedro Taques with that written in the late nineteenth century by Silva Leme.

Taques mentioned few Indians and emphasized the strains of Portuguese nobility in Paulista ancestry, whereas Silva Leme openly incorporates the native ancestors of the important families of São Paulo into his genealogy.

27. Silva Leme, *Genealogia*, vol. 1, p. 31, note.

28. For the Portuguese custom, see Mattos, *Manual de genealogia portuguesa*, p. 67. For the complexity of name usage in Brazil, see Marcílio, "Variation des noms."

29. Alfredo Ellis, Jr., in *Os Primeiros*, pp. 116–44, argues that most Portuguese immigrants of the first two centuries were of modest origins. Caio Prado, Jr., in *The Colonial Background*, pp. 92–93, states that most of the immigration to Brazil in the first half of the seventeenth century consisted of deportees.

30. See, for example, Clara Parenta, 1642, *IT*, vol. 13, whose brother, Manoel Alveres Pimentel, was also her son-in-law.

31. Of fifty-six families, twelve included marriages with relatives, of which six had several siblings marrying several siblings of another family, two were of a child of a previous marriage marrying the child of the stepfather or stepmother, one was of an uncle and niece, and three were between cousins. These statistics are probably too low, because relationship is not always obvious in the documents due to the use of different surnames for siblings.

32. Domingos Fernandes, 1652–1653, *IT*, vol. 27, p. 72.

33. Antonio Bicudo, 1648–1650, *IT*, vol. 15, p. 35; Taques, *Nobiliarquia*, vol. 3, p. 177.

34. See Domingos Cordeiro, 1643, *IT*, vol. 8; Silva Leme, *Genealogia*, vol. 8, p. 289; Francisco Carvalho Franco, *Dicionário de bandeirantes*, pp. 116 and 272; and Pedro de Oliveira, 1643, *IT*, vol. 14.

35. The information about Martim Rodrigues's family is based on the following inventários: Martim Rodrigues, 1603 (date of his will), *IT*, vol. 2; Damião Simões, 1578 (his wife's first husband), *IT*, vol. 1; Damião Simões (Martim's stepson), 1632, *IT*, vol. 8; Cornelio de Arzão, 1628 and 1638, *IT*, vol. 12; Braz Rodrigues de Arzão (Cornelio's son), 1692, *IT*, vol. 23; Clemente Alveres, 1641, *IT*, vol. 14; Maria Gonçalves (Clemente's first wife), 1599, *IT*, vol. 1; Maria Tenória (Clemente's second wife), 1620, *IT*, vol. 44; Luis Fernandes Folgado (Clemente's son-in-law), 1628, *IT*, vol. 7; Anna Tenória (Clemente's daughter, wife of Luis Fernandes Folgado), 1659, *IT*, vol. 12; Pedro Fernandes (Anna's second husband), 1653, *IT*, vol. 12; João Tenorio (Anna's brother), 1634, *IT*, vol. 9; Clemente Alveres o moço (Anna's brother), 1655, *IT*, vol. 43; Anna de Siqueira (Anna's sister-in-law), 1646, *IT*, vol. 33.

36. Clemente Alveres's inventário (*IT*, vol. 14) describes a *tenda de ferreiro* (forge) among his belongings. For his discoveries of mines, see Buarque de Holanda, *História*, vol. 2, p. 347.

37. Taunay, *História geral*, vol. 1, p. 173; Buarque de Holanda, *História*, vol. 2, pp. 250–51. Azevedo Marques, *Apontamentos históricos*, vol. 1, p. 206, quotes Cornelio's application for a sesmaria granted in 1627.

38. Martim Rodrigues, 1603, *IT*, vol. 2, p. 74. This foundry was built before the first foundry in Jamestown, Virginia. See Buarque de Holanda, *História*, pt. I, vol. 2, pp. 253–54.

39. Inventário da fazenda de Cornelio de Arzão, mandado fazer pela Inquisição,

1628, *IT*, vol. 12. Because of the community-property law and the Inquisition's belief in his wife's innocence, she retained her half of the property. See also Alcântara Machado, *Vida e morte*, p. 194.

40. Luis Fernandes is mentioned in the minutes of the municipal council in 1626, quoted in Monsenhor Camargo, *A Igreja*, p. 22.

41. Francisco Carvalho Franco, in *Dicionário de bandeirantes*, p. 27, maintains that Clemente Alveres built a foundry, *engenho de ferro*, in 1606 with his father-in-law. This interpretation is consistent with Martim's note in his account book, and the fact that the foundry appears in the inventário of one of Martim's and one of Clemente's sons-in-law. Yet if Clemente Alveres and Martim Rodrigues had in fact built and owned the foundry, it should have appeared in Martim's inventário (1612) and in that of his daughter, Clemente's wife, Maria Tenória, when she died in 1620, when Anna, their daughter, was still single and only eleven or twelve years old. That it did not appear in either inventário could be accounted for in two ways. The first is that it had been purposely omitted from the inventories so as to reserve it for a dowry. (I have found evidence of this practice in seventeenth-century São Paulo.) A better explanation is that it was not Clemente Alveres who built the foundry, but Cornelio de Arzão and Affonso Sardinha o moço, Clemente's companion in the discovery of gold and iron mines. Affonso Sardinha o moço is credited with building two foundries, called *fornos catalães* in some of the sources and *engenhos de ferro* in others. (See Buarque de Holanda, *História*, vol. II, pp. 250–51; Varnhagen, *História geral do Brasil*, vol. 2, pp. 51–52; Azevedo Marques, *Apontamentos históricos*, vol. 1, pp. 32–33; and Francisco Carvalho Franco, *Dicionário de bandeirantes*, p. 359.) Luis Fernandes could have bought the foundry from Francisco Lopes Pinto (who in his 1628 will stated that he had sold his share of a foundry [*IT*, vol. 7]), maybe with the help of his wife's dowry, because they had not been married long when he died in 1628, for Anna was expecting their first child.

42. Anna de Siqueira, 1646, *IT*, vol. 33, p. 29.

43. Manoel João Branco, 1641, *IT*, vol. 13, p. 284.

44. Manoel João Branco, 1641, and Maria Leme, 1663, *IT*, vol. 13, pp. 368 and 376.

45. Taques, *Nobiliarquia*, vol. 3, pp. 56–57. The surname of the grandniece was Leme, her mother's surname, also the surname of David Ventura's wife.

46. Messia Rodrigues, 1665, *IT*, vol. 17, pp. 119–20.

47. The appraised value may have been a little inflated. There is internal evidence within the inventário suggesting that some of Messia Rodrigues's heirs conspired to make it impossible for her will to be carried out; she bequeathed the remainder of her terça to the four natural (illegitimate) children of her deceased son, Jeronymo Pires, but her heirs managed things so that there was no remainder left. They arranged to have the appraisal carried out in São Paulo instead of on the farm, so that it is possible that the estate was undervalued. At the same time they had three dowries come in à colação and especially the very large dowry received by Antonio do Canto when he married Margarida. Since this dowry was five times the legítima, the remainder of the terça had to be used to cover the difference between the dowry and the legítima, thereby effectively eliminating the bequest to her illegitimate grandchildren. The heirs also invoked the fact that the family had noble blood,

which eliminated the legal claims of natural children, but did not eliminate the right of a testator to name beneficiaries to the remainder of the terça, which is probably why they resorted to the process of colação, so little practiced in the seventeenth century.

48. Legally the dowry described should have consisted only of what her mother gave her and not included Thomazia's paternal legítima, for the latter could not come in à colação, but if the word "dowry" was used in the sense of what she took to marriage, it could have included her inheritance.

49. When Belchior de Godoy died, he and his wife had net assets worth 81$300, plus a house in town without an appraisal; Thomazia's dowry consisted of a house in town plus either 62$560 or 90$000 in further assets (Belchior de Godoy, 1649, IT, vol. 39, and Messia Rodrigues, 1665, IT, vol. 17, p. 143). The lower number is my addition and the higher number is the notary's.

50. Catharina do Prado, 1649, IT, vol. 15.

51. João Gago da Cunha, 1639, IT, vol. 10. Both he and his son, the husband of Anna Pires, were famous bandeirantes (Francisco Carvalho Franco, *Dicionário de bandeirantes*, p. 133).

52. João Gago da Cunha, 1639, IT, vol. 10, pp. 380–81.

53. Ibid., pp. 372–73.

54. Catharina do Prado, 1649, IT, vol. 15, p. 115.

55. Mathias's maternal legítima was 17$390 plus two Indians, and his paternal inheritance was 16$014 and one Indian (Catharina de Medeiros, 1629, IT, vol. 8; Mathias Lopes o velho, 1651, IT, vol. 26). Mathias's father was a famous bandeirante who went with Antônio Raposo Tavares to Guairá in 1628 (Francisco Carvalho Franco, *Dicionário de bandeirantes*, p. 221).

56. Pedro de Araujo, 1638, IT, vol. 28. He was married in November 1637 at the age of 23, and he had been to the sertão at least once (see p. 251). His age was calculated from the fact that Pedro was three years old in 1617 in the inventário made after his father, also Pedro de Araujo, died in the sertão (IT, vol. 5, p. 171). Other references to his parents are in Francisco Carvalho Franco, *Dicionário de bandeirantes*, p. 35, and Taques, *Nobiliarquia*, vol. 3, p. 280, but Taques mistakes Pedro's wife and heirs.

57. When Pedro's mother died in 1644, Pedro's son received six Indians who would have been his father's had he lived long enough (Anna de Alvarenga, 1644, IT, vol. 29).

58. Pedro de Araujo, 1638, IT, vol. 29, p. 253.

59. Lavrin and Couturier, in "Dowries and Wills," p. 296, studied sixty marriages in seventeenth- and eighteenth-century Mexico, finding that in thirty the husband had no property or brought less to the marriage than his wife, in eighteen both partners brought approximately the same, and in only twelve was the husband the greater provider.

60. Deus, *Memorias*, pp. 83–84.

61. Antonio Raposo da Silveira, 1663, IT, vol. 16, p. 419. Anna Maria da Silveira married Salvador Cardoso de Almeida, who therefore became juiz dos órfãos, and the office was later held by Capitan Francisco de Camargo Pimentel, their son-in-law (See Silva Leme, *Genealogia*, vol. 1, p. 335).

CHAPTER 4

1. Boxer, *The Golden Age*, pp. 30–60; Buarque de Holanda, *História*, vol. 1, pp. 294–96; Antonil, *Cultura e opulência*, pt. 3, chaps. 2 and 3; Taunay, *História geral*, vol. 1, p. 216. One of the discoverers of gold was Antonio Rodrigues de Arzão, descendant of Martim Rodrigues, whose family with metallurgical expertise was described in Chapter 3. For the war between Paulistas and the interlopers, see Buarque de Holanda, *História*, vol. 1, chap. 3, and Boxer, *The Golden Age*, chap. 3.

2. Boxer, *The Golden Age*, pp. 254, 267.

3. Cassiano, *Marcha para oeste*, p. 91.

4. Of the nineteen inventários, seven had relatives in Minas Gerais, six in Goiás, five in Cuiabá, and one in both Goiás and Cuiabá. In "Clans," p. 208, Elizabeth Kuznesof describes the difficulty in tracing kin groups, such as the Prados who had members in Nossa Senhora do O, Santo Amaro, and the mines of Goiás.

5. Manoel João de Oliveira, AESP, INP, #ord. 537, c. 60.

6. Of the 84 inventários, 28 had connections to the mines.

7. The source is 69 estates with married daughters (1721–1790) for which the total value of the estate is known. Of the richest 17 estates, 10 had connections to the mines. Of the poorest 17, only 2 did. Using the number of African slaves owned as the index of wealth, we find that those estates having connections with the mines owned an average of 18.6 slaves, while those without connections to the mines owned an average of only 8.2 slaves.

8. See Goulart, *Tropas*; Alfredo Ellis, Jr., "O ciclo do muar"; and Myriam Ellis, "Estudo sobre alguns."

9. For the monções, see Boxer, *The Golden Age*, pp. 261–66, and Buarque de Holanda, *Monções*. For the way the mines were supplied, see Myriam Ellis, "Contribução," and Zemella, *O Abastecimento*. For the roads to the mines, see Caio Prado, Jr., *The Colonial Background*, pp. 284–90; for a contemporary's description, see Antonil, *Cultura e opulência*, pp. 159–66.

10. *DI*, vol. 23, pp. 329–63.

11. Bartholomeu de Quadros, 1722, *IT*, vol. 26, p. 271.

12. Metcalf, "Families of Planters," pp. 110–11.

13. Brazilians were not exceptional regarding illiteracy. For example, in Scotland in 1638, only 25 percent of adult men were literate, though men raised their literacy rate to 72 percent after 1700. Women, meanwhile, were 80 percent illiterate between 1630 and 1760, and it was the daughters and wives of lairds and professionals who were most likely to know how to read and write (see Houston, "Illiteracy in Scotland").

14. Taques, *Nobiliarquia*, vol. 2, p. 191.

15. Simonsen, *História econômica*, pp. 222–27; Taunay, *História da cidade* (1953), pp. 52–56.

16. As quoted in Boxer, *The Golden Age*, p. 34. Interesting enough, by 1694 the crown had decided to create a colonial coin with greater value than the Portuguese.

17. Simonsen, *História econômica*, p. 229.

18. Buarque de Holanda, *História*, vol. 1, pt. 2, pp. 34–36.

19. As quoted in Simonsen, *História econômica*, p. 230.

20. Manoel de Alvarenga, 1639, *IT*, vol. 14, p. xlix; see also Alcântara Machado, *Vida e morte*, p. 197.

21. Lourenço Fernandes, 1646–1666, *IT*, vol. 33, p. 135.

22. In the seventeenth century, either an ecclesiastic inspector (*visitador*) or the crown magistrate (*ouvidor geral*) checked whether wills had been carried out, but in the eighteenth century only the *ouvidor* did so.

23. The regular army remained small and unimportant until after the cutoff date of my eighteenth-century sample.

24. This interpretation is convincingly argued in Kuznesof, "Clans."

25. Leonzo, *As companhias*, p. 206.

26. See Taques, *Nobiliarquia*, vol. 3, pp. 118–19.

27. Manoel Mendes de Almeida, 1756, AESP, INP, #ord. 542, c. 55.

28. *DI*, vol. 23, p. 126.

29. The source is my sample. The highest rank of father, sons, or sons-in-law in each family was chosen for the data set. The lucrative position of juiz dos órfãos was also held by those already wealthy or high in the ranks of the militia. For example, in 1753 the juiz dos órfãos in Parnaíba was the captain major of the town (Escolastica Cordeiro Borba, 1758, AESP, INP, #ord. 533, c. 56). Since a substantial bond had to be posted to be named to the position of juiz dos órfãos, the possession of capital was also imperative. For example, in *Registro geral da câmara de São Paulo, 1750–1763*, p. 13, there is a document in which Dr. Luis de Campos puts up 400$000 to undo any damage orphans might suffer while he held the position.

30. See Aroldo de Azevedo, "Vilas e cidades," p. 49.

31. See Canabrava, "Uma economia." This trend was to reverse itself in the captaincy of São Paulo during the last third of the century, when sugar cane was increasingly cultivated and exported (see Petrone, *A lavoura canavieira*).

32. Contemporaries with such opinions were the Morgado de Mateus, 1767 (*DI*, vol. 33, pp. 380–81), and Governor Martim Lopes, 1775 (quoted in Paulo Prado, *Paulística*, p. 147).

33. Marcílio, "Crescimento," p. 293.

34. Such is Alcântara Machado's thesis in *Vida e morte*.

35. See, for example, Taques, *Nobiliarquia*, vol. 1, p. 117.

36. Alvará of May 8, 1758. Also see Caio Prado, Jr., *The Colonial Background*, p. 102.

37. My source is the estates in the sample in which the number of Indians or slaves is known.

38. For the importance of the renovation of the *caminho do mar* after 1780, see Kuznesof, "The Role of the Merchants."

39. In 1765 the free population of the city of São Paulo numbered 14,760 and the slave population 6,113 (in 1767) for a total population of 20,873. See Marcílio, *A cidade*, p. 98. This was, however, an increase in the proportion of African slaves. Alfredo Ellis, Jr., in *A economia paulista*, p. 130, n. 2, shows that the proportion of Africans to Indians in São Paulo was one African to every thirty-four Indians in the seventeenth century, and eight Africans to every seven Indians in the eighteenth.

40. Buarque de Holanda, "Movimentos," pp. 83–84.

41. Canabrava, "Uma economia," p. 103. Only 43.6 percent of households in the 1778 census owned slaves (see Kuznesof, "Household Composition," p. 85, n. 15).

42. The 1772 census of Sorocaba shows that only 30 percent of agricultural households owned the land they worked; the other 70 percent either paid a small rent for land belonging to the city council (9 percent), used *terras devolutas*, that is, land previously given in grants but that had been abandoned (26 percent), or worked land belonging to third parties, *planta em terras alheias* (35 percent). See Marcílio, "Crescimento," p. 286. For Parnaíba, see Metcalf, "Families of Planters," pp. 58–71.

43. Canabrava, "Uma economia," tables on pp. 101, 103.

44. My source is the 54 estates of my sample in which the net estate is known.

45. For the seventeenth century, see Table 1 in Chapter 1.

46. Only two of the wealthiest third of the sample did not own both a farm and a townhouse, and they were widows who probably had lost title to the houses they owned in town when their husbands died. For example, Maria de Lima de Siqueira died in the house of her daughter and son-in-law, situated in the center of São Paulo. The only real estate listed in her inventário were two sitios, one of which, in the parish of Cotia, was of sizable value. As her estate was quite large, over 4:000$000, it is probable that in the division of property after her husband died, the house or houses she and her husband had owned were allotted to their children. See Maria de Lima de Siqueira, 1769, AESP, INP, #ord. 545, c. 68.

47. In the inventário of Joanna Velozo (1758, AESP, INP, #ord. 539, c. 59), it explicitly states that she was allotted the house in the parish of Juquerí when the estate she had owned with her deceased husband was divided between her and their children.

48. See Canabrava, "Uma economia," pp. 115–16.

49. Kuznesof, "Household Composition," table III:3, p. 100. She found 29 businessmen in the strictly urban area of 568 households, or 5 percent.

50. *DI*, vol. 62, p. 70; Capitão José da Silva Ferrão, 1763, AESP, INP, #ord. 541, c. 64, also #ord. 54, c. 63. He had a brother who was *tenente-general* in Vila Rica, Minas Gerais. Since he was childless, his inventário is not in my sample. Not only was he one of the wealthiest people in São Paulo, but he had also been knighted with the Order of Christ, had twice been *juiz ordinário*, and had been a member of the city council. See Taques, *Nobiliarquia*, vol. 3, p. 114, and *Registro geral da câmara de São Paulo, 1750–1763*, p. 135.

51. For the complexity of eighteenth-century trade networks, see that of Francisco Pinheiro in Lisanti, *Negócios coloniais*. Two of the merchants in the sample were part of Francisco Pinheiro's network: Manoel Mendes de Almeida, captain major of the city of São Paulo, and Manoel Mendes Ferreyra Luctosa, son-in-law of Caetano Soares Viana. An analysis of the volume of merchandise Pinheiro's network sold throughout Brazil is in Levy, *História financeira*, pp. 94–100.

52. Most of these were of lower-middle-class origins. See Kuznesof, "The Role of the Merchants," p. 576. Buarque de Holanda claims in *Monções*, p. 117, that most of the merchants who made their fortunes in the traffic to the mines were not of the old Paulista families, but rather immigrants. This was also the situation in Bahia, where 83 percent of merchants were Portuguese. See Flory and Smith, "Bahian Merchants."

53. Martinho, "Organização do trabalho," p. 41.

54. Ibid. See also Lobo, "O comércio atlántico."

55. Tenente José Rodrigues Pereira, 1769, AESP, 1° Of., #ord. 686, c. 74, no. 14.533. This kind of partnership was called *de capital e indústria*.

56. 1767 census in *DI*, vol. 62, p. 261. José Rodrigues Pereira's inventário in 1769 shows the value of his assets as 26:196$200, close to the above estimate, but once his debts had been paid, his net estate was worth only 14:632$500 (AESP, 1° Of., #ord. 686, c. 74, no. 14.533).

57. Kuznesof, "The Role of the Merchants," p. 583. Almost three-fourths of the Portuguese merchants who served on the city council between 1767 and 1818 married into traditional Paulista families, and so had fifteen of the twenty Portuguese on the board of the Santa Casa de Misericórdia.

58. Escolástica Vellozo, 1753, AESP, INP, #ord. 530, c. 53. The total value of the goods for sale in Thomé's shop was 2:388$477. The inventory included 260$000 of gold bars and dust and 41$000 in cash. One male slave in his prime, worth 150$000 in São Paulo, was sold in Cuiabá for 420$000.

59. Manoel Vellozo, 1752, AESP, INP, #ord. 528, c. 51. Manoel is mentioned twice as a customer in Lisanti, vol. 4, p. 34, and vol. 3, p. 433. Among other dealings, Manoel had been one of the four Paulista partners and guarantors of the man who in 1722 bought the royal contract to collect the Cuiabá tithes (Taunay, *História da cidade . . . no século XVIII*, vol. 2, p. 7).

60. See *Registro geral da câmara de São Paulo, 1750–1763*, p. 88. For the struggles against merchants in the city council, see Taunay, *História da cidade* (1953), p. 118. For the importance of merchants on the city council, see Kuznesof, "The Role of the Merchants," pp. 580–91.

61. See Buarque de Holanda, *Monções*, p. 115.

62. Manoel Vellozo, 1752, AESP, INP, #ord. 528, c. 51. Pedro Taques, as the husband of Manoel's granddaughter, came in à colação with their share of his late mother-in-law's dowry.

63. For the same behavior in Bahia, see Flory and Smith, "Bahian Merchants," p. 576; for Mexico, see Brading, *Miners and Merchants*.

64. Silva Leme, *Genealogia*, vol. 8, p. 167.

65. Lourenço de Siqueira, 1665, *IT*, vol. 17, p. 37.

66. Raphael de Oliveira, 1648, *IT*, vol. 3, p. 310.

67. Pedro Fernandes, 1653, *IT*, vol. 12, p. 406.

68. Anastacio da Costa, 1651, *IT*, vol. 13, p. 226.

69. See Kennedy, "Bahian Elites," p. 420, for the requirement that merchants know double-entry bookkeeping to be registered with the Lisbon *Junta de Comércio*. I have found one or two instances of the use of double-entry bookkeeping in papers presented to document debt in eighteenth-century inventários.

70. Maria Bicudo, 1659, *IT*, vol. 16, p. 67.

71. Domingos Fernandes, 1653, *IT*, vol. 27.

72. Alcântara Machado, *Vida e morte*, p. 148.

73. Treslado dos Capitulos de Corecção do Desembargador Antonio Luis Pelleja ao Ouvidor Geral desta Comarca, 1722, Livros de Parnaíba 89:1–8; AESP, 6066-18, as cited in Metcalf, "Fathers and Sons," p. 470, n. 26.

CHAPTER 5

1. The source is my sample: a total of 68 families in the eighteenth century, of whom 55 gave dowries; 48 families in the seventeenth century, of whom one has missing information and 43 gave dowries.

2. João Fernandes da Costa, 1750, AESP, INP, #ord. 523, c. 46. His net estate, minus the half belonging to his widow, was worth 255$600, whereas the net estate of the widower José Rodrigues Pereira was worth 14:632$500.

3. Miguel Delgado da Cruz, 1758, AESP, INP, #ord. 535, c. 58.

4. Manoel Garcia, 1750, AESP, INP, #ord. 524, c. 65.

5. Manoel Soares de Carvalho, 1772, AESP, INP, #ord. 550, c. 1.

6. Aniceto Fernandes, 1762, AESP, INP, #ord. 540, c. 63.

7. According to Portuguese law, only illegitimate children who were born while both parents were unmarried (called *naturais*) would inherit from their father (or mother) after being recognized. Children born while one or both parents were married to third parties (called *adulterinos*) could never inherit, though they could receive bequests out of their father's (or mother's) terça.

8. See *Ordenações*, Liv. 4, Tit. 97, par. 1.

9. Maria Bueno de Oliveira, 1765, AESP, INP, #ord. 543, c. 66.

10. José Rodrigues Pereira, 1769, AESP, Inv. 1° Of., no. 14.533. His younger daughters married only with their maternal and paternal legítimas, thereby taking less property to marriage than their older sister who had received the remainder of his terça.

11. So had five widows in the sample who allowed their daughters to marry simply with their legítima. Besides Maria Bueno de Oliveira, the others were: Maria Rosa de Bicudo (1751, AESP, INP, #ord. 526, c. 49) with a small estate in Juquerí with no slaves; Joanna Vellozo (1758, AESP, INP, #ord. 539, c. 59) who owned only a house on Rua S. Bento; Izabel de Arruda Leite (1763, AESP, INP, #ord. 541, c. 64) who owned a house and four slaves; and Catharina de Lemos (1750, AESP, INP, #ord. 526, c. 49) with seven slaves, an urban house, and two sitios.

12. See Manoel Dultra Machado o velho, 1752, AESP, INP, #ord. 527, c. 50; Mariana Machado, 1759, AESP, INP, #ord. 536, c. 59; Ignes Dultra, 1763, AESP, 1° Of., no. 13.781.

13. My source is twenty-nine families with three or more married daughters, fourteen with dowries getting smaller, nine with dowries getting larger, and six in no particular order.

14. I divided the twenty-nine estates that had given three or more dowries into those in which the largest dowry was more than twice the smallest, and those in which it was less than twice.

15. Maria de Lima de Siqueira, 1769, AESP, INP, #ord. 545, c. 68. See also Appendix D.IV and VII.

16. Manoel Dultra Machado o Velho, 1752, AESP, INP, #ord. 527, c. 50; Mariana Machado, 1759, AESP, INP, #ord. 536, c. 59. They gave their first daughter 209$680, their second daughter 73$330, their third daughter nothing, their fourth daughter 49$400, and their fifth daughter 32$160. The total given in dowry was thus

364$570. The parents' net estate was 762$380, so their total divestment for dowries was 32 percent.

17. Diogo das Neves Pires was the great-grandson of João Pires and Messia Rodrigues. Diogo's first wife belonged to one of the old founding families, the Garcia Velhos family. His second wife was also a great-grandchild of João Pires and Messia Rodrigues. See Silva Leme, *Genealogia*, vol. 2, Tit. Pires.

18. He had eleven children. I calculated the net worth of his estate at the time of his first wife's death by working back from the value of the maternal legítima, mentioned in his inventário. When his daughter declined to inherit, the terça was not used, as in the seventeenth century. Diogo das Neves Pires, 1760, AESP, INP, #ord. 537, c. 60.

19. Izabel Dultra e seu marido Estevão de Lima do Prado, 1748, AESP, 1° Of., no. 13.781. For her dowry, see Manoel Dultra Machado o velho, 1752, AESP, INP, #ord. 527, c. 50. Izabel was the granddaughter of the couple who started the Dultra Machado family, and Estevão was of the old Prado family. See Silva Leme, *Genealogia*, vol. 9 for the Dultra Machados and vol. 3 for the Prados.

20. After Izabel's death, two of her sons used their horses to transport merchandise from Cubatão to São Paulo, earning barely enough to support themselves and feed their horses. One of her other daughters was taken in and raised by an uncle, who could not afford to give her a dowry, and instead made a dowry contract with her husband, promising that she would receive the remainder of his terça when he died. She had already received six steers as dowry, worth 1$900 each. (See AESP, 2° Tabelião de S.P., Liv. 2, 1753–1755, folhas 163, Escritura de dote, Doante André Teixeira Dias, doado Vicente Vieira dos Santos.)

21. Estevão remarried after Izabel died, but had no children with his new wife, and when he died, she only took back the things she had brought to the marriage, leaving everything else for his children.

22. See Appendix D.VI for further details.

23. Kuznesof, "Clans," pp. 209–11.

24. See Table 22 in Chapter 9.

25. Some inventários in which parents outfitted sons: Domingos Lopes de Oliveira, 1766, AESP, INP, #ord. 544, c. 67; Catharina Ribeiro, 1757, AESP, INP, #ord. 533, c. 56; Maria de Araujo, 1755, AESP, INP, #ord. 535, c. 58; Salvador Lopes de Medeiro, 1760, AESP, INP, #ord. 537, c. 60; Bartholomeu de Quadros, 1722, IT, vol. 26, p. 271.

26. Mariana Machado, 1759, AESP, INP, #ord. 536, c. 59; Bras Leme do Prado e Maria Domingues de Mattos, 1751, AESP, INP, #ord. 525, c. 48; Joanna da Cunha, 1766, AESP, INP, #ord. 544, c. 67.

27. My source is 21 complete dowries for the seventeenth century and 41 for the eighteenth.

28. An example is in Appendix D.I.

29. Spanish law must have had a procedure similar to colação because it also required that a dowry be subtracted from the legítima (Law XXVI of Toro). See Lavrin and Couturier, "Dowries and Wills," p. 286, n. 19.

30. This third is in fact one-sixth of the community property owned jointly by

both spouses. *Ordenações*, Liv. 4, Tit. 97, par. 3. A nineteenth-century jurist, Coelho da Rocha, explains that the purpose of colação was to preserve equality between children in relation to their parents' estate, only allowing the parents the free disposition of one-third of their estate. See *Ordenações*, Liv. 4, Tit. 97, par. 1, n. 4 on p. 968.

31. In Messia Rodrigues, 1665, *IT*, vol. 17, the terça was used, demonstrating seventeenth-century awareness of the law.

32. Maria Bueno de Araujo, AESP, INP, #ord. 544, c. 67. See Appendix D.III.

33. See Kuznesof, "Clans," p. 218.

34. *Ordenações*, Liv. 4, Tit. 97, par. 1.

35. See Appendix D.IV. The term used in the eighteenth century was *se levanta com seu dote*, and dowries were therefore classified for the partition as *levantados* or *conferidos* (brought in à colação). Because of the accounting process involved, both kinds of dowries had to be appraised. (Contrary to the situation in the seventeenth century, therefore, we know the value of all eighteenth-century dowries in the sample.) Most eighteenth-century daughters were married in the order of their birth, and the eldest daughter was the *primeira dotada* (first endowed) and therefore the first one to be given the choice of whether to *levantar* or *conferir* her dowry. Metcalf states that, by law, only the first dowry was protected by the terça ("Fathers and Sons," p. 470, n. 26). Yet the practice was clearly otherwise, since in Maria de Lima de Siqueira's case two daughters were protected by the terça.

36. Manoel Pacheco Gato, 1715, *IT*, vol. 26, p. 469.

37. Manoel João de Oliveira, AESP, INP, #ord. 537, c. 60; Ignacio Dinis Caldeyra, AESP, INP, #ord. 533, c. 56.

38. Taques, in *Nobiliarquia*, vol. 3, p. 124, mentions a ship being built by Luiz Dias Leme, Manoel João Branco's brother-in-law, when he died in 1659. The unfinished ship was appraised for 400$000, so Manoel João's ship would have been worth much more.

39. Constantino Coelho Leite, 1693, *IT*, vol. 25, pp. 141–42.

40. Pero Nunes, 1623, *IT*, vol. 6, p. 59.

41. See also Silva, "Sistema," p. 1258.

CHAPTER 6

1. Marcílio, A *cidade*, table 13, p. 119. See p. 122 for the hypothesis that men returned to São Paulo in their old age.

2. Letter, Jan. 31, 1768, in *DI*, vol. 23, p. 382.

3. See table 4 in Marcílio, A *cidade*, p. 105. In a later chapter Marcílio states that the 1798 census is the only one with reliable information regarding the sex, age, and civil status of the population of the parish of Sé. In that census, 45.5 percent of the men and 34.3 percent of the women over 50 in the parish of Sé were single (p. 163).

4. Women were the heads of 28.8 percent of urban households and 26.5 percent of rural ones (Kuznesof, "Household Composition," p. 86, table I, and p. 101).

5. Marcílio, A *cidade*, p. 159, tables 28 and 29 (1741–70).

6. Kuznesof, "Household Composition," p. 88, table III.

7. In the seventeenth century, only 2 families out of 58 in which ages were known had single daughters over 25 (6.7 percent). In the eighteenth century, there were single daughters over 25 in 21 families out of 82 in which ages were known (25.6 percent).

8. *DI*, vol. 23, pp. 380–81; Silva, *Sistema*, pp. 50–51.

9. Ramos, in "Marriage and the Family," demonstrates that in Vila Rica marriage was also only for the well-to-do.

10. Silva, *Sistema*, pp. 51–56.

11. For the single rate, see Marcílio, *A cidade*, pp. 164–65. For the percentage of female-headed households, see Kuznesof, "Household Composition," p. 100.

12. Deus, *Memorias*, pp. 83–84.

13. Russell-Wood, "Women and Society," p. 19.

14. The seventeenth-century São Paulo pattern of more women than men remarrying appears to be quite unusual. Studies of communities in France and Bavaria in the seventeenth and eighteenth centuries and in the United States in the early nineteenth century show that there was a much lower remarriage rate for women than for men except among the very young. There also appeared to be no direct or inverse correlation between remarriage and wealth. See Grigg, "Toward a Theory of Remarriage."

15. Marcílio, *A cidade*, p. 166, demonstrates that between 1728 and 1770 in the Sé parish, 9.6 percent of men were remarrying versus only 8 percent of women (887 marriages).

16. Metcalf, "Fathers and Sons," pp. 476–78.

17. Thomé Alves de Crasto, 1772, AESP, INP, #ord. 549, c. 72. See also *DI*, vol. 62, pp. 9, 28, 71, 257, 305, 306.

18. I have found misrepresentation of worth to the census taker. For example, Maria da Silva Leite, the widow of the wealthy merchant José da Silva Ferrão, reported property worth only 10 contos to the 1765 census, when her half of their community property had been over 28 contos when he died two years earlier. (See *DI*, vol. 62, p. 70; Capitão José da Silva Ferrão, AESP, INP, #ord. 541, c. 64, and #ord. 54, c. 63.)

19. Letter of Captain General Martim Lopes Lobo de Saldanha, 1777. *DI*, vol. 23, p. 348.

20. Since the paternal legítima of Thomé's children amounted to 1:630$900, their maternal legítima, which both sons had received long before, was at least that large. Therefore, his eldest son, who had received property worth 642$000 on top of his maternal legítima probably owned much more property than the 200$000 his wife reported to the census taker, for she was living in her mother's home, and he was absent, maybe in the gold-mining region. Her husband probably had with him slaves and/or merchandise worth a considerably greater amount, but still probably not as large as his sisters' fortunes. Thomé's second son declared property worth 2:000$000, just a little more than his legítima, indicating that his wife brought no important dowry to marriage.

21. We can be more confident of the statistics in this case than in the preceding one, since all data come from inventários and not from the 1765 census.

22. Ignacio Soares de Barros, AESP, 1° Of., no. 14.328.

23. Licenciado Manoel José da Cunha was both a chemist and a merchant, and when he died they owned a pharmacy (*botica*), contents valued at 80$000, and a shop selling housewares, such as china from Macao and gold jewelry, contents valued at 3:844$855. His inventory included a substantial library of 48 books, most of them about medicine and surgery. They owned three houses in the center of São Paulo. After he died in 1746, his widow married Dr. Luis de Campos, a lawyer and later juiz dos órfãos, who in the 1765 and 1767 censuses was living with his wife on Rua Direita (maybe in the house she had owned with her former husband) and declared capital of 7:700$000. (See Licenciado Manoel José da Cunha, AESP, 1° Of., no. 14.123, and *DI*, vol. 62, pp. 59 and 269.)

24. His property included a house in the parish of Cotia and three sitios. The largest of these was probably his parents' because he received half his mother's farm when she died. It had a good house, *senzalas* (slave quarters), a small sugarmill, and sugar cane that was distilled to make rum. He owned eleven slaves, counting the three taken by two of his three single sons (one a priest in Minas Gerais). Joseph Ortiz de Camargo, AESP, 1° Of., no. ord. 689, c. 77.

25. 1767 census in *DI*, vol. 62, p. 268.

26. Manoel Vellozo married Ignacia Vieira of the Maciel family (Silva Leme, *Genealogia*, vol. 8, Maciéis, p. 167).

27. Silva Leme, *Genealogia*, vol. 8, Maciéis, p. 167. One of Anna's aunts, Angela Vieira, another of Manoel's daughters, married the captain major of the Mato Grosso mines and had prominent descendants, including two coffee barons, the Barão de Itapetininga and his son-in-law, the Barão de Rio Claro.

28. Manoel Vellozo's son became a priest.

29. See João de Siqueira Caldeira e sua mulher Catharina Rodrigues Cardoso, 1750, AESP, INP, #ord. 523, c. 46, and Catharina Ribeiro de Siqueira, 1749, AESP, 1° Of., no. 13.737.

30. Bento Gomes de Oliveira, 1729, AESP, 1° Of., no. 14.304. The murder is described in Silva Leme, *Genealogia*, vol. 8, p. 167 (Ignacia Vieira and Captain Manoel Vellozo).

31. The second dowry came out of his terça. Manoel Vellozo, 1752, AESP, INP, #ord. 528, c. 51.

32. Manoel João de Oliveira, 1760, AESP, INP, #ord. 537, c. 60.

33. See Appendix D.II for the division of Manoel João's property.

34. The law was especially concerned with widows, who were viewed as prone to alienate their property imprudently, thereby dissipating their heirs' inheritance. Men could also be declared spendthrifts, and if they were married, the law considered their wives the best choice as administrators (if they had the ability and desire to take on the job) because there was no conflict of interest between husband and wife, while there was between father and son. (On widows, see *Ordenações*, Liv. 4, Tit. 107. On male married spendthrifts, see *Ordenações*, Liv. 4, Tit. 103.)

35. His children responded by offering to pay for the masses from their inheritance (Thomé Alves de Crasto, 1772, AESP, INP, #ord. 549, c. 49). The law stating that children could sue a father who was dissipating his property is in *Ordenações*, Liv. 3, Tit. 9.

36. Taques, *Nobiliarquia*, vol. 1, p. 131.

CHAPTER 7

1. Petrone, A lavoura canavieira; Caio Prado, Jr., História econômica, chaps. 10 and 12. For a summary of economic and political change in São Paulo up to 1850, see Buarque de Holanda, História, pt. 2, vol. 2, pp. 415–72.

2. Kuznesof, "The Role of the Merchants."

3. For the expansion of coffee plantations in São Paulo, see Millet, Roteiro do café.

4. See Richard Graham, Britain and the Modernization of Brazil, chap. 2, for the importance of the railroad for the exportation of São Paulo's coffee.

5. See José Camargo, Crescimento da população.

6. See Willems, "Social Differentiation," for a study of several censuses taken in 1820 in ten localities of the captaincy of São Paulo, finding that there were more agriculturalists who owned no slaves than there were slaveholding agriculturalists, and that within both groups there was great heterogeneity in income, confirming the existence of an intermediate class between the large plantation owner and the slave.

7. Kuznesof, Household Economy, table IV: 5, p. 82.

8. For the decline in numbers of slaves in São Paulo, see José Camargo, Crescimento da população, table 2.

9. Inventários had to be carried out judicially after the Alvará of June 17, 1809, and the Regimento of April 28, 1842, when the state (Fazenda Pública) commenced the taxation of inheritance and bequests. (See Ordenações, Liv. 4, Tit. 96, par. 18; Buarque de Holanda, História, vol. 6, p. 62.) All bequests to persons or institutions other than necessary heirs were taxed 10 percent by the province of São Paulo. One of the ways the law was enforced was by encouraging denunciations of families that had not made inventários at the death of a parent. This happened in the case of José Rodrigues Machado, whose inventário was made in 1868, 30 years after his death (AMJ, 2° O. da F., no. 549), and in the case of Doctor Hypolito José Soares de Souza, whose death was reported by a creditor in 1869 (AMJ, 2° O. da F., no. 570).

10. In the 44 volumes of the published inventários, only two women knew how to sign. See Alcântara Machado, Vida e morte, p. 103. Some men had little education and only knew how to sign. For example, Clemente Alveres, who did sign, once declared that he did not know how to figure, fazer contas.

11. Diretoría geral, Recensamento do Brasil, pt. 4, pp. xvi–xvii.

12. Catharina Gotfriet, 1852, AMJ, 2° O. da F., no. 219.

13. José Pereira, 1862, AMJ, 2° O. da F., no. 411.

14. Documentos com que o illustrissimo, p. 23.

15. An exception: Joanna da Cunha's heirs declared a farm on someone else's land (1766, AESP, INP, #ord. 544, c. 67).

16. Canabrava, "Uma economia," p. 101.

17. See Dean, "Latifundia," and Costa, "Land Policies." Usage did not change immediately, however, for many continued to squat on land and even sell their "rights" to such land. Agregados also continued to have rights.

18. Words used in a sesmaria granted June 26, 1726: "and he must not sell the land without His Majesty's explicit authorization" (Sesmarias [1720–1736], vol. 3).

19. Dariz Abreu, "A terra e a lei." The law that land given in sesmaria must be cultivated was specifically applied to Brazil in the Alvará of January 5, 1785.

20. Novais, *Portugal e Brasil*, p. 262.

21. *Ordenações*, Liv. 4, Tit. 103 and 107.

22. Decreto de 23 de maio de 1821, about freedom against arbitrary arrest, later incorporated into the Imperial Constitution of 1824, art. 179, together with other individual liberties and the protection of private property. See Trípoli, *História*, vol. 4, pp. 129, 140, 162, and 179–80; see also Buarque de Holanda, *História*, vol. 3, p. 254.

23. Trípoli, *História*, vol. 2, p. 143.

24. *Ordenações*, Liv. 4, Tit. 107, n. 1.

25. The birthplaces of the deceased in the nineteenth-century sample (for the 170 known) were: the city or province of São Paulo, 144 (84.7 percent); other regions of Brazil, 8 (4.7 percent); Portugal, 5 (2.9 percent); Germany, 10 (5.9 percent); Denmark, 1 (0.6 percent); Italy, 1 (0.6 percent); and Uruguay, 1 (0.6 percent). The total sample was 178 people, of whom 8 had unknown birthplaces.

26. João Soares de Camargo, 1858, AMJ, 2° O. da F., no. 324.

27. Five of the eleven inventários of Germans in the sample were of families living in rural areas: Jacob Heindrich, 1862, AMJ, 2° O. da F., no. 413; João Hattenback, 1866, AMJ, 2° O. da F., no. 497; João Julio, 1863, AMJ, 2° O. da F., no. 431; João Pedro Schmidt, 1868, AMJ, 2° O. da F., no. 547; and Maria Margarida Kristin e seu marido, 1864, AMJ, 2° O. da F., no. 472.

28. Canabrava, "A repartição."

29. See Petrone, *A lavoura canavieira*, p. 82, on the importance of *matas*, or bush, for fuel for sugarmills, leading to the search for new lands when existing matas were used up.

30. There were three coffee plantations, 24 mule-breeding establishments, and a few small sugarmills in the rural areas of the city of São Paulo in 1823. Taunay, *História da cidade . . . sob o império*, p. 179.

31. There were 48 estates that owned mules out of 142 estates in which we have the necessary information, and they owned from 1 mule to 96, an average of 10.

32. Of 169 estates in which the kinds of livestock owned are known, 116 owned horses, mules, oxen, or cattle.

33. Of 111 estates where the kinds of crops planted are known, 66 (59 percent) planted subsistence crops.

34. Kuznesof, "Household Composition," p. 187.

35. Levi, *A família Prado*, p. 58.

36. This category was used to classify heads of household in São Paulo in the *Almanak 1858*, together with other categories such as *propietário*, *advogado*, and *vendeiro*.

37. See *Almanak 1858*, p. 108, and Barão de Antonina, 1875, AMJ, 2° O. da F., no. 669. His net estate was worth over 359 contos and he owned 180 contos worth of apólices, or bonds.

38. Wealthy nineteenth-century plantation owners tended to live much of the time in the city and spend only a part of the year on their plantations (Candido, "The Brazilian Family," p. 307).

39. For example, the inventário of José Rodrigues da Silva Menezes, 1859, AMJ, 2° O. da F., no. 344, lists a house beside the Monastery of São Bento, in a state of some disrepair, worth 1:500$000, and seven quartos, contiguous to the above house, each with one door and a piece of garden, worth 1:750$000. This practice of renting

semi-independent rooms had begun in the eighteenth century in Buenos Aires (Johnson and Socolow, "Population and Space").

40. José Francisco de Andrade, 1866, AMJ, 2° O. da F., no. 506.

41. José Gomes Segurado e sua mulher D. Anna Benedicta de Azevedo Segurado, 1866, AMJ, 2° O. da F., no. 509.

42. See *Almanak 1858*, p. 107.

43. Dr. João Thomaz de Mello, 1859, AMJ, 2° O. da F., no. 357. Their gross estate was over six contos, with debts exceeding that amount. The trip cost 35$000 for the ship from Rio to Santos, plus 27$000 for animals and men to take her from Santos to São Paulo. To get an idea of these prices, the monthly rent for their two-story house was 40$000, and their horse and saddle was appraised for 50$000. Among their unpaid bills was tuition for two daughters, 16$000 per month, and 150$000 owed a doctor for 30 visits to the sick man at the court in Rio de Janeiro.

44. See Candido, "The Brazilian Family," p. 307.

45. See *Codigo penal do imperio*, art. 179, par. 20; also Trípoli, *História*, vol. 2, p. 216.

46. Law of October 31, 1831. See *Colecção das Leis*; Trípoli, *História*, vol. 2, p. 316. See also *Codigo commercial do imperio*, pt. 1, tit. 1, cap. I, art. 1, par. 3, note explaining that the *filho-família* over 21 no longer existed legally, since parents' legal authority automatically ceased when children reached 21.

47. Manoel Pacheco Gato, 1715, IT, vol. 26.

48. "Autuação de uma petição de João Pacheco Gato, Manoel Pacheco Gato, Francisco Xavier Paes, and José Gonçalves da Costa," IT, vol. 26.

49. Antonio Azevedo, *Primeira parte*, p. 637.

50. Article 12 of *Código de posturas 1829*, as cited in Canabrava, "Evolução," p. 51.

51. *Ordenações*, Liv. 4, Tit. 97, par. 16.

52. Emancipation was a legal process that in colonial times only concerned people with property. Both men and women who had no property left their families easily to try their fortune elsewhere or set up their own households (as can be seen in the great number of female-headed households in late eighteenth-century São Paulo; see Kuznesof, "The Role of the Female-Headed Household").

53. Suzanna Rodrigues de Arzão, 1754, AESP, INP, #ord. 542, c. 55.

54. Caetano Soares Viana, 1757, AESP, INP, #ord. 538, c. 61, and #ord. 535, c. 58.

55. Maria de Lima de Siqueira, 1769, AESP, INP, #ord. 545, c. 68.

56. For example, see Justificação de Manoel Pires (emancipation from his widowed mother), 1673, IT, vol. 26.

57. *Codigo commercial do imperio*, pt. 1, tit. I, cap. I, art. 1, par. 3, note commenting on *Ordenações*, Liv. 4, Tit. 50, par. 3.

CHAPTER 8

1. Polanyi, *The Great Transformation*; Tawney, *Religion and the Rise of Capitalism*.

2. For example, José da Silva Ferrão, 1763, AESP, INP, #ord. 541, c. 64, and #ord. 54, c. 63.

3. A detailed inventário of a dry goods store is in Ignacia Maria Rodrigues, 1768, AESP, INP, #ord. 546, c. 69: "990 covados of different colored serge, at 520 réis a covado, 514$000, 74 more pink covados, 640 réis per covado, etc."

4. D. Cándida Maria Miquelina de Oliveira, 1859, AMJ, 2° O. da F., no. 352. When the widower died five years later, the business had still not been liquidated.

5. *Codigo commercial do imperio*, section 7, art. 335, par. 4, n. 491.

6. See *Ordenações*, Liv. 4, Tit. 44, p. 828, n. 6. See also Sweigart, *Coffee Factorage*, p. 91, for a partnership liquidated at the death of the main silent partner.

7. *Codigo commercial do imperio*, cap. III, section 1, art. 308, n. 431.

8. Sweigart, *Coffee Factorage*, p. 254.

9. They required legislative permission, however. See Kuznesof, "Property Law," p. 6.

10. *Codigo commercial do imperio*, section 7, "Da dissolução da sociedade," n. 1272.

11. Alfredo Ellis, Jr., *Um parlamentar paulista*, pp. 80–83.

12. Bento José Martins da Cunha, 1858, AMJ, 2° O. da F., no. 343. In *Almanak 1858*, p. 123, the partnership is listed as one of five saddle-makers in the center of São Paulo: "Martins & Sobrinho, canto da rua do Ouvidor."

13. Luis Bernardo Pinto Ferraz, 1856, AMJ, 2° O. da F., no. 284.

14. Freitas, *Paulistas*, p. 180.

15. Sweigart, *Coffee Factorage*, chap. 3.

16. Antonio Bento de Andrade, 1868, AMJ, 2° O. da F., no. 553.

17. When Anna Josepha de Lima died in 1864 (AMJ, 2° O. da F., no. 464), her husband declared that he had inherited a part of a sitio worth three contos from his father, but he did not know how much was his. In Anna Francisca Bueno's inventário (1867, AMJ, 2° O. da F., no. 531), the property listed included: "1 part of the lands inherited from João Carvallo dos Santos (still undivided) 500$000, 4/6 parts of the land bought from . . . (still undivided) 800$000." In Maria José's inventário (1859, AMJ, 2° O. da F., no. 344): "1 part of the large fenced site inherited from her parents, 50$000."

18. D. Anna Maria de Souza Queiros, 1867, AMJ, 2° O. da F., no. 520.

19. The juizo de órfãos in the seventeenth century kept the funds belonging to orphans and lent them out at 8 percent interest, in that way acting as a bank. Inventários from that century frequently contain pages and pages documenting who had borrowed the money belonging to an estate, with what security, and when it was returned. See also Alcântara Machado, *Vida e morte*, p. 146.

20. Pedro Fernandes, 1653, *IT*, vol. 12, pp. 394, 436–38.

21. The source is my sample. I used the distribution of debtors only from the seventeenth-century sample because it is the only one in which masses and funeral expenses were not considered debts. They came out of the terça, whereas in the eighteenth century funeral expenses were included in the category "debts," so that practically everybody in the sample had outstanding debts. By the mid-nineteenth century, some estates paid the funeral expenses first so that they did not even appear in the inventário, while others included them in the outstanding debts.

22. Levy, *História financeira*, pp. 94–100. She found that the interest charged for merchandise sold with credit usually went from 8 to 12 percent, but in some promissory notes it reached 30 percent.

23. In his inventário, only half of each credit carried since his wife's death was credited to his estate, since the other half had been credited to his wife's heirs (José Rodrigues Pereira, 1769, AESP, 1° Of., no. 14.533).

24. Buarque de Holanda, Monções, p. 116.

25. Maria de Lima de Siqueira, 1769, AESP, INP, #ord. 545, c. 68.

26. Silva Leme, Genealogia, vol. 1, p. 192.

27. Levi, A família Prado, p. 53.

28. Brigadeiro Luis Antonio de Souza was a merchant who functioned as a banker (see Taunay, História colonial, vol. 3, pp. 313–20).

29. Alcântara Machado, Vida e morte, p. 129. In the United States the complete prohibition of the imprisonment of debtors did not come about until the second half of the nineteenth century. See Coleman, Debtors and Creditors in America, pp. 249–69.

30. Loans from the juizo de órfãos in the seventeenth century were secured with words in the following tenor, "for which he obliged his person and goods, both movable and immovable, which he now possesses or may later possess" (Simão Sutil Oliveira, 1650, IT, vol. 15, p. 275).

31. Ordenações e leys do reyno, Liv. 3, Tit. 41.

32. See Codigo commercial do imperio, tit. 13, cap. I, including Lei hypothecas n. 1237 de 1864, art. 10; and cap. II. See also Sweigart, Coffee Factorage, chap. 4, esp. pp. 125–31.

33. This was also still the case in Rio de Janeiro. Sweigart, Coffee Factorage, p. 143, has a table showing that 31.6 percent of the mortgages on coffee plantations registered in Rio in 1878 were held by individuals or coffee factors and the rest were held by mortgage banks.

34. Antonio de Paiva Azevedo, 1849, AMJ, 2° Ofício Civel, c. 185, whose only son, Tenente José Elias de Paiva Azevedo, is listed as a capitalista in the 1858 Almanak, p. 108.

35. Commendador José Manoel de França, 1853, AMJ, 2° O. da F., no. 243. Also, Captain José de Araujo Novaes (1865, AMJ, 2° O. da F., no. 483) owned a farm in Cutia, two-thirds of an important coffee plantation in Guaratinguetá, several houses in Sorocaba, and slaves, but 79 contos out of his estate of 136 contos were letters of credit and promissory notes at 12 percent. Other examples of specialization in banking are the Barão do Tieté (1877, AMJ, 2° O. da F., no. 711) who was listed as a capitalista in the 1858 Almanak, p. 108, and Martinho Prado (see Levi, A família Prado, p. 162), who in 1864 received interest amounting to 35 contos, an enormous amount of money when we compare it with the 183 inventários I studied, of which only 21 had gross estates of over 35 contos.

36. For the creation of banks see Taunay, História colonial, vol. 3, pp. 313–30, and Foot and Leonardi, História da indústria, pp. 73–79. There was a branch of the Bank of Brazil in São Paulo by the mid-nineteenth century and several private commercial banks such as the Banco Mauá e Cia., Banco Teodoro Richert, and the Caza Bancaria de Bernardo Gavião, Ribeiro e Gavião (banks mentioned in Manoel José de Moraes, 1868, AMJ, 2° O. da F., no. 541, and José de Araujo Novaes, 1865, AMJ, 2° O. da F., no. 483).

37. Alexandre Antonio dos Reis, 1867, AMJ, 1° O. da F., no. 143. (He and his wife had made a joint will in which they left each other the remainder of their terça in view of the efforts they had both put in to develop their business.) Other inventários

in which credits were the debts of clients: Maria Robertola das Dores, 1862, AMJ, 2°
O. da F., no. 416, and D. Leocardia Maria de Jesus, 1862, AMJ, 2° O. da F., no. 421.
38. Levi, *A família Prado*, p. 58.

CHAPTER 9

1. Maria Clara Pedroza, 1860, AMJ, 2° O. da F., no. 381.
2. That is, 48 out of 55 families.
3. That is, 30 out of 47 families.
4. That so few nineteenth-century families gave all their married daughters dowries does not appear to be related to demographic changes. The mean number of daughters and married daughters holds remarkably steady for the samples of the three centuries (see accompanying table).

	17th cent.	18th cent.	19th cent.
Daughters per family (mean)	3.51	3.52	3.36
Married daughters (mean)	2.17	2.35	1.87

5. For the eighteenth century see Table 8 in Chapter 5. The nineteenth-century average would be considerably less if I had not counted the slave that Josefa Joaquina Bueno received as a dowry, for the current price of her slave was over seven times the value of her *legítima*.
6. Anna Roza de Moraes, 1860, AMJ, 2° O. da F., no. 362.
7. Barão de Limeira, 1873, AMJ, 2° O. da F., no. 622. The total amount spent on the four dowries was 160:066$000, while his net estate amounted to 2,751:537$000.
8. The source is my sample: 36 inventários in the eighteenth century and 48 in the nineteenth in which both the net estate and total value of dowries given are known.
9. My finding is corroborated by the nineteenth-century jurist T. de Freitas, who states in a note to *Ordenações*, Liv. 4, Tit. 97, art. 119, that people no longer used the right given by the law to refuse to inherit.
10. We will define means of production as the natural resources and tools that labor uses to make a product to be consumed or exchanged. Means of consumption, on the other hand, are usually consumed, yet they can also be sold, thereby providing for another type of consumption or becoming the capital necessary to buy the means of production.
11. Labor is of course always a factor of production, but Marx considered slaves a part of the means of production themselves (Marx, *Capital*, vol. 1, p. 714).
12. See Schneider, "Trousseau as Treasure."
13. Alfredo Ellis, Jr., *Um parlamentar paulista*, p. 87.
14. For example, the dowry received in 1758 by Anna Maria da Horta had as its trousseau: a scarlet damask bedspread; another bedspread; a bed canopy with curtains of fine cotton with lace; a bed with a wool mattress; three pairs of sheets with pillowcases; two tablecloths with twelve napkins; six towels; six silver spoons and six silver

forks; and two jacaranda chests, one large and one small. See Catharina da Silva Dorta, 1774, AESP, INP, #ord. 548, c. 71, and #ord. 551, c. 74.

15. Anna Rita de Oliveira, 1858, AMJ, 2° O. da F., no. 335; Barão de Limeira, 1873, AMJ, 2° O. da F., no. 622; João Biemback, 1855, AMJ, 2° O. da F., no. 268.

16. Ignacio Correa de Lemos, 1787, AESP, 1° Of., no. 14.412 and no. 14.768.

17. What I have categorized as money in seventeenth-century dowries almost always consisted of commodities for sale.

18. I have found several nineteenth-century testators that manumitted female slaves because they had been very "productive"—that is, produced many children.

19. For example, the daughters of the Barão de Limeira, Note 7 above, received about 70 percent of their dowries in cash. The averages used are of only those dowries that included money and in which the amount is known: eight for the eighteenth century and ten for the nineteenth. I found only three dowries in the seventeenth century in which both the value of the dowry and the amount of commodities for sale are known; the average for those is 51 percent.

20. Pedro José Machado, 1861, AMJ, 2° O. da F., no. 407.

21. Maria Francisca do Rosario, 1851, AMJ, 2° O. da F., no. 206.

22. Captain-Major Caetano Soares Viana, 1760, AESP, INP, #ord. 538, c. 61, and #ord. 535, c. 58.

23. *Ordenações*, Liv. 4, Tit. 97, par. 7.

24. Bento José Martins da Cunha, 1858, 2° O. da F., no. 343.

25. José Mathias Ferreira de Abreu, 1851, AMJ, 2° O. da F., no. 200. Fewer Paulistas made wills in the nineteenth century than in colonial times, a fact that I attribute to the process of secularization of society. The most important part of seventeenth-century wills was the testator's statement of faith and the religious bequests he or she made from the terça. Deceased who made wills in the seventeenth century: 41 (out of 48; 85.4 percent); in the eighteenth century: 41 (out of 68; 60.3 percent); and in the nineteenth century: 38 (out of 178; 21.3 percent).

CHAPTER 10

1. *Ordenações*, Liv. 4, Tit. 88, par. 1, n. 1 (for Assento 5° de 9 de abril de 1772); also *Additamentos ao Liv. 4*, Lei de 19 de junho de 1775. The scope of these laws was limited somewhat by the law of November 29, 1775, that empowered judicial authorities to allow a marriage they judged convenient without parents' consent, since some parents refused even good marriages for their children, and the law of October 6, 1784, that permitted persons who had reached the age of 25 to marry without their parents' consent, without having to wait to be judicially emancipated. The 1775 law had applied to sons and daughters who were filhos-família of whatever age, since emancipation did not come automatically upon reaching the age of 25.

2. See Arrom, *The Women*, pp. 69, 77.

3. See Rebelo, *Discurso sobre*. Flandrin, *Families in Former Times*, pp. 130–35, notes that in France, from the sixteenth century on, patriarchal power over children increased, and that this is generally attributed to the revival of Roman law and the rise of the absolute state. He also shows that Protestants were scandalized at the Catholic

insistence on the right of people to marry without their father's consent, and explains that when the Council of Trent reaffirmed this right, it was concerned principally with ending forced religious vocations.

4. *Ordenações, Additamentos ao Liv. 4*, Lei de 19 de junho de 1775.

5. Dantas, *O Amor em Portugal*, p. 71. For the way in which love became the pre-eminent decider of marriage in England, see Trumbach, *The Rise of the Egalitarian Family*.

6. *Ordenações*, Liv. 4, Tit. 88, par. 3.

7. *Ordenações, Additamentos ao Liv. 4*, Assento 5° de 19 de abril de 1772.

8. *Ordenações, Additamentos ao Liv. 4*, Lei de 17 de agosto de 1761, *Regulando os dotes das filhas das pessôas da primeira grandesa*, pars. 1–7.

9. *Codigo penal do imperio*, art. 247.

10. Lewin found families of Paraíba arranging their sons' marriages until the beginning of the twentieth century (see *Politics*, p. 198).

11. The Catholic church always asked both bride and groom whether they were marrying voluntarily, and this requirement was reinforced at the Council of Trent (1545–63). See Seed, *To Love*, pp. 32–34.

12. Western society adapted to the new emphasis on love, finding ways to manipulate behavior so people still tended to marry their peers. See Goode, "The Theoretical Importance of Love."

13. See Brotero, *A família Monteiro*, pp. 116, 120–21; Levi, *A família Prado*, p. 64.

14. Brotero, *A família Monteiro*, p. 122; Levi, *A família Prado*, p. 65.

15. Alfredo Ellis, Jr., *Um parlamentar paulista*, pp. 50–51, 61, 75.

16. Gaspar Cubas o velho, 1648, *IT*, vol. 37.

17. Cándida Maria Miquelina de Oliveira, 1859, AMJ, 2° O. da F., no. 352.

18. *Codigo penal do imperio*, art. 247. Both this article and the law of 1775 were cited by a lawyer in a petition to marry in 1855 (Cap. Joaquim Theodoro Leite Penteado, 1855, AMJ, 2° O. da F., no. 259).

19. Alcântara Machado, *Vida e morte*, p. 153.

20. Angela de o Campo e Medina, 1641, *IT*, vol. 13, p. 99.

21. Taques, *Nobiliarquia*, vol. 1, p. 139.

22. Gertrudes Lourenço de Jesus, 1752, AESP, INP, #ord. 527, c. 50.

23. Francisco de Godoy Preto, 1752, AESP, INP, #ord. 550, c. 73, and #ord. 523, c. 46.

24. This interpretation is contrary to Seed's, in *To Love* (see esp. pp. 227–33). She argues that after the 1776 Royal Pragmatic there was in Mexico greater control of children's marriages by their parents than in the sixteenth and seventeenth centuries. I have concluded that in previous centuries the dowry served as the instrument of control by the older generation, not only over women, but mainly over men, because men required a dowry to marry. Dowry was a system of economic inducement to get men to marry the right kind of person (of course, some men and women still made their own choices, and it is this part of the population that Seed studies). Once men had other ways of supporting a wife than through a dowry, they became increasingly independent in their marriage choices, and laws became necessary to continue controlling marriage. That these laws were ineffective is borne out in my nineteenth-century sample in which so many daughters married before their older sisters.

25. Silva, *Sistema*, p. 66.

26. Mello, *Carta de guia de casados*, p. 8.

27. Hermann, "Evolução da estrutura social," p. 41. Of the majority of marriages—between younger women and older men—44 percent had more than ten years' difference.

28. Silva, *Sistema*, pp. 67–68.

29. See petitions in Antonio Francisco Lima, 1758, AESP, INP, #ord. 535, c. 58; Balthazar Rodrigues Fam, 1758, AESP, INP, #ord. 536, c. 59; Izabel Dultra e seu marido, 1748, AESP, 1° Of., #ord. 618, c. 6; João Rodrigues Barboza, 1771, AESP, INP, #ord. 548, c. 71; José Rodrigues Pereira, 1769, AESP, 1° Of., #ord. 686, c. 74; and Maria Rodrigues Pires, 1751, AESP, INP, #ord. 525, c. 48.

30. Pedro Ortiz de Camargo, 1764, AESP, INP, #ord. 542, c. 65.

31. He did marry. See Balthazar Rodrigues Fam, 1758, AESP, INP, #ord. 536, c. 59; also Metcalf, "Families of Planters," pp. 116–17.

32. Izabel Dultra e seu marido Estevão de Lima do Prado, 1748, AESP, 1° Of., #ord. 618, c. 6.

33. Autuação de uma petição de José de Góes e Moraes e Anna Ribeiro de Almeida, 1710, IT, vol. 27.

34. Anna Eufrosina Jordão de Araujo e seu marido Dr. Raphael de Araujo Ribeiro, 1865, AMJ, 2° O. da F., no. 485. The date of the first petition was June 5, 1876, and of the second, June 20, 1876. She married in January of the following year.

35. Bento Joaquim de Souza e Castro, 1857, AMJ, 2° O. da F., no. 320; Joaquim Mathias Bicudo, 1862, AMJ, 2° O. da F., no. 412; Luis Antonio Machado, 1865, AMJ, 2° O. da F., no. 486.

36. Firmiano Leme da Cunha, 1851, AMJ, 2° O. da F., no. 210.

37. The deceased of the seventeenth-century sample had 341 children, of which 205 carried their father's name. Besides 23 children with no surname, there were 392 children in the eighteenth-century sample of which 257 used their father's name. Besides 186 with no surname, there were 702 children in the nineteenth century of which 575 bore their father's name.

38. See *Ordenações*, Liv. 4, Tit. 88, n. 1.

39. *Ordenações*, Liv. 4, Tit. 97, par. 4, p. 974, n. 1.

40. Professions also gave sons greater leverage in arranging their own marriages. See Lewin, *Politics*, pp. 195–96.

41. Caio Prado, Jr., *The Colonial Background*, p. 411; and Ramos, "Marriage and the Family," pp. 208–15.

42. See Marcílio, "Crescimento," p. 157. Arrom, in *The Women*, p. 120, shows that the proportion of never-married in Mexico City also decreased from 19.5 percent of men and 16.6 percent of women over 40 in 1790 to 8.4 percent of men and 12.3 percent of women over 40 in 1848.

43. Zaira Americana, in *Mostra as immensas vantagens*, lamented that there appeared to be fewer marriages in Brazil than in Argentina and Uruguay, and she correlates it with the continued custom of dowry in Brazil. Since she was obviously writing for the elites, it was probably among the elites that she observed fewer marriages. Some families who were willing to give dowries might have had trouble marrying off the daughters at a time when men were more frequently marrying for love.

44. Sandra Graham, *House and Street*, table 10, p. 192.

45. Silva, *Sistema*, p. 98, found few *contratos de dote e arras* in colonial São Paulo.
46. *Ordenações*, Liv. 4, Tit. 46.
47. Bevilaqua, *Direito da família*, pp. 184–86.
48. Silva, *Sistema*, pp. 99–100; Samara, "O dote."
49. João Correa de Lemos, 1731, AESP, 1° Of., #ord. 668, c. 68.
50. Guarda Mor Francisco de Godoy Preto, 1750, AESP, INP, #ord. 550, c. 73, and #ord. 523, c. 46; and Ana Maria de Silveira (his first wife), 1728, AESP, INP, #ord. 508, c. 31.
51. Joanna Soares de Siqueira, 1776, AESP, INP, #ord. 548, c. 71. She was knowledgeable about her affairs, listing precisely what her property consisted of and also the amount of capital she had given her second husband to administer, adding that he should duly account for how he had used it and the profits received. He may not have been very wealthy, as she also left him 30$000 for his funeral expenses.
52. Autos Civis de Petição para Consentimento de Casamento que ha o Alferes João Carlos da Silva Rangel, 1853, AMJ, 2° O. da F., no. 244.
53. See José Maria de Souza Queiroz, 1868, AMJ, 2° O. da F., no. 532, and D. Anna Maria de Souza Queiroz, 1867, AMJ, 2° O. da F., no. 520.
54. Samara, "O dote," pp. 42–45.
55. Ibid., pp. 45–46. Samara shows how, though the amount the bride received was called *arras*, it was not in fact arras because arras presupposes a dowry. Instead she considers it *dotalício*, an institution for nobles.
56. Ibid., p. 48.
57. Their grandson, the historian Alfredo Ellis, Jr., does not appear to have known about the marriage contract between his grandparents, for he wonders why Dr. William Ellis did not seem to inherit as much as his brothers-in-law when their father-in-law died (*Um parlamentar paulista*, p. 22). Since the contract stipulated that any inheritance received would remain separate, the widower was not his father-in-law's heir as he would have been if he and his wife had had community property.
58. Maria do Carmo Ellis, 1867, AMJ, 2° O. da F., no. 528. As she did in fact predecease him, her possessions—a slave, some jewels, and a thirteen-conto promissory note her brother held at interest—were inherited by her children.
59. Although a premarital contract could arrange a system of property other than community property, it could not disinherit necessary heirs (see *Ordenações*, Liv. 4, Tit. 70, about the rights of children as heirs).
60. Francisco Arnelung, 1858, AMJ, 2° O. da F., no. 328, and D. Maria Elizabeth Schuenck, 1856, AMJ, 2° O. da F., no. 281.
61. Luis Manoel da Paixão Branco, 1866, AMJ, 2° O. da F., no. 507.
62. Maria das Dores, 1860, AMJ, 2° O. da F., no. 374.
63. Joaquim Elias da Silva, 1863, AMJ, 2° O. da F., no. 430.
64. Antonio Francisco Baruel, 1859, AMJ, 2° O. da F., no. 351-A.
65. The nineteenth-century jurist Teixeira de Freitas says in *Ordenações*, Liv. 4, Tit. 47, n. 5, that husbands routinely dowered wives who had not received dowries.
66. See Samara, "O dote," p. 48.
67. Bento Joaquim de Souza e Castro, 1857, AMJ, 2° O. da F., no. 320. He is listed under "Proprietarios e Capitalistas" in *Almanak 1857*, p. 132. His estate was worth 43 contos, and he might have married with this contract because of his earlier marriage in Portugal, which had been duly annulled, and his first wife remarried. By

stipulating that his second wife was not *meeira* they might avoid litigation after his death that sought to invalidate their marriage.

CHAPTER 11

1. See Maxwell, "Pombal." For an excellent analysis of the influence of the ideas of the Enlightenment on Portuguese society and government, see Novais, *Portugal e Brasil,* esp. pp. 213–24.

2. *Ordenações, Additamentos ao Liv. 4,* Lei de 17 de agosto de 1761, *Regulando os dotes das filhas das pessôas da primeira grandesa,* pars. 1–7. Silva summarizes this law in "A legislação pombalina."

3. *Ordenações, Additamentos ao Liv. 4,* Decreto de 17 de julio de 1778.

4. *Ordenações, Additamentos ao Liv. 4,* Alvara de 4 de fevereiro de 1765.

5. *Ordenações, Additamentos ao Liv. 4,* Lei de 17 de agosto de 1761, n. 1.

6. *Ordenações, Additamentos ao Liv. 4,* Lei de 17 de agosto de 1761.

7. Pombal himself appears to have been married under this law, for his wife brought no dowry to the marriage, nor did she inherit from her family. See Samara, "O dote," pp. 47–48.

8. *Ordenações, Additamentos ao Liv. 4,* Lei de 17 de agosto de 1761.

9. See Chapter 9.

10. *Ordenações, Liv. 4,* Tit. 97, par. 4. The code was entirely sex-neutral in this respect, for it defined the privileged category as a gift given at marriage, whether a dowry to a daughter or a gift to a son.

11. In 1821 slaves cost between 250$000 and 440$000, by 1855 they cost between 500$000 and 1:000$000, and by 1875 the maximum price had reached 2:500$000. Food prices had also risen. See Costa, *Da Senzala à colonia,* pp. 40 and 117–18. For inflation, see Buescu, "A Inflação brasileira" and Onody, *A inflação no Brasil,* chap. 1.

12. Manoella Joaquina Gomes de Assiz, 1865, AMJ, 2° O. da F., no. 493. An example of the valorization of land can be found in the *inventário* of the Barão de Antonina, 1875, AMJ, 2° O. da F., no. 669. Some plots of land he owned in the Villa of Apiahy showed the following increases in value:

Year bought	Value	Appraised value in 1875
1849	120$000	400$000
1849	150$000	600$000
1850	60$000	400$000
1853	140$000	250$000
1853	600$000	630$000
1857	80$000	150$000
1857	132$000	250$000

13. Francisco Vieira de Paula, 1857, AMJ, 2° O. da F., no. 308.

14. Job Antonio de Moraes, 1868, AMJ, 2° O. da F., no. 543. Each heir received 1:000$000 worth of land, later sold for 1:300$000. If the 600$000 dowry had come in

à colação, the daughter and her husband would have received only 400$000 worth of the property and only 120$000 profit when it was sold.

15. Dean, *Rio Claro*, p. 74, shows that giving slave children at marriage was a frequent practice in Rio Claro plantation society.

16. Gertrudes Branca de Siqueira, 1863, AMJ, 2° O. da F., no. 448.

17. Alexandre José Rodrigues, 1850, AMJ, 2° O. da F., no. 184.

18. Anna Roza de Moraes, 1860, AMJ, 2° O. da F., no. 362.

19. I counted these as dowry in the data set; of the 47 families in the sample who gave their daughters dowries, six considered them "debts."

20. *Ordenações*, Liv. 4, Tit. 97, par. 1.

21. José Manoel Godinho, 1863, AMJ, 2° O. da F., no. 441.

22. José Domingues Moreira, 1861, AMJ, 2° O. da F., no. 391.

23. *Codigo civil*, art. 236, established the continuing validity of dowries or gifts made to sons when they married or when they established themselves separately.

24. Alencar, *Senhora*, pp. 14–15.

25. Alencar, *A viuvinha*.

26. As quoted in Hahner, *Women in Latin American History*, p. 53, from *O Sexo Feminino* (Campanha), Oct. 25, 1873, pp. 1–2.

27. Americana, *Mostra as immensas vantagens*, p. 5.

28. Ibid., pp. 101–2.

29. Ibid., pp. 107–8.

30. Ibid., pp. 108–9.

31. John Mawe, quoted by Maria Carvalho Franco in *Homens Livres*, p. 135.

32. Thomas and Znaniecki, *The Polish Peasant*, vol. 1, p. 117.

33. Hahner, *Women in Latin American History*, p. 53.

34. *Documentos com que o illustrissimo*, p. 23.

35. For example, Antonio Bento de Andrade, 1868, AMJ, 2° O. da F., no. 553. The daughters had not learned to read and write because they were too far from school, and the two minor sons had not learned, one because he was deaf, and the other because his father had wanted him to help on the farm instead.

36. They were probably also in the more urban families. Dean, in *Rio Claro*, p. 113, found that in the 1850's in rural areas eight out of ten planters' wives did not know how to sign their names.

37. See Table 15 in Chapter 7.

38. Bevilaqua, *Direito da familia*, chap. 7, p. 229. He couched it in universal terms, but the sequence he described is precisely the one described for Europe by Hughes in "From Brideprice to Dowry."

39. See, for example, Kaplan, *The Marriage Bargain*, p. 3.

40. Rubin, "The Traffic in Women."

41. AESP, Livro de Notas 1640–1642. See also Alcântara Machado, *Vida e morte*, p. 157, on the dowry promised his daughter by Garcia Rodrigues o velho.

42. In England the marriage portion was also an inducement for men to marry (see Stone, *Crisis of the Aristocracy*, pp. 599 and 621).

43. Lockhart and Otte, eds., *Letters*, p. 129.

44. See Mello, *Carta de guia de casados*, p. 223.

45. See, for example, Taques, *Nobiliarquia*, vol. 1, p. 139.

46. AESP, Livros de Notas, #ord. 459, c. 1, Notas Parnaíba 1685, 8/22/1685.

CONCLUSION

1. *Colecção das Leis*, Law of October 6, 1835. See also Trípoli, *História*, vol. 2, p. 272.

2. Quoted by Ariès, *Centuries of Childhood*, p. 121.

3. Friedl, in "The Position of Women," documents the greater power within marriage of rural endowed wives in Greece compared to urban unendowed ones. Hughes says that families "secured a daughter's inheritance in a dowry that gave her rights and status in her husband's home" ("From Brideprice to Dowry," p. 42).

4. See Leacock, "Introduction"; Sacks, "Engels Revisited"; and Ryan, *Womanhood in America*.

5. Montesquieu, in *The Spirit of Laws*, p. 2, describes marriage as an institution that serves to oblige husbands to support children.

6. Hermenegildo Almeida, "Direito romano."

7. *Colecção das Leis*, Decree no. 181 of January 24, 1890, art. 56, pars. 4–5. This law also decreed obligatory civil marriage.

8. See *Ordenações*, Liv. 4, Tit. 99. If the parents separated, the mother was responsible for raising the child until he or she was three, and the father thereafter.

9. *Codigo civil*, art. 240 and 233. See also Hernani, *Direitos da mulher*, p. 70, and Pimentel, "Communicação docente," p. 39.

BIBLIOGRAPHY

Portuguese orthography has changed more than once in the twentieth century. I have retained the original spelling in the titles of books published in the nineteenth or early twentieth century.

Abreu, Dariz Bizzocchi de Lacerda. "A terra e a lei: Estudo de comportamentos socio-econômicos em São Paulo nos séculos XVI e XVII." Master's thesis, University of São Paulo, 1981.

Abreu, J. Capistrano de. *Caminhos antigos e povoamento do Brasil*. Rio de Janeiro: Briguiet, 1960.

Albuquerque, Rui H. P. L. *Capital comercial, indústria têxtil e produção agrícola*. São Paulo-Brasília: Hucitec, 1982.

Alcântara Machado, José de. *Vida e morte do bandeirante*. Belo Horizonte: Itatiaia; São Paulo: Universidade de São Paulo, 1980.

Alden, Dauril. "Black Robes Versus White Settlers: The Struggle for 'Freedom of the Indians' in Colonial Brazil." In Howard Peckham and Charles Gibson, eds., *Attitudes of Colonial Powers Toward the American Indian*. Salt Lake City: University of Utah Press, 1969.

Alencar, José de. *A viuvinha*. São Paulo: Atica, 1981.

———. *Senhora*. São Paulo: Atica, 1982.

Almanak administrativo, mercantil e industrial da provincia de São Paulo para o anno de 1857. São Paulo: Imparcial, 1856.

Almanak administrativo, mercantil e industrial da provincia de São Paulo para o anno de 1858. São Paulo: Imparcial, 1857.

Almeida, Cândido Mendes de, ed. *Codigo philippino ou ordenações do reino de Portugal.* 14th ed. Rio de Janeiro: Typographia do Instituto Philomatico, 1870.

Almeida, Hermenegildo Militão de. "Direito romano: O pae e obrigado a dotar a filha emancipada?" *O direito: Revista mensal de legislação, doutrina e jurisprudencia,* Anno X, vol. 29 (1882).

Alvarez Lopez, José Luis, trans. and ed. *Historia del derecho germánico.* Barcelona, 1936.

Amaral, J. J. A. Ginzel de. "Como se constitue o dote." Thesis, Facultade de Direito de São Paulo, 1879.

Americana, Zaira. *Mostra as immensas vantagens que a sociedade inteira obtem da Illustração, Virtudes e Perfeita Educação da mulher como mãi e esposa do homen.* Rio de Janeiro: Dous de Dezembro-de Paula Brito, 1853.

Andrade e Silva, Raul de, ed. *A evolução urbana em São Paulo.* São Paulo, 1955.

———. "São Paulo nos tempos coloniais." In Andrade e Silva, *A evolução urbana em São Paulo.*

Antonil. *Cultura e opulência do Brasil por suas drogas, e minas.* Recife: Universidade Federal de Pernambuco, 1969.

Ariès, Philippe. *Centuries of Childhood: A Social History of Family Life.* Trans. Robert Baldick. New York: Vintage Books, 1962.

Arrom, Silvia M. "Changes in Mexican Family Law in the Nineteenth Century: The Civil Codes of 1870 and 1884." *Journal of Family History* 10, no. 3 (Fall 1985): 304–17.

———. "Marriage Patterns in Mexico City: 1811." *Journal of Family History* 3, no. 4 (Winter 1978): 376–91.

———. *The Women of Mexico City, 1790–1857.* Stanford, Calif.: Stanford University Press, 1985.

Atas da câmara da villa de São Paulo, 1640–1652. São Paulo: Arquivo Municipal de São Paulo, Publicação Official, 1913.

Azevedo, Antonio Luis de, ed. *Primeira parte das cartas familiares de D. Francisco Manoel de Mello (1608–1668).* Rome, 1644.

Azevedo, Aroldo de. "Vilas e cidades do Brasil colonial." Boletim no. 208. São Paulo: Facultade de Filosofia, Ciências e Letras da Universidade de São Paulo, 1956.

Azevedo, Thales de. "Família, casamento e divórcio no Brasil." *Journal of Inter-American Studies* 3 (1961): 213–37.

Azevedo Marques, Manuel Eufrazio de. *Apontamentos históricos, geográficos, biográficos, estadísticos e noticiosos da província de São Paulo.* 2 vols. São Paulo and Belo Horizonte: Itatiaia, 1980.

Balmori, Diana, and Robert Oppenheimer. "Family Clusters: Generational Nucleation in Nineteenth-Century Argentina and Chile." *Comparative Studies in Society and History* 21, no. 2 (1979): 231–61.

Balmori, Diana, Stuart F. Voss, and Miles Wortman. *Notable Family Networks in Latin America.* Chicago and London: University of Chicago Press, 1984.

Berlinck, Manoel Tosta. "The Structure of the Brazilian Family in the City of São Paulo." Ph.D. diss., Cornell University, 1969.

Bevilaqua, Clovis. *Direito da família*. 1895. 5th ed. Rio de Janeiro: Freitas Bastos, 1933.
Bordieu, Pierre. "Marriage Strategies as Strategies of Social Reproduction." In Elborg Forster and Patricia Ranum, eds., *Family and Society: Selections from the Annales*. Baltimore: Johns Hopkins University Press, 1976.
Bossen, Laurel. "Toward a Theory of Marriage: The Economic Anthropology of Marriage Transactions." *Ethnology* 28, no. 2 (1988): 127–44.
Boxer, Charles R. *The Golden Age of Brazil, 1695–1750*. Berkeley: University of California Press, 1962.
———. *Mary and Misogyny: Women in Iberian Expansion Overseas, 1415–1815. Some Facts, Fancies and Personalities*. London: Duckworth, 1975.
Brading, Charles. *Miners and Merchants in Bourbon Mexico, 1763–1810*. Cambridge, Engl.: Cambridge University Press, 1971.
Brotero, Frederico de Barros. *A família Jordão*. São Paulo: Gráfica Paulista, 1948.
———. *A família Monteiro de Barros*. São Paulo: João Bentivegna, 1951.
Bruno, Ernani Silva. "O que revelam os inventários sobre escravos e gente de serviço." *Revista do Arquivo Municipal* (São Paulo) 188 (1976): 63–70.
Buarque de Holanda, Sergio. *Monções*. São Paulo: Alfa-Omega, 1976.
———. "Movimentos da população em São Paulo no século XVIII." *Revista de Estudos Brasileiros* 1 (1966): 55–111.
———, ed. *História geral da civilização brasileira*. 7 vols. São Paulo: Difel/Difusão, 1981.
Buescu, Mircea. "A Inflação brasileira de 1850 a 1870: Monetarismo e estruturalismo." *Revista Brasileira de Economia* 26, no. 4 (Oct./Dec. 1972): 125–47.
———. *Evolução econômica do Brasil*. Rio de Janeiro: Apec, 1974.
Camara, José Gomes B. *Subsídios para a história do direito patrio*. Rio de Janeiro: Brasiliana, 1965.
Camargo, José Francisco de. *Crescimento da população no estado de São Paulo e seus aspectos econômicos (Ensaio sobre as relações entre a demografia e a economia)*. São Paulo: Universidade de São Paulo, 1952.
Camargo, Monsenhor Paulo Florêncio da Silveira. *A Igreja na história de São Paulo, 1624–1676*. São Paulo: Instituto Paulista de História e Arte Religiosa, 1952–53.
Canabrava, Alice P. "A repartição da terra na capitania de São Paulo, 1813." *Estudos Econômicos* (São Paulo) 2, no. 6 (Dec. 1972): 77–130.
———. "Esboço da história econômica de São Paulo." In Ernani Silva Bruno, ed., *São Paulo, terra e povo*. Porto Alegre: Globo, 1967.
———. "Evolução das posturas municipais de Sant'Ana de Parnaíba, 1829–1867." *Revista de Administração* 3, no. 9 (Mar. 1949): 34–62.
———. "Uma economia de decadência: Os níveis de riqueza na capitania de São Paulo, 1765/1767." *Revista Brasileira de Economia* 26, no. 4 (Oct./Dec. 1972): 95–123.
Cancian, Francesca M., Louis W. Goodman, and Peter H. Smith. "Capitalism, Industrialization and Kinship in Latin America: Major Issues." *Journal of Family History* 3, no. 4 (Winter 1978): 319–36.
Candido, Antônio. "The Brazilian Family." In T. Lynn Smith and Alexander Marchant, eds., *Brazil: Portrait of Half a Continent*. Westport, Conn.: Greenwood Press, 1972.

———. Os Parceiros do Rio Bonito. São Paulo: Duas Cidades, 1979.

Carvalho Franco, Francisco de Assis. Dicionário de bandeirantes e sertanistas do Brasil. São Paulo: Indústria Gráfica Siqueira, 1953.

———. Os Camargo de São Paulo. São Paulo: Spes, 1937.

Carvalho Franco, Maria Sylvia de. Homens Livres na Ordem Escravocrata. São Paulo: Instituto de Estudos Brasileiros, 1969.

Cassiano, Ricardo. Marcha para oeste (a influência da bandeira na formação social e política do Brasil). Rio de Janeiro: José Olimpio, n.d.

Chevalier, François. "New Perspectives and New Focuses on Latin American Research." Newsletter: Conference on Latin American History 21, no. 1 (Apr. 1985).

Chojnacki, Stanley. "Dowries and Kinsmen in Early Renaissance Venice." Journal of Interdisciplinary History 5, no. 4 (Spring 1975): 571–600.

Chowning, Margaret. "A Mexican Provincial Elite: Michoacán, 1810–1910." Ph.D. diss., Stanford University, 1985.

Codigo civil dos Estados Unidos de Brasil. Comentado por Clovis Bevilaqua. Rio de Janeiro: Francisco Alves, 1917.

Codigo commercial do imperio do Brazil. Annotado pelo Desembargador Salustiano Orlando de Araujo Costa. 4th ed. Rio de Janeiro: Laemmert, 1886.

Codigo penal do imperio de Brasil. Rio de Janeiro: Perseverança, 1877.

Colecção das leis do imperio de Brasil. Rio de Janeiro: Nacional, 1864, 1875, and 1890.

Coleman, Peter J. Debtors and Creditors in America. Madison: State Historical Society of Wisconsin, 1974.

Congresso Nacional—Annaes da Camara dos Deputados—Sessões de 1907. Rio de Janeiro: Imprensa Nacional, 1908.

Cooke, Edward. An Inquiry into the State of the Law of Debtor and Creditor in England. London, 1829.

Corrêa, Mariza. "Repensando a família patriarcal brasileira." In Maria Suely Kofes de Almeida, ed., Colcha de retalhos: Estudos sobre a família no Brasil. São Paulo: Brasiliense, 1982.

"Correspondencia do Capitão-General Dom Luiz Antonio de Souza Botelho Mourão, 1766–1768." In Documentos Interessantes. Vol. 23. São Paulo: Arquivo do Estado de São Paulo, 1896.

Costa, Emilia Viotti da. The Brazilian Empire: Myths and Histories. Chicago: University of Chicago Press, 1985.

———. Da Senzala à colonia. São Paulo: Ciências Humanas, 1982.

———. "Land Policies: The Land Law, 1850, and the Homestead Act, 1862." In Costa, The Brazilian Empire.

Costa, Iraci del Nero da. "A estrutura familial e domiciliária em Vila Rica no alvorecer do século XIX." Revista do Instituto de Estudos Brasileiros 19 (1977): 17–34.

Costa Pinto, Luiz de Aguiar. Lutas de famílias no Brasil. São Paulo: Brasiliana, 1980.

Couturier, Edith. "Women and the Family in Eighteenth-Century Mexico: Law and Practice." Journal of Family History 10, no. 3 (Fall 1985): 294–303.

Dantas, Julio. O Amor em Portugal no Século XVIII. 3d ed. Lisbon, n.d.

Dean, Warren. "Latifundia and Land Policy in Nineteenth-Century Brazil." Hispanic American Historical Review 51, no. 4 (Nov. 1971): 606–25.

———. *Rio Claro: A Brazilian Plantation System, 1820–1920.* Stanford, Calif.: Stanford University Press, 1976.

Deus, Frei Gaspar da Madre de. *Memorias para a historia de São Vicente hoje chamada de São Paulo.* 1797. Reprint. São Paulo: Martins, 1953.

Dias, Maria Odila da Silva. "Aspectos da ilustração no Brasil." *Revista do Instituto Histórico Geográfico Brasileiro* (Rio de Janeiro) 278 (1968): 105–70.

———. *Quotidiano e poder em São Paulo no século XIX: Ana Gertrudes de Jesus.* São Paulo: Brasiliense, 1984.

Dimaki, Jane Lambiri. "Dowry in Modern Greece: An Institution at the Crossroads Between Persistence and Decline." In Kaplan, *The Marriage Bargain.*

Diretoría geral de estatística. *Recensamento do Brasil realizado em setembro 1920.* Rio de Janeiro: Imprensa Nacional, 1922.

Documentos com que o illustrissimo e excellentissimo Senhor Senador José Joaquim Fernandes Torres Presidente de São Paulo instruio o relatorio da abertura da assembleia legislativa provincial no dia 2 de Fevereiro de 1858. São Paulo, 1858.

Documentos interessantes para a história e costumes de São Paulo. 93 vols. São Paulo: Arquivo do Estado de São Paulo, 1897–1980.

Dumont, Louis. *Homo Hierarchicus: An Essay on the Caste System.* Tr. Mark Sainsbury. Chicago: University of Chicago Press, 1970.

———. "The Modern Conception of the Individual: Notes on Its Genesis and that of Concomitant Institutions." *Contributions* 8 (1965): 13.

Elder, Glen H., Jr. "History and the Family: The Discovery of Complexity." *Journal of Family History* 6, no. 2 (Aug. 1981): 489–519.

Ellis, Alfredo, Jr. *A economia paulista no século XVIII.* São Paulo: Academia Paulista de Letras, 1979.

———. "O ciclo do muar." *Revista de História* 1, no. 1 (Jan./Mar. 1950): 73.

———. *Os primeiros troncos paulistas.* São Paulo: Nacional, 1936.

———. *Raça de gigantes.* São Paulo: Helios, 1926.

———. *Um parlamentar paulista da república.* São Paulo: João Bentivegna, 1949.

Ellis, Myriam. "Contribução ao estudo do abastecimento das zonas mineradoras do Brasil no século XVIII." *Revista de História* 17, no. 36 (1958): 429–67.

———. "Estudo sobre alguns tipos de transporte no Brasil colonial." *Revista de História* 1, no. 4 (Oct./Dec. 1950): 495–516.

Engels, Frederick. *The Origin of the Family, Private Property and the State.* Ed. Eleanor Burke Leacock. New York: International Publishers, 1972.

Faoro, Raymundo. *Os donos do poder, Formação do patronato político brasileiro.* 2 vols. Porto Alegre: Globo, 1979.

Felstiner, Mary Lowenthal. "Kinship Politics in the Chilean Independence Movement." *Hispanic American Historical Review* 56, no. 1 (Feb. 1976): 58–80.

Ferreira, Waldemar Martins. *História do direito brasileiro.* São Paulo: Max Limonad, 1956.

———. *O casamento religioso de efeitos cíveis.* São Paulo: Sigueiras Salles Oliveira, 1935.

Flandrin, Jean-Louis. *Families in Former Times: Kinship, Household and Sexuality.* New York: Cambridge University Press, 1979.

Flory, Rae Jean Dell, and David Grant Smith. "Bahian Merchants and Planters in the Seventeenth and Early Eighteenth Centuries." *Hispanic American Historical Review* 58 (1978): 571–94.

Fonseca, Padre Manoel da. *Vida do veneravel Padre Belchior de Pontes da Companhia de Jesus*. Lisbon, 1752.

Foot, Francisco, and Victor Leonardi. *História da indústria e do trabalho no Brasil*. São Paulo: Global, 1982.

Freitas, Divaldo Gaspar de. *Paulistas na Universidade de Coimbra*. Coimbra: Coimbra Editora, 1958.

French, John. "Riqueza, poder e mão-de-obra numa economia de subsistência: São Paulo, 1596–1625." *Revista do Arquivo Municipal* 45, no. 195 (1982): 79–107.

Freyre, Gilberto. *The Masters and the Slaves*. New York: Knopf, 1956.

———. "The Patriarchal Basis of Brazilian Society." In Joseph Maier and Richard Weatherhead, eds., *Politics of Change in Latin America*. New York: Praeger, 1964.

Friedl, Ernestine. "The Position of Women: Appearances and Reality." *Anthropological Quarterly* 40, no. 3 (July 1967): 97–108.

Fukui, Lia F. K. "Riqueza do pobre: relações pais e filhos entre sitiantes tradicionais brasileiros." *Revista do Instituto de Estudos Brasileiros* 14 (1973): 67–77.

———. *Sertão e bairro rural*. São Paulo: Atica, 1979.

Furtado, Celso. *Economic Development of Latin America: A Survey from Colonial Times to the Cuban Revolution*. Trans. Suzette Macedo. Cambridge, Engl.: Cambridge University Press, 1970.

———. *The Economic Growth of Brazil*. Trans. Ricardo W. de Aguiar and Eric Charles Drysdale. Berkeley: University of California Press, 1965.

Gandavo, Pero de Magalhães. *História da província Santa Cruz*. São Paulo: Itatiaia, 1980.

Gillis, John R. *For Better, For Worse: British Marriages, 1600 to the Present*. New York: Oxford University Press, 1988.

———. "Peasant, Plebeian, and Proletarian Marriage in Britain, 1600–1900." In David Levine, ed., *Proletarianization and Family History*. Orlando, Fla.: Academic Press, 1984.

Goode, William J. "The Theoretical Importance of Love." *American Sociological Review* 24 (1959): 38–47.

———. *World Revolution and Family Patterns*. New York: The Free Press, 1963.

Goody, Jack. *The Development of the Family and Marriage in Europe*. New York: Cambridge University Press, 1983.

———. "Strategies of Heirship." *Comparative Studies in Society and History* 15, no. 1 (Jan. 1973): 3–20.

Goody, Jack, and S. J. Tambiah. *Brideprice and Dowry*. Cambridge, Engl.: Cambridge University Press, 1973.

Goody, Jack, Joan Thirsk, and E. P. Thompson, eds. *Family and Inheritance: Rural Society in Western Europe, 1200–1800*. Cambridge, Engl.: Cambridge University Press, 1976.

Goulart, José Alipio. *Tropas e tropeiros na formação do Brasil*. Rio de Janeiro: Conquista, 1961.

Graham, Richard. *Britain and the Modernization of Brazil, 1850–1914*. Cambridge, Engl.: Cambridge University Press, 1968.

Graham, Sandra Lauderdale. *House and Street: The Domestic World of Servants and Masters in Nineteenth-Century Rio de Janeiro*. Cambridge, Engl.: Cambridge University Press, 1988.

Grigg, Susan. "Toward a Theory of Remarriage: A Case Study of Newburyport at the Beginning of the Nineteenth Century." In Robert I. Rotberg and Theodore K. Rabb, eds., *Marriage and Fertility: Studies in Interdisciplinary History*. Princeton, N.J.: Princeton University Press, 1980.

Guimarães, Alberto Passos. *Quatro séculos de latifúndio*. 6th ed. São Paulo: Paz e Terra, 1989.

Hahner, June E. *Women in Latin American History: Their Lives and Views*. Los Angeles: University of California Press, 1976.

Hareven, Tamara K. "Modernization and Family History: Perspectives on Social Change." *Signs: Journal of Women in Culture and Society* 2, no. 1 (1976): 190–206.

Harrell, Stevan, and Sara A. Dickey. "Dowry Systems in Complex Societies." *Ethnology* 24, no. 2 (1985): 105–20.

Herlihy, David. *Medieval Households*. Cambridge, Mass.: Harvard University Press, 1985.

Hermann, Lucila. "Evolução da estrutura social de Guaratinguetá num período de trezentos anos." *Revista de Administração* 2 (Mar./June 1948): 3–316.

Hernani, Estrella. *Direitos da mulher*. Rio de Janeiro: Konfino, 1975.

Hill, Christopher. "Sex, Marriage, and the Family in England." *Economic History Review* 31, no. 3 (Aug. 1978): 450–63.

Hoornaert, Eduardo, Riolando Azzi, Klaus van der Grijp, and Benno Brod. *História da Igreja no Brasil: ensaio de interpretação a partir do povo*. Petrópolis: Editora Vozes, 1977.

Houston, Rab. "Illiteracy in Scotland, 1630–1760." *Past and Present* 96 (Aug. 1982): 81–102.

Hughes, Diana Owen. "From Brideprice to Dowry in Mediterranean Europe." In Kaplan, *The Marriage Bargain*.

Inventários e Testamentos. 44 vols. São Paulo: Arquivo do Estado de São Paulo, 1926–1975.

Johnson, Harold B., Jr. "A Preliminary Inquiry into Money, Prices, and Wages in Rio de Janeiro, 1763–1823." In Dauril Alden, ed., *Colonial Roots of Modern Brazil*. Berkeley: University of California Press, 1973.

Johnson, Lyman L., and Susan M. Socolow. "Population and Space: Eighteenth-Century Buenos Aires." In David Robinson, ed., *Social Fabric and Spatial Structure in Colonial Latin America*. Syracuse, N.Y.: Microfilms International, 1979.

Kaplan, Marion A. "For Love and Money: The Marriage Strategies of Jews in Imperial Germany." In Kaplan, *The Marriage Bargain*.

———, ed. *The Marriage Bargain: Women and Dowries in European History*. New York: Harrington Park Press, 1985.

Kennedy, John Norman. "Bahian Elites, 1750–1822." *Hispanic American Historical Review* 53, no. 3 (1973): 415–39.

Kicza, John E. "The Great Families of Mexico: Elite Maintenance and Business Practices in Late Colonial Mexico City." *Hispanic American Historical Review* 62, no. 3
(1982): 429–57.
———. "The Role of the Family in Economic Development in Nineteenth-Century
Latin America." *Journal of Family History* 10, no. 3 (Fall 1985): 235–46.
Korth, Eugene H., and Della M. Fleuche. "Dowry and Inheritance in Colonial Span-
ish America: Peninsular Law and Chilean Practice." *The Americas* 43, no. 4 (April
1987): 395–410.
Kuznesof, Elizabeth. "Household Composition and Headship Rates as Related to
Changes in Mode of Production: São Paulo, 1765–1836." *Comparative Studies in
Society and History* 22, no. 1 (Jan. 1980): 78–108.
———. "Clans, the Militia, and Territorial Government: The Articulation of Kin-
ship with Polity in Eighteenth-Century São Paulo." In David J. Robinson, ed.,
Social Fabric and Spatial Structure in Colonial Latin America. Syracuse, N.Y.: Micro-
films International, 1979.
———. "From Family Clans to Class Alliance: The Relationship of Social Structure
to Economic Development in 19th Century São Paulo." *Revista da Sociedade
Brasileira de Pesquisa Histórica* (São Paulo) 3 (1986–87): 29–46.
———. "Household Composition and Economy in an Urbanizing Community: São
Paulo, 1765 to 1836." Ph.D. diss., University of California, Berkeley, 1976.
———. *Household Economy and Urban Development, São Paulo, 1765 to 1836.* Boul-
der, Colo.: Westview Press, 1986.
———. "Property Law and Family Strategies: Inheritance and Corporations in Brazil,
1800–1960." Paper presented at the American Historical Association meetings,
Dec. 1984.
———. "The Role of the Female-Headed Household in Brazilian Modernization: São
Paulo, 1765 to 1836." *Journal of Social History* 13, no. 4 (June 1980): 589–613.
———. "The Role of the Merchants in the Economic Development of São Paulo,
1765–1850." *Hispanic American Historical Review* 60, no. 4 (1980): 571–92.
Ladurie, E. Le Roy. "Système de la coutume: Structures familiales et coutumes d'heri-
tage en France au XVI siècle." *Annales* 27, no. 4–5 (July–Oct. 1972): 825–46.
Lantz, Herman R. "Romantic Love in the Pre-modern Period: A Sociological Com-
mentary." *Journal of Social History* (Spring 1982): 349–70.
Laslett, Peter. *Household and Family in Past Time.* Cambridge, Engl.: Cambridge Uni-
versity Press, 1972.
Lavrin, Asunción, and Edith Couturier. "Dowries and Wills: A View of Women's So-
cioeconomic Role in Colonial Guadalajara and Puebla, 1640–1790." *Hispanic
American Historical Review* 59, no. 2 (1979): 280–304.
Leacock, Eleanor. Introduction to Engels, *The Origin of the Family.*
Leite, Aureliano, ed. *Homens de São Paulo.* São Paulo, 1955.
Leite, Mario. *Paulistas e mineiros, plantadores de cidades.* São Paulo: EdArt, 1961.
Leite, Serafim. *História da Companhia de Jesus no Brasil.* 10 vols. Rio de Janeiro: Civi-
lização Brasileira, 1938–45.
Leonzo, Nanci. *As companhias de ordenanças na capitania de São Paulo: Das origens ao
governo do Morgado de Matheus.* São Paulo: Coleção Museu Paulista, Serie de His-
tória, 1977.

Levi, Darrell E. *A família Prado*. São Paulo: Cultura 70, 1977.

Levy, Maria Bárbara. *História financeira do Brasil colonial*. Rio de Janeiro: IBMEC, 1979.

Lewin, Linda. "Natural and Illegitimate Children in Brazilian Inheritance Law from Colony to Empire: A Methodological Note." Unpublished manuscript.

———. *Politics and Parentela in Paraíba*. Princeton, N.J.: Princeton University Press, 1987.

———. "Some Historical Implications of Kinship Organization for Family-Based Politics in the Brazilian Northeast." *Comparative Studies in Society and History* 21, no. 2 (April 1979): 262–92.

Lima, Heitor Ferreira. *História político-econômica e industrial do Brasil*. São Paulo: Brasiliana, 1976.

Lima, Ruy Cirne. *Pequena história territorial do Brasil*. Pôrto Alegre: Livraria Sulina, 1954.

Lisanti Filho, Luís. *Negócios coloniais (uma correspondência comercial do século XVIII)*. 5 vols. São Paulo: Visão, 1973.

Lobo, Eulalia Maria Lhameyer. "O comércio atlántico e a comunidade de mercadores no Rio de Janeiro e em Charleston no século XVIII." *Revista de História* 51, no. 101 (1975): 49–106.

Lockhart, James. *Spanish Peru, 1532–1560*. Madison: University of Wisconsin Press, 1968.

Lockhart, James, and Enrique Otte, eds. *Letters and People of the Spanish Indies: Sixteenth Century*. New York: Cambridge University Press, 1976.

Lopez Ortiz, P. José. *Derecho musulman*. Barcelona: Labor, 1932.

Lorenzo-Fernandes, O. S. *A evolução da economia brasileira*. Rio de Janeiro: Zahar, 1976.

Love, Edgar. "Marriage Patterns of Persons of African Descent in a Colonial Mexico City Parish." *Hispanic American Historical Review* 51, no. 1 (Feb. 1971): 71–91.

Macfarlane, Alan. *The Origins of English Individualism: The Family, Property, and Social Transition*. Oxford: Blackwell, 1978.

Maine, Sir Henry. *Ancient Law: Its Connection with the Early History of Society and its Relation to Modern Ideas*. New York: Holt, 1906.

Marchant, Alexander. *From Barter to Slavery: The Economic Relations of Portuguese and Indians in the Settlement of Brazil, 1500–1580*. Baltimore: Johns Hopkins University Press, 1942.

Marcílio, Maria Luiza. *A cidade de São Paulo, povoamento e população, 1750–1850*. São Paulo: Pioneira, 1974.

———. "Crescimento demográfico e evolução agrária paulista, 1700–1836." Livre-Docência thesis, University of São Paulo, 1974.

———. "Evolução da população brasileira através dos censos até 1872." *Cadernos CEBRAP* 16 (1973): 115–37.

———. "Mariage e remariage dans le Brésil traditionnel: Lois, intensité, calendrier." In Jacques Dupaquier, ed., *Marriage and Remarriage in Populations of the Past*. London: Academic, 1981.

———. "Variation des noms et prénoms au Brésil." *Annales de démographie historique* (1972): 345–53.

Martinez-Alier, Verena. *Marriage, Class and Colour in Nineteenth-Century Cuba: A Study of Racial Attitudes and Sexual Values in a Slave Society.* London: Cambridge University Press, 1974.

Martinho, Lenira Menezes. "Organização do trabalho e relações sociais nas firmas comerciais do Rio de Janeiro (primeira metade do século XIX)." *Revista do Instituto de Estudos Brasileiros,* no. 18 (1976): 41–62.

Marx, Karl. *Capital.* 3 vols. New York: International Publishers, 1967.

Mattos, Armando de. *Manual de genealogia portuguesa.* Porto: F. Machado, 1943.

Maxwell, Kenneth. "Pombal and the Nationalization of the Luso-Brasilian Economy." *Hispanic American Historical Review* 48, no. 4 (Nov. 1968): 608–31.

McCaa, Robert. "*Calidad, Clase,* and Marriage in Colonial Mexico: The Case of Parral, 1788–90." *Hispanic American Historical Review* 64, no. 3 (Aug. 1984): 477–501.

Mello, D. Francisco Manoel de. *Carta de guia de casados.* Coimbra, 1747.

Merrick, Thomas W., and A. H. Graham. *Population and Economic Development in Brazil: 1800 to the Present.* Baltimore: Johns Hopkins University Press, 1979.

Mesgravis, Laima. *A Santa Casa da Misericórdia de São Paulo (1559?–1884).* São Paulo: Conselho Estadual de Cultura, 1976.

Metcalf, Alida C. "Families of Planters, Peasants, and Slaves: Strategies for Survival in Santana de Parnaíba, Brazil, 1720–1820." Ph.D. diss., University of Texas at Austin, 1983.

———. "Fathers and Sons: The Politics of Inheritance in a Colonial Brazilian Township." *Hispanic American Historical Review* 66, no. 3 (1986): 455–84.

———. "Recursos e estruturas familiares no século XVIII, em Ubatuba, Brasil." *Estudos Econômicos* 13 (1983): 771–75.

Millet, Sérgio. *Roteiro do café e outros ensaios.* São Paulo: Hucitec/Pró-Memória, 1982.

Monteiro, John. "São Paulo in the Seventeenth Century: Economy and Society." Ph.D. diss., University of Chicago, 1985.

———. "Vida e morte do indio: São Paulo colonial." In Comissão pro Indio, ed., *Indios no estado de São Paulo: resistência e transfiguração.* São Paulo: Yankatú, 1984.

Montesquieu, Charles de Secondat. *The Spirit of Laws.* Vol. 2. New York: The Colonial Press, 1949.

Morse, Richard. *From Community to Metropolis: A Biography of São Paulo.* Gainesville: University of Florida Press, 1958.

Moura, Margarida Maria. *Os herdeiros da terra: Parentesco e herança numa área rural.* São Paulo: Hucitec, 1978.

Nazzari, Muriel. "The Disappearance of the Dowry: The Case of São Paulo." Forthcoming in *Revista da Sociedade Brasileira de Pesquisa Histórica.*

———. "Dotes Paulistas: Composição e Transformações (1600–1870)." Trans. Lina Gorenstein Ferreira da Silva. *Revista Brasileira de História* 9, no. 17 (Sept. 88/Feb. 89): 87–100.

———. "Parents and Daughters: Change in the Practice of Dowry in São Paulo (1600–1770)." *Hispanic American Historical Review* 70, no. 4 (Nov. 1990): 639–65.

———. "The Significance of Present-Day Changes in the Institution of Marriage." *Review of Radical Political Economics* 12, no. 2 (Summer 1980): 63–75.

————. "Women, the Family, and Property: The Decline of the Dowry in São Paulo, Brazil, 1600–1870." Ph.D. diss., Yale University, 1986.

Neme, Mario. "Apossamento do solo e evolução da propriedade rural na zona de Piracicaba." *Coleção Museu Paulista.* Série de História, vol. 1. São Paulo: Fundo de Pesquisas do Museu Paulista da Universidade de São Paulo, 1974.

————. "Dados para a história dos indios Caiapó." *Anais do Museu Paulista* 23 (1969).

Novais, Fernando A. "O código commercial brasileiro: principaes emendas approvadas pelo senado em 1848." *Revista da Faculdade de Direito* 17 (1979).

————. *Portugal e Brasil na crise do antigo sistema colonial (1777–1808).* São Paulo: Hucitec, 1981.

Okin, Susan Moller. "Patriarchy and Married Women's Property in England: Questions on Some Current Views." *Eighteenth-Century Studies* 17 (Winter 1983/84): 121–38.

Oliveira, Dom Oscar de. *Os dízimos eclesiásticos do Brasil nos períodos da colônia e do império.* Belo Horizonte: Universidade de Minas Gerais, 1964.

Oliveira, J. J. Machado d'. *Quadro historico da provincia de São Paulo.* São Paulo, 1897.

Oliveira Viana, F. J. *Populações meridionais do Brasil.* São Paulo: Monteiro Lobato, 1920.

Onody, O. *A inflação no Brasil (1820–1958).* Rio de Janeiro, 1960.

O primeiro-quinto livro das ordenações. Lisbon, 1521.

Ordenações e leys do reyno de Portugal confirmadas e estabelecidas pelo Senhor rey D. João IV. Lisbon, 1747.

Outhwaite, R. B., ed. *Marriage and Society: Studies in the Social History of Marriage.* New York: St. Martin's, 1982.

Paiva, José Maria de. *Colonização e catequese (1549–1600).* São Paulo: Autores Associados, Cortez, 1982.

Pereira de Queiroz, Maria Isaura. *Bairros rurais paulistas.* São Paulo: Livraria Duas Cidades, 1973.

Petrone, Maria Thereza Schorer. *A lavoura canavieira em São Paulo.* São Paulo: Difusão Europeia do Livro, 1968.

Pimentel, Silvia. "Communicação docente: Evolução dos direitos da mulher—norma—fato—valor." Diss., Facultade de Direito, São Paulo, 1976.

Pinto, Virgilio Noya. "Balanço das transformações econômicas no século XIX." In Carlos Guilherme Mota, ed., *Brasil em perspectiva.* São Paulo: Difel, 1968.

Polanyi, Karl. *The Great Transformation.* New York: Rinehart, 1944.

Prado, Caio, Jr. *The Colonial Background of Modern Brazil.* Trans. Suzette Macedo. Berkeley: University of California Press, 1967.

————. *História econômica do Brasil.* São Paulo: Brasiliense, 1983.

Prado, Paulo. *Paulística, história de São Paulo.* Rio de Janeiro: Ariel Editora, 1934.

Priore, Mary del. *A mulher na história do Brasil.* São Paulo: Pinsky, 1988.

Ramos, Donald. "City and Country: The Family in Minas Gerais, 1804–1838." *Journal of Family History* 3, no. 4 (Winter 1978): 361–75.

————. "Marriage and the Family in Colonial Vila Rica." *Hispanic American Historical Review* 55, no. 2 (May 1975): 200–225.

Rapp, Rayna, Ellen Ross, and Renate Bridenthal. "Examining Family History." In Judith L. Newton, Mary P. Ryan, and Judith R. Walkowits, eds. *Sex and Class in Women's History.* London: Routledge and Kegan Paul, 1983.

Rebelo, Bartolomeu Coelho Neves. *Discurso sobre a inutilidade dos esponsais dos filhos celebrados sem consentimento dos pais.* Lisbon, 1773.

Registro geral da câmara de São Paulo, 1750–1763. Vol. 10. São Paulo: Arquivo Municipal de São Paulo, 1920.

Ribeiro, Maria da Conceição Martins. "A vida urbana paulistana vista pela administração municipal: 1560–1828." Diss., University of São Paulo, 1972.

Rocha, Manoel Antonio Coelho da. *Instituções de direito civil português.* Rio de Janeiro: H. Garnier, 1907.

Roussel, Louis. *La famille après le mariage des enfants.* Paris: Presses Universitaires de France, 1976.

Rubin, Gayle. "The Traffic in Women: Notes on the 'Political Economy' of Sex." In Rayna R. Reiter, ed., *Toward an Anthropology of Women.* New York: Monthly Review Press, 1975.

Russell-Wood, A. J. R. "Female and Family in Colonial Brazil." In Asunción Lavrin, ed., *Latin American Women: Historical Perspectives.* Westport, Conn.: Greenwood Press, 1978.

———. *Fidalgos and Philanthropists: The Santa Casa da Misericórdia of Bahia, 1550–1755.* Berkeley: University of California Press, 1968.

———. "Women and Society in Colonial Brazil." *Journal of Latin American Studies* 9, no. 1 (1977): 1–34.

Ryan, Mary P. *Womanhood in America, from Colonial Times to the Present.* New York: New Viewpoints, 1975.

Sá, Joseph Barbosa de. "Relação das povoações do Cuyabá e Mato groso de seos principios thé os prezentes tempos." *Anais da Biblioteca Nacional do Rio de Janeiro* 23 (1901): 5–58.

Sacks, Karen. "Engels Revisited: Women, the Organization of Production, and Private Property." In Michelle Z. Rosaldo and Louise Lamphere, eds., *Woman, Culture, and Society.* Stanford, Calif.: Stanford University Press, 1978.

Saffiotti, Heleieth B. *Women in Class Society.* New York: Monthly Review Press, 1978.

Samara, Eni de Mesquita. "A Família na sociedade paulista do século XIX, 1800–1860." Diss., University of São Paulo, 1980.

———. *As Mulheres, o poder e a família, São Paulo, século XIX.* São Paulo: Marco Zero e Secretaria de Estado da Cultura de São Paulo, 1989.

———. "Casamento e papéis familiares em São Paulo no século XIX." *Cadernos de Pesquisa* 37 (May 1981): 17–25.

———. "Estatégias matrimoniais no Brasil do século XIX." *Revista Brasileira de História* 8, no. 15 (Sept./Feb. 1987): 91–106.

———. "Família, divórcio e partilha de bens em São Paulo no século XIX." *Estudos Econômicos* 13, special no. (1983): 787–97.

———. "O dote na sociedade paulista do século XIX: legislação e evidências." *Anais do Museu Paulista* 30 (1980–81): 41–53.

———. "O papel do agregado na região de Itú 1798–1830." *Coleção Museu Paulista* (Serie de História, São Paulo) 6 (1977): 1–105.

———. "Uma contribuição ao estudo da estrutura familar em São Paulo durante o período colonial: a família agregada em Itú de 1780 a 1830." *Revista de História* (São Paulo) 105, no. 53 (1976): 33–45.

Sampaio, Teodoro, ed. *São Paulo no século XIX e outros ciclos históricos*. São Paulo: Editora Vozes, 1978.

Schneider, Jane. "Trousseau as Treasure: Some Contradictions of Late Nineteenth-Century Change in Sicily." In Eric B. Ross, ed., *Beyond the Myths of Culture: Essays in Cultural Materialism*. London and San Francisco: Academic Press, 1980.

Schwartz, Stuart B. *Sovereignty and Society in Colonial Brazil*. Berkeley: University of California Press, 1973.

Searle, Eleanor. "Seigneurial Control of Women's Marriage: The Antecedents and Function of Merchet in England." *Past and Present* 82 (1979): 3–43.

Seed, Patricia. "The Church and the Patriarchal Family: Marriage Conflicts in Sixteenth- and Seventeenth-Century New Spain." *Journal of Family History* 10, no. 3 (Fall 1985): 248–57.

———. *To Love, Honor, and Obey in Colonial Mexico: Conflicts over Marriage Choice, 1574–1821*. Stanford, Calif.: Stanford University Press, 1988.

Segalen, Martine. *Nuptialité et Alliance*. Paris: G. P. Maissoneuve et Larose, 1973.

Sesmarias (1720–1736). São Paulo: Arquivo do Estado de São Paulo, 1937.

Silva, Maria Beatriz Nizza da. "A legislação pombalina e a estrutura da família no antigo regime português." Separata da colectânea *Pombal Revisitado*. São Paulo: Editorial Estampa, 1984.

———. "Educação feminina e educação masculina no Brasil colonial." *Revista de História* (São Paulo) 109, no. 40 (1977): 149–64.

———. "Sistema de casamento no Brasil colonial." *Ciência e Cultura* 28, no. 11 (Nov. 1976): 1250–63.

———. *Sistema de casamento no Brasil colonial*. São Paulo: T. A. Queiroz Editor, 1984.

Silva Leme, Luis Gozaga da. *Genealogia paulistana*. 9 vols. São Paulo: Duprat, 1903–5.

Simonsen, Roberto. *História econômica do Brasil (1500–1820)*. São Paulo: Companhia Editora Nacional, 1978.

Slater, Miriam. "The Weightiest Business: Marriage in an Upper-Gentry Family in Seventeenth-Century England." *Past and Present* 72 (1976): 25–53.

Socolow, Susan. *The Merchants of Buenos Aires, 1778–1810*. Cambridge, Engl.: Cambridge University Press, 1978.

Soeiro, Susan. "The Feminine Orders in Colonial Bahia, Brazil: Economic, Social and Demographic Implications, 1677–1800." In Asunción Lavrin, ed., *Latin American Women*. Westport, Conn.: Greenwood Press, 1978.

Stearns, Peter N., and Carol Z. Stearns. "Emotionology: Clarifying the History of Emotions and Emotional Standards." *The American Historical Review* 90, no. 4 (Oct. 1985): 813–36.

Stone, Lawrence. *Crisis of the Aristocracy*. Oxford: Clarendon Press, 1965.

———. "Family History in the 1980's." *Journal of Interdisciplinary History* 12, no. 1 (Summer 1981): 51–87.

———. *The Family, Sex and Marriage in England, 1500–1800*. New York: Harper and Row, 1977.

———. "The Rise of the Nuclear Family in Early Modern England: The Patriarchal Stage." In Charles E. Rosenberg, ed., *The Family in History*. Philadelphia: University of Pennsylvania Press, 1975.

Stuard, Susan Mosher. "Dowry Increase and Increments in Wealth in Medieval Ra-
gusa (Dubrovnik)." *Journal of Economic History* 41, no. 4 (Dec. 1981): 795–811.

Swartz, W. R. "Codification in Latin America: The Brazilian Commercial Code of
1850." *Texas International Law Journal* 10, no. 347 (1975): 347–56.

Sweigart, Joseph E. *Coffee Factorage and the Emergence of a Brazilian Capital Market,
1850–1888.* New York: Garland, 1987.

Taques de Almeida Paes Leme, Pedro. *Historia da capitania de S. Vicente (com um esboço
biographico do autor por Affonso de E. Taunay).* São Paulo: Melhoramentos, n.d.

———. *Nobiliarquia paulistana histórica e genealógica.* 3 vols. São Paulo: Universidade
de São Paulo, 1980.

Taunay, Affonso d'E. *História administrativa e econômica do Brasil.* Rio de Janeiro: Fo-
rense, 1972.

———. *História colonial da cidade de São Paulo no século XIX.* 3 vols. São Paulo: Publicação da Divisão do Arquivo Histórico, 1956.

———. *História da cidade de São Paulo.* São Paulo: Edições Melhoramentos, 1953.

———. *História da cidade de São Paulo no século XVIII.* 2 vols. São Paulo: Publicação
da Divisão do Arquivo Histórico, 1931–1934.

———. *História da cidade de São Paulo sob o império.* São Paulo: Publicação da Divisão
do Arquivo Histórico, 1956–1977.

———. *História geral das bandeiras paulistas.* 11 vols. São Paulo: Ideal, H. L. Canton,
1951.

———. *São Paulo nos primeiros annos (1554–1601).* Tours: Impr. de Arrault, 1920.

Tawney, Richard Henry. *Religion and the Rise of Capitalism.* New York: Penguin Books,
1938.

Thomas, W. I., and F. Znaniecki. *The Polish Peasant in America.* Vol. 1. New York:
Dover, 1958.

Tilly, Charles, and L. A. Tilly. "Stalking the Bourgeois Family." *Social Science History*
4, no. 2 (Spring 1980): 251–60.

Trípoli, César. *História do direito brasileiro.* 2 vols. São Paulo: Revista dos Tribunaes,
1936.

Trumbach, Randolph. *The Rise of the Egalitarian Family: Aristocratic Kinship and Domestic Relations in Eighteenth-Century England.* New York: Academic Press, 1978.

Tutino, John. "Family Economies in Agrarian Mexico, 1750–1910." *Journal of Family
History* 10, no. 3 (Fall 1985): 258–71.

———. "Power, Class and Family: Men and Women in the Mexican Elite, 1750–
1810." *The Americas* 39 (July 1982–Apr. 1983): 359–82.

Varnhagen, Francisco. *História geral do Brasil antes de sua separação e independência.* 2
vols. São Paulo: Melhoramentos, 1975.

Villasboas, Antonio de. *Nobiliaria portuguesa.* Lisbon, 1676.

Wagley, Charles. *An Introduction to Brazil.* New York: Columbia University Press,
1963.

———. "Kinship Patterns in Brazil: The Persistence of a Cultural Tradition." In
Charles Wagley, ed., *The Latin American Tradition: Essays on the Unity and Diversity of Latin American Culture.* New York: Columbia University Press, 1968.

Weber, Max. *The Protestant Ethic.* New York: Scribner, 1952.

Willems, Emilio. "Social Differentiation in Colonial Brazil." *Comparative Studies in
Society and History* 12, no. 1 (Jan. 1970): 31–49.

Wilson, Fiona. "Marriage, Property, and the Position of Women in the Peruvian Central Andes." In Raymond T. Smith, ed., *Kinship Ideology and Practice in Latin America*. Chapel Hill: University of North Carolina Press, 1984.

Wormald, Jenny. "The Blood Feud in Early Modern Scotland." In John Bossy, ed., *Disputes and Settlements: Law and Human Relations in the West*. Cambridge, Engl.: Cambridge University Press, 1983.

Yver, Jean. *Egalité entre héritiers et exclusion des enfants dotés*. Paris: Sirey, 1966.

Zemella, Mafalda P. *O Abastecimento da capitania das Minas Gerais no século XVIII*. Boletim no. 118 da FFCL da USP. São Paulo: University of São Paulo, 1951.

INDEX

In this index an "f" after a number indicates a separate reference on the next page, and an "ff" indicates separate references on the next two pages. A continuous discussion over two or more pages is indicated by a span of page numbers, e.g., "57–59." *Passim* is used for a cluster of references in close but not consecutive sequence.

Library of Congress Cataloging-in-Publication Data

Nazzari, Muriel, 1924–
    Disappearance of the dowry : women, families, and social change in
São Paulo, Brazil (1600–1900) / Muriel Nazzari.
        p.   cm.
Includes bibliographical references and index.
ISBN 0-8047-1928-4 (alk. paper)
1. Dowry—Brazil—São Paulo—History.   2. Women—Brazil—São
Paulo—Social conditions.   3. Family—Brazil—São Paulo—History.
4. São Paul (Brazil)—Social conditions.   I. Title.
HQ1017.N39   1991
306'.0981'61—dc20
91-9737
CIP

⊗ This book is printed on acid-free paper.